Portraits of White Racism

DAVID T. WELLMAN

ASSISTANT PROFESSOR OF SOCIOLOGY
THE UNIVERSITY OF OREGON

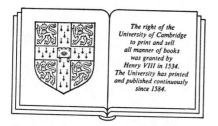

The right of the
University of Cambridge
to print and sell
all manner of books
was granted by
Henry VIII in 1534.
The University has printed
and published continuously
since 1584.

CAMBRIDGE UNIVERSITY PRESS

CAMBRIDGE
LONDON NEW YORK NEW ROCHELLE
MELBOURNE SYDNEY

Published by the Press Syndicate of the University of Cambridge
The Pitt Building, Trumpington Street, Cambridge CB2 1RP
32 East 57th Street, New York, NY 10022, USA
10 Stamford Road, Oakleigh, Melbourne 3166, Australia

First published 1977
Reprinted 1978, 1979, 1980, 1982, 1983, 1984, 1985

Printed in the United States of America

Library of Congress Cataloging in Publication Data
Wellman, David T
Portraits of white racism.
Includes bibliographical references and index.
1. Racism – United States.
2. United States – Race relations. I. Title.
E185.615.W35   301.45'1'042   76-47187
ISBN 0 521 21514 5 hard covers
ISBN 0 521 29179 8 paperback

Contents

Foreword by Robert Blauner   ix

Preface   xviii

1 Prejudiced people are not the only racists in
   America   1
  Introduction   1
  Racist beliefs seen as prejudice: conceptual and
    empirical difficulties   4
  Racial prejudice: assumptions and measurements   14
  Toward an alternative perspective   35
  White racism as a strategy for maintaining
    privilege   40

2 From theory to research and back again — a
   methodological discussion   45
  Introduction   45
  Organizing a research project: original interests
    and intentions   49
  Research strategy   52
  The data "talk back"   56
  What does it all mean?   58
  Character portraits   64
  A note on methodological orthodoxy   66

3 "I favor anything that doesn't affect me person-
      ally." Gene Danich   74
   Prologue   74
   "I've got the last job I'm ever gonna have."   77
   "I never met a single colored person in
      conversation until I was over eighteen years
      old!"   84
   "Equality means ain't nobody better than
      anybody else."   90
   Epilogue   102

4 "The trouble is all this suspicion between us."
      Darlene Kurier   108
   Prologue   108
   Growing up unaware   111
   Coming to grips with the 1960s   118
   Education is the solution   124
   But there's all this suspicion between the races   127
   Epilogue   130

5 "If I could do it, why can't they do it?"
      Dick Wilson   138
   Prologue   138
   Making it the hard way   141
   Getting off Oregon Hill   145
   Finding rewarding work   148
   "I can relate to people whose backgrounds are
      similar to mine."   152
   "Blacks need pride in themselves and genuine
      jobs — not the indiscriminate use of ideological
      phrases like black power."   154
   "Change has to occur within the law — and people
      have to be motivated to do that."   157
   Epilogue   163

6 "Convincing people that this is a racist country is

like selling soap — if agitators say it enough
times people will believe it." John Harper 168
Prologue 168
Having to work for what you get: a
three-generation California tradition 170
"Aside from skin color there's no difference
between black and white people." 177
The problem is agitators, not inequality 182
Epilogue 189

7 "There wouldn't be any problems if people's
heads were in the right place." Roberta 194
Prologue 194
"I want to devote my whole life to like spiritual
things." 196
"Spades want to see you defend yourself a lot of
times. Like that's their trip." 204
"Like it's a drag to have as your whole trip
trying to get your race equal to another." 207
Epilogue 211

8 Toward a sociology of white racism 216
Introduction: the contradiction 216
Getting off the hook 218
Legitimacy of grievance and receptivity to
change: some differences 222
The pulls of race and the pushes of class 225
Personal concerns and the commitment to
individualism 228
Conclusion 234

Appendix: interview guide 237

References 243

Index 250

Foreword
by Robert Blauner

David Wellman's book is a study of racial consciousness. It is about the conflicts of the 1960s as experienced by ordinary white Americans. Until then most whites outside the South could escape an awareness of involvement in racism because white and black lives so rarely touched. Suddenly, race exploded on the domestic scene, and Americans of African descent began to impinge on white lives. Blacks could no longer be confined to the margins of whites' perceptual screens, for these formerly "invisible" men and women had seized history's center stage.

Not only the big voices were heard — the sounds of ghetto revolt and calls for black power — but the little voices, previously silent, were heard on the job, in the classroom, and on the streets. Most white people at least squirmed a little as comfortable "resolutions" of racial questions were shaken up. The new black consciousness — certainly not monolithic, with its various shades and hues — forced a greater self-consciousness about race, and many larger questions were raised about social justice and how we all live our lives.

Although Professor Wellman is a sociologist, he illuminates these social processes out of the texture of personal experience much like the fine novelist. In this book you

ix

will meet five people of diverse backgrounds who grappled in unique ways with the racial crisis. First is Gene Danich, Wellman's one-man rebuttal to the Archie Bunker stereotype of the American worker. Danich is a longshoreman and a member of the ILWU, a fifty-percent black union. The racial electricity of his story is intensified by the probing questions of interviewer Alex Papillon, a black fellow worker. Danich is a study in contradictions. Although his baptismal introduction to dark-skinned people while a raw recruit in the Marines was a black fist in the mouth, he believes that police *are* really brutal to blacks. At the same time that he was admiring the Black Panthers and their project of arming the black community, he "fairly" could not tolerate the aggressive, "arrogant" stance of Stokely Carmichael and seemingly would have done anything to get rid of him. I believe the sketch of Danich is the most brilliant chapter in the book and should be required reading for all college students who have been assigned Seymour Martin Lipset's classic portrait of the worker as an authoritarian, simplistic thinker. (There are similar portraits. Reportedly Professor Lipset has since disclaimed this position.)

Next we encounter Darlene Kurier painfully trying to make sense of the changing racial climate of the 1960s. When she took a job as an assistant in a Head Start program black people became prominent in her life. As Wellman deftly characterizes her poignant dilemmas and confusions: "Just as she was coming to evaluate black people as individuals, they demanded to be treated as a group. When she came to recognize that black people needed equal opportunities, they were demanding political power. As she began to locate the issues of discrimination in individual prejudice, black people were speaking of the entire society as a racist one. At the time she recognized that blacks needed help, they didn't want any." Because she is unusually honest about her feelings and because she evidently struggled with her prejudices and tried to listen to her black co-workers, the pathos of always being out of synchronization with the changing times is all the more underscored.

Dick Wilson, on the other hand, experiences none of the doubts and confusions that beset Kurier; this businessman's views of law, order, and procedures for social redress are indeed "authoritarian." Born in Virginia in extreme poverty, his whole life has been a struggle to escape his origins, to achieve the solid middle-class status provided by his position as supervisor of a large manufacturing plant. Whereas black people were distant and irrelevant when he was growing up, in 1968 (when the interview took place) they made up a sizeable proportion of his work force. Seven of these workers took time off the job to lend solidarity to Huey Newton, the Black Panther Minister of Defense, who was on trial for the murder of a white police officer. Wilson was furious, and frustrated because the racial climate prevented him from invoking the discipline in which he so strongly believed. C. Wright Mills said that sociology should examine the interplay of public events and private troubles, but how often do we have an opportunity to see this in action? *Portraits of White Racism* is dense with such social history: the interviews overflow with references to the assassination of King, to Malcolm X, Carmichael and Black Power, the Panthers, and above all "the riots."

John Harper, the next actor in this drama, is also remarkably sure of himself and of the correctness of his viewpoints. An unusually articulate scion of an old and prosperous California family, he achieved wealth and financial security from an earlier career as an engineering entrepreneur. He is a financial manager for an East Bay city and deals with black people as employees and consumers of the city services. Dedicated to nineteenth-century principles of individualism, hard work, and testing one's mettle, he is especially antagonistic to black studies programs, which he feels undermine society's values. Harper professes a "color-blind" attitude about race, and like so many of the others in this book, social class — and not race — is the criterion he would use to exclude people from his personal world of friendship and neighborhood.

Finally we meet Roberta, a young, almost pampered middle-class teenager who brought her romantic idealization of black people all the way from Louisiana to San Francisco's Haight-Ashbury district. Roberta exemplifies how many young whites in the counterculture identified with blacks and black culture perhaps as an antidote to their own sense of inner emptiness. Romantic rebel turned hippie, her views of "spades" went through a series of changes as she was more and more "hassled in the Haight." The story of Roberta's loss of innocence is at the same time a glimpse of the relations between white hippies and urban blacks in San Francisco in the 1960s.

The interviews from which Wellman's portraits are drawn cover a vast range of topics, focusing particularly on the history of the subjects' encounters with people of color. The ultimate interest was to cut through conventional truisms, stereotypes, and political rhetoric in order to confront the depth and complexity of actual feelings about blacks and other minorities. Wellman and his field workers were looking for what Winthrop Jordan has called the "sense of difference" between whites and blacks, and for how their white respondents perceived Afro-Americans. Beyond this Wellman was curious about the person's mental picture of American society and its race relations. To what extent do people recognize racial hierarchy, inequality, and injustice? And, if recognized, how are they explained? This led him to the question of how white people come to terms with their *racial privilege*, that is, the advantages they all share that are denied members of minority groups because skin color is so fateful in our society. For example, to what degree do white people recognize their complicity in, their participation in, and personal responsibility for, the subordination of people of color?

The case study method is especially suited to deal with these hard and sensitive questions. Quantitative research — like opinion surveys — requires that answers and positions be formulated with some precision. On the level of depth and nuance where Wellman is working, however, the very essence of racial consciousness is ambiguity and contradiction. Qualitative research, whether based on observation, the clinical or focused interview, or the life-history, makes it possible to confront the special features and subtleties of each particular case, and to view the person or the social process in some larger context or situation.

It is true that life-history interviews are difficult and indeed frustrating to analyze because they are not as standardized as other techniques. Wellman's interviews emphasize each person's unique story and life themes, as well as his or her "racial" history. With Gene Danich the larger context was his tortuous work history and his finally successful search for that "freedom job"; in the case of Roberta it was her search for a community of love. Although this lack of comparable data limits certain kinds of analysis, it makes it possible to view the person as a total entity, and in particular to link specific attitudes (for example, responses to the riots) to larger themes of personality and consciousness. Thus we can understand why Gene Danich is able to empathize with angry blacks taking to the streets when we see how violence has been such a prominent, upfront theme in his own life. Roberta's response to rioting is clearly linked to her own precarious sense of public safety — she was living on the fringes of San Francisco's Fillmore District. Similarly, the powerful aversions expressed by Wilson and

Harper make more sense when we see them in the context of their generally rigid socio-political views and their apparently successful mastery of their own aggressive impulses. Contrast this with the more conventional surveys of the 1960s that gave us reams of public opinion data on how population cross-sections felt about ghetto insurrections — their causes, possible justifications, and appropriate responses — but that come to us in stark, mechanical percentages that inevitably abstract the data from the framework of personal and political experience.

Roberta and her co-respondents were interviewed as part of a larger study of racism and racial attitudes conducted at the University of California in the late 1960s. I was the principal investigator of this research, which means that I wrote the grant proposal and provided many of the guiding ideas. David Wellman was the sparkplug of the study, which means he did most of the work and assumed the major responsibilities, especially for what turned out to be more than 300 depth interviews. (More than 200 of these interviews were with blacks and do not play a direct part in this book.)

Our project sacrificed randomness in drawing its sample in order to maximize rapport between interviewer and interviewee. Although a conscientious attempt was made to systematically include a demographic cross-section, there is no way to know whether Wellman's findings are representative of a larger population. The author has discussed these issues at length in Chapter 2.

Portraits of White Racism is based on the 107 interviews with white people that Wellman and his fellow field workers collected. Even though only five of these persons appear directly in the book the others form the backdrop against which the foreground figures come to life. For it was in poring over the tape-recorded transcripts of the entire sample that Professor Wellman formulated his theoretical approach to the phenomenology of white racism. The specific five "Portraits" were then selected because they were, in a sense, *exemplary* cases. Either because a respondent was particularly insightful and articulate or because she or he had experienced conflicts of race especially intensely, or for whatever reason — these subjects exemplified themes that were common to a much larger group of respondents. Thus, their very particularity highlighted generic social realities. Needless to say, another criterion of selection was diversity. Women and men, young and old, working-and middle-class are included.

Each of the portrait chapters opens with a brief prologue which places the interview in context. Here Wellman vividly exposes the inner life of the research project, its day-to-day problems. Then comes the heart of the matter, the sketch of the informant based on a creative synopsis of the interview materials. Finally, in the process of interpreting the interview, he introduces his own ideas and theories of racism. These ideas come in the epilogue, after we have experienced the interview on its own terms. The reader who has already gotten a sense of Roberta or John Harper or Gene Danich can make his or her own judgments as to whether or not the author's theoretical leaps are firmly grounded in the empirical materials, whether or not they cast fresh light on the subjects. Like Robert Coles and Studs Terkel, David Wellman lets people speak for themselves.

After they have spoken, David Wellman goes to work on them. Like the good sociologist he is — and my aim here is to question the sociological method — our author approaches with considerable skepticism Roberta's vision of the community of love, Harper's Protestant ethic values, Kurier's pathos, and Wilson's ideals of right living. He wants to chip away at them, to point out their contradictions and inconsistencies, to show how consistently self-serving they are, how they mask racial privilege and cloud the true structure of society. It is true that people's beliefs, in some very general way, are connected to their positions in society. But beliefs and their seriousness vary from one person to another, indeed from one time of life to another. They can be canned from ready-made formulae easily available in the cultural/ideological supermarket. Or they can be, with all their confusions and contradictions, the product of hard-fought battles to make sense out of our lives. These are the extremes. The five who sat for David Wellman's portraits, like most of us I suppose, are somewhere in between, but I experienced their views more as deeply-felt attempts to comprehend social reality than as ideology, rationalization, or the automatic playback of public opinion. Although I have exaggerated a tendency in Wellman's approach to underscore my own polemic, I think the author comes closest to such reductionism in the epilogue to Darlene Kurier. Whereas he seems especially hard on her, he seems to take Gene Danich's ideas most seriously. I read this as an expression of a certain working class bias in Wellman, intimations of which may also be found in the comparison of middle class and working class racism in Chapter 8.

One of the most engaging — and important — aspects of this book is its frankness and openness. With the exception of ethnographic work, it is difficult in much of social science to get a sense of the concrete human situation in which the drama of research is played out: the final report seems so "reified," so cut off from the actual point of data production, often from personal experience itself. Wellman's remarkably candid discussion of methodology in Chapter 2 goes far to demystify social research, as he shows the difference between textbook expectations and the way a real-life sociological study unfolded. In the prologue to Roberta's chapter, he speculates about why her interview "worked," thus dismissing the closely guarded professional secret that most interviews don't. Later he notes that Darlene Kurier wasn't one of Hardy Frye's best interviews. He tells us what he thinks of his staff, of his own weaknesses and hangups and those of Alex, Hardy, Lincoln, Ed, — what they missed as well as what they got. When you read this book you can see that interviewing is no neutral encounter, but a problematic, often painful human situation which changes the interviewer as well as the respondent. In talking to Dick Wilson, for example, Dave Wellman shed some of his own prejudices against business people. This gives this study a flavor of authenticity that is all too rare in sociology.

Portraits of White Racism is a sensitive and multifaceted book. The reader can expect to engage in some provocative dialogues with the author and his research subjects, dialogues that will help clarify his or her own relationship to the system of racial privilege in this country.

Preface

This book is about white racism. Unlike most books on the subject, however, it is not about prejudice. For reasons that I make clear in the first chapter, I find that concept troublesome: It does not adequately explain the pervasiveness and subtlety of racist beliefs in American life. Thus, instead of assuming that racist sentiments are expressed as prejudice, I explore an alternative: Racism can mean culturally sanctioned beliefs which, regardless of the intentions involved, defend the advantages whites have because of the subordinated position of racial minorities. Viewed through these lenses, racism need not be restricted to the obvious hostilities expressed by bigots, nor found solely among the ranks of lower- and working-class people. It is seen to be more pervasive, existing throughout the American class structure.

I am suggesting that racism is much more subtle, elusive, and widespread than sociologists have acknowledged. Part of the reason they have been unable to see racism in this light is conceptual: They have not "looked" for these expressions of it. The other part is methodological: Traditional instruments used by sociologists in large-scale surveys are not yet sensitive to these manifestations of racism. The structured questions asked in highly systematic research designs also assume a great deal of knowledge about the subject *before* the questions are posed. Since we know relatively little about that face of racism that I am exploring, traditional sociological methodologies are not much help; in fact they probably get in the way of understanding.

Thus my research departs from orthodox procedures. This book is grounded in five "sociohistories," case studies based on in-depth, qualitative interviews. The case studies reflect five different ways in which white Americans defend racial advantage; they show how people without prejudice continue to think in terms that maintain the racial status quo. Focusing intensely on a few people may limit the extent to which I can generalize, but it enhances my ability to show the subtleties and complexities of racism and to place racism within social, cultural, and biographical contexts. These contexts are crucial to my argument. As long as racial sentiments are evaluated independently of the contexts within which they occur, only the most obvious kinds of racism are detectable: the prejudiced kinds.

The arguments made in this book are not based on statistical "proof": I do not pretend to measure how widespread the racism I am analyzing is, nor do I assess the quarters in which it is most prominent. The purpose of this book is not to show how racism is distributed throughout the population. In fact, since the data were not collected in a random sample, that is not possible. Thus, I have neither the basis nor the reason to use statistical evidence. What this book does provide are the tools and the perspective with which to see racism in sentiments that are usually considered nonracist. That *is* possible with the data at hand.

Writing is a solitary project, books are not. However, most of the people who contribute to the making of a book never see their names on title pages. This book is the product of many different efforts. Were it not for two people in particular it would never have seen the light of day. Professor Robert Blauner taught me a great deal about race relations. Through his example I have also learned irreverence, although not disrespect, for traditional ways of looking at the world; he has given me the courage to try new formulations. Bob read this book in many forms; his comments always pushed me farther than I thought was possible. As a friend and colleague he has always been around when I needed to be told "enough," or "more," or "great," or "not quite." He made this book possible in yet another way: He was principal investigator of the research project that collected the data on which it is based.

The other person I feel especially indebted to is Professor Jan Marie Newton. There is not one draft of this book she has not seen and put long hours of work into; there is not an idea in it which we have not discussed at great length. Trying to please Jan is not easy; but that is what I have tried to do. The extent to which I achieve theoretical and literary clarity is largely due to her influence. Jan is more than a teacher and colleague: She is one of my most intimate friends. She administered emotional first aid when it was required and infected me with spirit when I was caught with my confidence down. She also taught me how to relax and celebrate when there was cause. Without her love and friendship this book would have been impossible.

Other people have been instrumental in the making of this book. Throughout the writing of it Professor Troy Duster has been an insightful critic, a persistent advocate, and a dear friend; sometimes simultaneously, always at the right time. Professor Jan E. Dizard carefully read draft after draft, persistently but not belligerently insisting I refine one or another idea. When I did not, he did not give up; when I did, he pushed anyway. Professor Steven Deutsch read beginning drafts; he has offered me encouragement, constructive criticism, and a friendly ear. Professor Richard Hill read Chapter 2 with a magnifying glass. I did not expect an endorsement; I know it is richer because of his contribution. Todd Gitlin's sympathetic, suggestive reading of an earlier draft came at the right time; his questions, suggestions, and friendship were necessary. I probably would never have written a book if I had not known Buddy Stein. As fan and teacher he has helped me become a writer during the last ten years. The encouragement and questions offered by Professors William Tabb and John Leggett helped me reformulate one chapter and feel comfortable about another. Judy Small read the next-to-the-last draft with a fine-tooth comb. I am grateful for her contagious excitement and the literary polish she graciously offered. Barbara Hill took time from her already too-busy schedule to help me smooth the final rough edges on the book. I am an indebted and hopefully better writer for it. Pat Mazzeo patiently listened as I agonized over this project. When he could get a word in edgewise, he made many fine suggestions and helpful observations. I am also grateful to Professor John Gumperz, who took time from his busy schedule to carefully read an early draft.

I have a special debt to the research staff with which I worked in collecting the data for this study. Without Lincoln Bergman, Hardy Frye, Alex Papillon, Ed Price, and Lynn Turner there would have been no study to write about. I have also benefited from discussions with William Dorsey and Jeffrey Prager, other members of the staff.

One of the painful dilemmas of "doing" sociology is that there is no real payment of the debt one owes to the people about whom he or she writes. Acknowledgment may not be compensation. It is necessary nonetheless. I am deeply grateful to the people who agreed to share their lives with us. I hope I do them justice.

I have an enormous intellectual debt to Professor Herbert Blumer. It goes considerably beyond this book. Right now I can only acknowledge the obligation; I am currently in the process of assessing it. Professor Blumer read drafts of Chapter 1. Since I am quite familiar with his critical side, I was especially encouraged by his supportive readings of it.

I am grateful to Jennifer Neaves and Dina Wills, who did excellent jobs typing early drafts of some chapters. I am indebted to Jan O'Connor, who patiently and proficiently transformed a mass of inserts and crossed-out words into a cleanly typed and complete manuscript. Twice.

There is another group of people to whom I am indebted. Without their warmth and support I could not have written a book. They are my family — immediate and extended: Saul Wellman, Vickie and Henry Shein, Joan Acker, Marguerite Adams, Mike and Vera Baylin, Ron and Susan Bloom, Betty Bonham, Beth and Steve Deutsch, Kris Dymond, Hardy Frye, Barbara and Dick Hill, George Hill, Jeff Lustig, Pat Mazzeo, Suzy Nelson, Frank Soracco, Buddy Stein, all the Takagis.

I wish there was some way I could implicate each of the people I have mentioned in whatever mistakes might follow, but, because I have probably ignored their advice on crucial issues, that would not be fair to them. I therefore reluctantly accept full responsibility for whatever shortcomings the reader may find.

The research upon which this book is based was supported in part by NIMH Grant 1-449495-29121, and in part by PHS Research Grant No. 17216 from the Center for Urban Ethnography at the University of Pennsylvania.

David T. Wellman

Berkeley, California
March, 1977

1 Prejudiced people are not the only racists in America

Introduction

In the late 1960s a television series titled "All in the Family" became extremely popular among Saturday night viewers in the United States. The leading character of the show, Archie Bunker, is supposedly a caricature of working-class men in America: heavyset and not very bright, usually the victim of his own inadequacies, Archie is really laughable. He is also a racist, though by liberal standards he is a relatively benign one: he does not call black people "niggers," he refers to them as "jungle bunnies"; he certainly would not want his daughter to marry "one of them," however, and he worries about them moving into his neighborhood. Archie is also authoritarian: people who disagree with him are "dingbats."

As a composite picture of the average American worker the character of Archie Bunker is hardly accurate. Archie is not typical of American workers. As one labor publication states the case: "There are a lot of workers who are thin, think everyone deserves a truly equal opportunity, are sincerely compassionate and essentially intelligent" (*Focus,* April 1972; cited in *Eugene (Ore.) Register Guard,* April 25, 1972). However, as a television portrayal of

1

sociological theories about racism, the Archie Bunker
character *is* accurate. He is a walking, talking, real-life
depiction of how the sociological imagination portrays
racists. Who other than an Archie Bunker type would af-
firmatively answer the following survey questions designed
to measure ethnocentrism?

> Negroes have their rights, but it is best to keep them
>   in their own districts and schools and prevent too
>   much contact with whites.

> It would be a mistake ever to have Negroes for fore-
>   men and leaders over whites.

> Manual labor and unskilled jobs seem to fit the Negro
>   mentality and ability better than more skilled or
>   responsible work.

> The only people who raise all the talk about putting
>   Negroes on the same level as whites are
>   radical agitators trying to stir up conflict [Adorno
>   et al., 1950; cited by Allport, 1958: 69].

The only people who will agree with these clichés are,
of course, people to whom liberal, middle-class ideals
about race relations have little meaning. Unlike the social
scientists formulating the questions, the people answering
them in an ethnocentric manner hold one thing in
common: Black demands for racial parity pose basic threats
to their often insecure position in American society. Given
the nature of racial stratification in America, such persons
stand to gain very little from racial equality. It should not
be surprising, then, that studies of ethnocentrism, authoritarianism or prejudice find these attitudes disproportionately among those people with biographies that resemble
Archie Bunker's. Thus Stewart and Hoult (1959: 277)
found that most studies locate the highest levels of authoritarianism among the following groups: the poorly edu-

cated; the aged; those living in rural areas; poor minorities; dogmatic religious groups; those of low socioeconomic status; social isolates; and the people raised in authoritarian family situations. If Archie Bunker is fiction, sociological theories about prejudice have helped create him.

Yet as events of the last decade indicate, Archie Bunker is hardly the typical American racist. For example, a study conducted by the University of Michigan Survey Research Center concluded that there were no important attitude differences on matters of race between white people living in cities and those living in suburbs, *except* that the suburbans "are somewhat sensitive to the prospect of having black people move into these neighborhoods" (Campbell, 1972; cited in *Trans-action*, March 1972: 10–12). Suburbanites, needless to say, are not Archie Bunker types. And if Archie Bunker is a racist, how are we to label the white people in a 1972 Gallup poll, 69 percent of whom were opposed to compulsory busing even though 66 percent believed that schools should be desegregated? (*Newsweek*, March 13, 1972: 24). Call them confused if you will. The real confusion, however, exists in the sociology of racist beliefs. The Archie Bunker prototype of racial bigotry — the idea that prejudiced people are the Archie Bunkers of America — no longer conforms with reality, if it ever did. Thus the sociological perspectives and assumptions that led to the conclusion that prejudiced people constitute a special type and that prejudice is concentrated among working-class people are equally inadequate and inaccurate. It seems quite clear that we need a more adequate sociological perspective on racist beliefs than the current one.

This study is concerned with how white Americans cope with the demands black people make for equality and with the troubles these demands present for whites. It is a study in white racism. But instead of assuming that racism manifests itself as prejudice, I will explore another possibility:

that racist beliefs are culturally sanctioned, rational responses to struggles over scarce resources; that they are sentiments which, regardless of intentions, defend the advantages
that whites gain from the presence of blacks in America.
Such beliefs are a pervasive phenomenon which can be
found throughout the class structure.

This chapter provides the theoretical spectacles necessary
to see racism in this light. Toward that end, I will first
consider in more detail some of the obvious problems with
the dominant sociological perspective that views racist
beliefs as a form of prejudice. Then I will explore the
assumptions that prevent this perspective from adequately
capturing the meaning of racism. Finally, I will outline my
approach to white racism.

Racist beliefs seen as prejudice: conceptual and empirical difficulties

Sociologists generally consider the attitudes of white
Americans to be a major cause of racism. The great mass of
writing devoted to the subject of prejudice indicates the
extent to which sociologists have been preoccupied with
attitudinal dimensions of racism. Rarely is a book written
about racism that does not explain America's racial problems in terms of one sort of prejudice or another. Racism
and prejudice usually mean the same thing.

Despite the variety of interpretations attached to attitudes based on racial considerations, almost without exception people studying prejudice describe it as a combination
of *hostility* toward and *faulty generalizations* about racial
groups. The definition of prejudice suggested by Simpson
and Yinger (1972: 24) captures the essential elements of
what nearly all sociologists mean when they study racial
prejudice. "We shall define prejudice," they state, "as an

emotional, rigid attitude . . . toward a group of people. [It] involves not only prejudgment but . . . misjudgment as well. It is categorical thinking that systematically misinterprets the facts." Generally speaking this has been the operating sociological definition of racial prejudice for at least the last half-century. There has been sufficient time, then, to assess the adequacy of this notion. What are some of the problems that stem from this approach to racism? What kinds of things can we say about it in light of recent events?

Limited focus

By definition, the kinds of attitudes this approach is concerned with are restricted to two types: to be prejudiced, attitudes must (1) be rigid and emotional and/or (2) reflect prejudgment or misjudgment of a racial group. One of the characteristics of a rigid and emotional attitude is that it is usually quite obvious. If people feel strongly about something they are usually overt about it, express their feelings in rather explicit terms, and more than likely are intolerant of those who disagree with them. Thus one of the characteristics of an attitude presumed to be prejudiced is that it is usually *overt* or *explicitly stated*.

Prejudiced attitudes are also misinterpretations of the social world. But they are not "honest" mistakes in judgment. They are categorical and they systematically misinterpret "facts." People who think in categorical terms are usually *hostile,* consciously or unconsciously, toward someone or something. That is why they systematically misrepresent issues. Thus hostility is another characteristic of prejudiced attitudes.

The most critical feature of prejudiced attitudes, however, is that they reflect incorrect thinking. Prejudice is misjudgment as well as prejudgment. The definition of a "correct" judgment, of course, is not relative. If an attitude expresses a judgment which *from the researcher's perspective is accurate,* it is not racial prejudice.

How sociologists define a problem is directly related to the conclusions they reach. If the attitudinal dimension of racism is defined as explicitly racial, hostile, and inaccurate — that is what will be found. Studies of racism guided by this conception have been severely limited. They have been able to focus only on those attitudes having the characteristics of prejudice. If these were the only kinds of racially motivated attitudes then the limitation would not be a liability: it would accurately mirror racial feeling in America. However, it has become increasingly obvious in recent years that many American attitudes about racial issues are not expressed in obvious ways, do not reflect hostility, and are not always misjudgments of the problem. These kinds of attitudes, however, cannot be detected or adequately interpreted as long as racial feelings are conceptualized as prejudice.

Defining racist attitudes as prejudice limits sociological analysis in another way. If, in the researcher's eyes, prejudiced beliefs do not accurately reflect racial issues, prejudiced people will be the ones who do not share the sociologist's racial world view. Thus the sociological "net," with which we go fishing for racists, is really capable of catching only those whose racial facts differ from our own. When we "catch" people like ourselves, we are without a systematic theory to explain why they are in our net. But our usual catch of prejudiced people has been limited to poor and working-class people — the Archie Bunkers. They are the people who, because of their class origins, have either not learned the proper ways of presenting racial views to sociological questioners or find middle-class ideals about race relations irrelevant to their situation.

Empirical inadequacies

We see, then, that attitudes based on racial considerations are not so limited as the notion of prejudice would lead us to think. They are neither restricted to Archie Bunker types nor expressed in openly hostile terms. In the last ten years, many white people who are not "prejudiced" have defended the status quo in the face of black demands for institutional reorganization. These whites say they are not hostile toward black people. Moreover, their defense of traditional arrangements is not based on misperception.

For example, in 1966 black and Puerto Rican leaders in East Harlem, New York City, demanded that their schools either be integrated or community controlled. The New York City School Board responded with an experiment that altered relationships of power over education in the city: The administration of schools was decentralized and community-run school boards were established in three predominantly black communities. In the fall of 1968, traditionally liberal white teachers went on strike, protesting the actions of the black unit administrator and his school board in one of these areas – Brooklyn's Ocean Hill-Brownsville ghetto. The teachers did not express racial hostility toward the black administrator or the community board; prejudice was not the issue, they argued. They felt their rights and interests as teachers were at stake. Their opposition to changes in the status quo was not articulated in racial terms. They defended their position, and the status quo, "in the rhetoric of the preservation of professionalism" (Gittell, 1969: 331). In another context, when racial minorities insisted upon new relationships with local police departments and proposed that civilian review boards or community control boards be established as steps in that direction, the resistance to these proposals was expressed in similar terms (Brooks, 1966: 36–7; *Nation*, 1966: 468; *New Yorker*, 1966: 50–1).

Opposition to these reforms is rarely stated in explicitly racial terms. The issue, argue supporters of continued police autonomy, is "efficiency," "standards," and the facilitation of normal operations. Middle-class white Americans who oppose school busing to achieve racial balance rarely voice their opposition in racial categories. They tell us they are concerned with buses, not blackness: The issue is that children spend too much time in transit. In institutions of higher education the situation is not much different. A racial vocabulary is not used by professors who oppose open enrollment programs or black-studies departments. They say they are concerned that these programs will lower academic standards and that selective recruitment of black faculty or subprofessionals will violate universalistic academic norms (Blauner, 1972a: 256–94).

The terms in which middle-class professionals defend traditional institutional arrangements are, strictly speaking, not examples of racial prejudice. They are neither overtly racial nor, given these people's *interests*, misinterpretations of "facts." However, while the sentiments may not be prejudiced, they justify arrangements that in effect, if not in intent, maintain the status quo and thereby keep blacks in subordinate positions. Whether the demands and responses are legitimate or illegitimate is not at issue here. The question is whether implementation of black demands would decrease the unequal relationship between blacks and white. If the consequence of whites acceding to a black demand reduces black–white inequality and if whites choose to oppose it, then regardless of the principle invoked that opposition perpetuates the status quo. The consequence of negative attitudes toward community control, busing, and open enrollment is then the same as if the attitudes were prejudiced. However, people expressing these ideas seldom show up in opinion polls as being prejudiced because they do not speak in an explicitly prejudiced way. Thus the focus on prejudice is empirically inadequate. It presents an inaccurate picture of racism since it can detect only the racism of people who are prejudiced.

Unfulfilled expectations

The empirical limitations of studies of prejudice are not restricted solely to detectable racism: They have also failed in predicting the development of racist thinking. Most people studying prejudice have been singularly optimistic in the belief that, measured as prejudice, racism will decrease. This prediction or expectation can be discerned in the writings of Robert Park (1950) and possibly even W. I. Thomas (1904), both of whom argued that caste beliefs would give way to beliefs based on class position. The studies of caste relations in the South conducted by Dollard (1957) and Davis et al. (1941) also predict this evolution. In their estimation, northern migration by blacks and southern industrialization would replace caste feelings with class ones. Myrdal was especially hopeful. In his words, "the biological inferiority dogma threatens to become *the lone surviving ideological support* of color caste in America" (1944: 97; emphasis added).

In the 1950s and '60s many studies supported this expectation. Bettelheim and Janowitz (1964) concluded that prejudice was declining among the young. Erskine (1962: 130–48) argued that the percentage of whites favoring desegregated facilities was increasing. Public housing studies showed that integrated living led to a decrease in prejudice (Deutsch and Collins, 1951). Sheatsley, writing in the late 1960s, claimed to demonstrate that "revolutionary changes" had taken place in white attitudes toward blacks. Whites were becoming less prejudiced, he argued;

and paraphrasing Barry Goldwater, he concluded, "In their hearts they know that the American Negro is right" (1966: 323).

In traditional terms, it may be that prejudice has been decreasing; but people's attitudes continue to reflect their experiences as members of racial groups. Opinion polls that divide respondents by race typically indicate little consensus between the races on social issues. Blacks and whites see the world quite differently on many questions. In a 1968 Gallup poll, for example, black people viewed the United States as "sick" by a ratio of 8 to 7, while white people held an opposing view by a ratio of more than 3 to 2 (*New York Times,* July 3, 1968). Another Gallup poll found that a person's views on the demonstrations at the Chicago Democratic Party Convention in 1968 depended in large part on his or her race: Six in ten whites approved of the actions of police, while six in ten blacks disapproved (*San Francisco Chronicle,* September 19, 1968). Racial experience thus still heavily influences how people view the world. Caste-based sentiments have not been replaced by class-based ones.

One of two interpretations is possible: either (1) feelings based on racial experience are not declining, in which case a major expectation of the focus is unfulfilled; or (2) prejudice — in the strict sense of the word — is declining while feelings based on race continue. If either is the case then there are serious difficulties with analyzing racism as prejudice.

Inconsistencies

Explaining racism in terms of prejudiced attitudes is not only limited by its poor fit with American racial realities; it is also beset with inconsistencies. Rigid thinking is ostensibly a characteristic of prejudice. However, both prejudiced and unprejudiced people are often inconsistent in their thinking. The Gallup poll on busing referred to above is a case in point. The first question is a standard one in research on prejudice: "Do you believe that schools in this country, both North and South, should be desegregated so that black and white pupils attend the same school?" If a person agrees, this is usually considered an indication that he or she is not prejudiced. In the Gallup poll 66 percent of the whites agreed with the statement. However, when they were asked the question, "Do you favor or oppose compulsory busing of some children, both black and white, so that school desegregation can be achieved?" only 20 percent answered yes. The two responses are hardly consistent; as neighborhoods in America are currently organized there cannot be meaningful desegregation without busing. Thus a negative response to the second question appears to be an indication of "prejudice."

Inconsistent thinking is nothing new among whites and there are many examples of it. Angus Campbell (1972: 23), studying racial attitudes in fifteen major American cities, found that most white people accept the rights of blacks to equal job treatment. Two-thirds of them (67%) were in favor of legislation that would prevent discrimination against blacks in job hiring and promotion; only four percent believed that whites should have job preference. When the same people were asked about housing issues, however, a different picture emerged. Less than half (40%) favored legislation to prevent discrimination against blacks in buying or renting houses and apartments and nearly one-third (30%) felt that whites had a right to keep black people out of their neighborhoods. Hamilton (1972: 413) found similar "inconsistencies" among the majority of nonsouthern white workers. In an article about southern businessmen and school desegregation, Cramer (1963: 384–9) points out that the "moderate" attitudes of these men are specific to particular issues. While they might favor school desegregation, they would not favor residential desegregation. They are moderates only insofar as they think it necessary to attract new industry or to preserve peace and harmony. In each of these examples, the differences between expressed attitudes indicates that people can develop less prejudiced attitudes in one sphere of social life without changing their attitudes on other issues. Thus people are quite likely to express contradictory or inconsistent attitudes concerning racial matters.

The fact that people adhere to inconsistent beliefs on racial matters is only one aspect of a two-pronged problem. Sometimes inconsistencies also emerge between people's beliefs and their behaviors. Discriminatory behavior does not always correspond neatly with prejudiced attitudes. Recognizing this, Robert Merton (1949) developed a classification which suggests that the discrepancy between prejudiced attitudes and discriminatory behavior produces four possible types of people: (1) the "all-weather liberal," the person who neither expresses prejudiced attitudes nor engages in discriminatory behavior; (2) the "fair-weather liberal," someone who is not prejudiced but who may discriminate if group pressure or self-advantage so dictate; (3) the "fair-weather illiberal," the person who is prejudiced but might not discriminate if such behavior were costly or painful; (4) the "all-weather illiberal," the consistent person who is both prejudiced and discriminates against certain groups.

Determining whether or not someone is prejudiced, then, is not always very helpful in predicting how they will respond to issues posed by black people. Other factors may be influencing their thoughts and actions. Examples of this sort require us to seriously question the usefulness of explaining racism mainly in terms of prejudice.

Meaningless distinctions

Contradictions in research findings are not per se criticisms of an approach. The approach *is* seriously weakened, however, when there is no systematic theory by which the inconsistencies can be explained. This is apparently the situation with research on prejudiced attitudes. The distinction between prejudiced and unprejudiced attitudes becomes almost meaningless when sociologists address themselves to the issue of middle-class white opposition to black demands for change in institutional priorities. Selznick and Steinberg, for example, found that while educated whites rejected "anti-Negro prejudice" and expressed support of civil rights, on the critical issue of defending property rights rather than ideals, "the educated were as likely as the uneducated to come to the defense of property rights" (1969: 178). In other words, when it comes to a choice between ideals and the interests represented by property rights, both educated and uneducated whites turn up in the same camp. According to the authors the only difference between the two groups is that:

> ... the attitudes of the uneducated toward Negroes and toward property rights are congruent and mutually reinforcing. In contrast, more of the educated are ambivalent; they defend *both* the civil rights of Negroes *and* what they perceive to be the rights of individual property owners [1969: 178–9; emphasis added].

It is, of course, becoming increasingly impossible to defend both property rights and civil rights. The two often come into conflict with each other. The conflict is difficult to explain, however, when prejudice is used to account for racist thinking. Thus Selznick and Steinberg come to the amazing conclusion that, "*When the unprejudiced claim a right to discriminate* in private spheres, they reflect an *unresolved dilemma of our normative order*" (1969: 183; emphasis added).

The concept of prejudice is meaningless in this context. If people who claim the right to discriminate are not prejudiced, of what use is the concept? If both the prejudiced and the unprejudiced claim the right to discriminate in private affairs, the concept explains nothing about racism. I will argue that the explanation of racism as prejudice is limited because the very assumptions that inform the perspective prevent it from adequately coming to grips with the nature of racism.

Racial prejudice: assumptions and measurements

The inadequacies that follow from the analysis of racism as prejudice are tied to assumptions that suggest that racist attitudes are very rarely rational. Even in those cases where the attitudes are regarded as rational, they are not considered to be in the interests of the person expressing them. In both instances prejudice is misperception – if people saw the world "correctly" there would be no prejudice. Since racism presumably reflects something other than rational interests, most sociologists see it as a reflection of psychological problems of the individual or group expressing racist sentiments. Other social scientists see prejudice as "false consciousness" resulting from the ideological manipulations of ruling groups. Regardless of the perspective, most social scientists define racist attitudes in psychological, nonrational terms and evaluate them accordingly. The problem is not merely definitional or restricted to conceptions of attitudes. Prejudiced attitudes are defined as such because of the theoretical context within which they are analyzed. In this scheme, prejudice appears to have a life of its own which is somehow independent of or causally prior to social structure. The racial organization of society is thus seen as a consequence of, rather than a cause of, people's racial beliefs. The sociological cart is placed before the horse.

The order needs to be reversed. Sociologically it makes much more sense to anchor attitudes in social contexts and organization. Without an understanding of the structural context within which attitudes occur, we cannot grasp their meaning. Their importance is also exaggerated; it seems as though the attitudes "cause" the structures. Sociologists traditionally recognize this relationship when they analyze an issue. An example is Bendix's (1956) classic study of managerial ideologies in which he shows how in the late eighteenth and early nineteenth centuries, belief systems surfaced as attitudes to explain and justify class-based privileges.

Sentiments based on racial position must be placed in the same framework; racial beliefs need to be situated in a sociological context. Attitudinal manifestations of racial inequality have to be related to the political and economic forms of stratification which give rise to and perpetuate them. The alternative is to be mired endlessly in psychological explanations which, while perhaps allowing hope to spring eternal, preclude accurate sociological understandings of racial beliefs. This is the problem with sociological accounts of racist attitudes; they lead directly to the previously discussed inadequacies. What, then are some of the assumptions that inform the dominant perspective on prejudice?

Assumption: racial subordination is not a fundamental principle of stratification in industrial society

With few exceptions, social scientists studying racism as prejudice do not consider racial division as a form of stratification built into the structure of society. In this view the roots of racial division are not located in the structure of the division of labor or in the organization of political power. Racial stratification is not considered essential to the functioning of modern society; the primacy of race as an aspect of social structure in America is not recognized. Rather, modern racial divisions are considered "holdovers" or remnants from past forms of social organization in which racial differences were crucial to societal development. Racial division in industrial society is not systematically generated in the way that, for example, class divisions are. Blacks are not "produced" in the same way as are workers. This is the point from which most sociological analyses of racism begin.

The "founding fathers" of sociology attributed racial subordination to many things, but they never explained it in terms of the functions it may have served for society as a whole. Racial division was explained by Sumner (1906) as mores; Giddings (1908) attributed it to "consciousness of kind"; Cooley (1918) argued that racial groups had different temperaments and capacities; E. A. Ross (1921) held the opinion that white people possessed a "celtic temperament," superior to other temperaments, which accounted for their superordinate social position. W. I. Thomas was one of the first sociologists to explain the inferior social position of blacks in terms of race prejudice, which he defined as "a horror of the external aspect of the Negro" (1904: 610). Racial divisions existed because whites had socially and mentally isolated blacks from full participation in society. And Robert Park (1924), for whom human relationships evolved from unconscious competition to consensus based on assimilation, saw racial problems as a temporary phenomenon: prejudice, "fear of the unfamiliar and uncomprehended," was a subjective barrier that would soon give way to the forces of assimilation.

Even sociologists who related racial stratification to structural determinants did not consider it a structurally generated aspect of modern society. As mentioned above, the caste-class "school" of race relations suggested that caste relations would give way to industrial relations when blacks moved north and/or the South became industrial (Davis et al., 1941; Dollard, 1957). And for Myrdal, the status of blacks in the United States " . . . presents nothing more and nothing less than a century-long lag of public morals. In principle the Negro problem was settled long ago" (1944: 24). Not all sociologists accepted this framework. Notable exceptions were two black sociologists, St. Clair Drake and Horace Cayton. In their classic study *Black Metropolis* (1945), they argue that Chicago's black ghetto is in large part a creation of the white world that surrounds it. In this instance, racial stratification is analyzed as a product of structural conditions. But for the bulk of sociologists, as Blauner observes, the most important assumption guiding their theories " . . . is the idea that as industrial societies develop and mature, race and ethnicity become increasingly irrelevant as principles for group formation, collective identity, and political action" (1972a: 3).

Given this assumption, sociologists writing prior to the late 1960s were relatively optimistic that racial barriers in the United States would be undermined. The influence of racism on one's social position was expected to decrease. Most sociologists assumed America was a loosely structured, relatively open society which promoted upward mobility for groups that were properly motivated. According to Talcott Parsons (1953), for example, the dominant value orientations of industrialized societies like America are "universalism" and "achievement." Universalism refers to an ethic by which all people are evaluated by the same criteria. The achievement orientation insists that people be evaluated in terms of what they do rather than who they are. These value orientations were assumed by most sociologists to be characteristic of modern societies like America.

Thus race and ethnicity, as bases of stratification, were expected to decrease as America continued to industrialize and blacks moved to the urban North. In Parson's terms:

> Its [race and ethnicity] importance would, in the normal course of development of our type of society, be expected to decrease. . . . [T]here are very powerful forces of acculturation at work which tend to break down distinctive ethnic traditions. Broadly we may regard the ethnic factor as a secondary basis of modification of the stratification pattern. . . . [1953: 118]

While certainly not Parsonians, Simpson and Yinger also suggest that racial status is no longer a necessary determinant of one's position in American society. In their words:

> It seems doubtful that belonging to racial, ethnic, or religious groups is a primary criterion or determinant of position in a system of social stratification. There is no reason to suppose that a member of a given racial, ethnic, or religious group within a society cannot learn to fill any social role found in that society. [1965: 396]

In this view, then, racism is not generated by social structural arrangements. The dominant value orientations of an industrial society assure that people who wish to be mobile can be so. People are expected to relate to each other on the basis of universalistic rather than particularistic standards and with respect to achieved rather than ascribed characteristics. Instances in which the value orientations are not lived up to — where people are discriminated against on the basis of race — can be analyzed in one of two ways. They can be explained either in terms of poor socialization — cases in which the orientations have not been internalized — or as a reflection of incomplete social development, for example, the effects of modernization have not yet taken hold. But regardless of the explanation, racism is not the result of structural arrangements. The relationship between American institutions and racial stratification is not adequately explored.

As Robert Blauner points out, many orthodox Marxists also deny the autonomy of race and racism; they reduce race to class.[1] While recognizing that racial prejudice is a product of capitalism, most Marxists do not understand that,

> . . . *racial realities have a material basis.* They are built into the economic structure as well as the culture of all colonial societies, including those capitalist nations which developed out of conquest and imported African slaves to meet labor needs [Blauner, 1972c: 32–3, emphasis in original].

For many Marxists, prejudice is "sold" to white workers by ruling groups. It is not generated structurally; instead, it represents "false consciousness." Since racial minorities are mainly workers, they have the same interests as white workers. Racism is then a mistaken outlook. It is also a relatively temporary one for the assumption is that once white workers recognize their class interests their racism will dissipate. " . . . [T]he race prejudice of modern whites," state Baran and Sweezy, "is not only a unique but also a transi-

---

[1]This paragraph relies heavily on the unpublished ideas of Robert Blauner (1972b and c).

tory historical phenomenon" (1966: 265). Critical of this approach, the Marxist historian Eugene Genovese summarizes it in the following terms:

> Until recently, American Marxists like many others viewed racism as simply a class question. They regarded racial discrimination as a "mask for privilege" — a technique by which the ruling class exploits minorities and divides the working class [1971: 55].

The underlying theoretical assumption of orthodox Marxism, writes Blauner in a similar vein, "is that race and ethnicity are epiphenomena which only modify the form, but not the content, of the overall society and class struggle" (1972c: 31).

This voice of Marxism is not without its Marxist critics. Some Marxists emphasize the complexity involved in the relationship between racist institutions and ideology. They see interaction between values and material interests. Depending upon the historical period, racist ideology is both a consequence and a cause of racist structures. As Genovese states the relationship, "once an ideology arises it alters profoundly the material reality and in fact becomes a partially autonomous feature of that reality" (1969: 244).

Assumption: racism is an attitudinal or ideological problem

If the sources of racism are not located in structural dimensions, that is, the economic, political, and social arrangements of modern society, then it follows that its origins are in people's minds. In this regard Blauner's evaluation of Marxian treatments of race relations is applicable to most perspectives on racism: "The basic strategy has been to place prejudice, racism and ethnic loyalties into the superstructure, particularly the sphere of culture and psychology" (1972c: 10).

In fact, racism is usually studied in terms of the *attitudes* that white people hold toward minority groups. When people speak of racism they usually mean attitudes rather than institutionally generated inequality. Given this perspective, the crucial feature of race relations in America becomes the *ideas* that whites have about others; not their own superior position, the benefits following from their position, or the institutions that maintain this relationship.

The study of attitudes is obviously a legitimate area for sociological investigation. The problem, as mentioned above, is that when sociologists analyze race relations they tend to attribute causal significance to attitudinal variables, nearly precluding the effect of other factors. A recent example of this is Jack Levin's study, *The Functions of Prejudice*, in which he explicitly treats prejudice as an *independent* variable: "a causal factor that has certain consequences for society and its members" (1975: 103).

Classically, Myrdal is among the more explicit of those who assume that prejudice is the primary determinant in race relations. In his words: "the chief hindrance to improving the Negro is the white man's firm *belief* in his inferiority" (1944: 101; emphasis added). While Myrdal notes that discrimination may be rooted in the tradition of economic exploitation, he does not offer a socioeconomic explanation of prejudice: "The eager intent to explain away race prejudice and caste in simple terms of economic competition . . . is an attempt to escape from caste to class" (1944: 792). He contends that the "white man's rank order of discrimination" undercuts any structural explanation. In his estimation white people are more concerned about racial purity — as indicated by their fears of intermarriage —

than they are about competing with blacks. Thus, for Myrdal, the beliefs that whites hold about blacks are the key to explaining racial dynamics in America.

The causal significance that Myrdal attributes to racial attitudes is found in the writings of other social scientists, including some who share little else in common with him. Writing from a Marxist perspective, Oliver Cox (1959) relates prejudice to the rise of capitalism, but maintains that " . . . all racial antagonisms can be traced to the *policies* and *attitudes* of the leading capitalist people . . . " (1959: 322; emphasis added). Cox and Myrdal see different functions performed by prejudiced attitudes; but for Cox, as well as Myrdal, racial antagonisms are set in motion by racist ideas rather than institutionally generated conflict. Cox seems to assume that if people were *aware* of the motivation behind racist ideas they would cease to use them. In his words, "It is possible that most of those who propagate and defend race prejudice are not conscious of its fundamental motivation" (1959: 333).

It would be mistaken to suggest that all sociologists relegate racism to the ideological sphere. While never establishing hegemony in social science thinking, a number of sociologists have consistently opposed the notion that individual prejudiced attitudes are the determinants of racist institutions. Arnold Rose (1956), for example, argues that prejudiced attitudes have little effect on intergroup relations. To understand the process of desegregation, he contends, one must analyze legal, political, economic, and social structural facts. Raab and Lipset suggest that "the pattern of *community practices* is the fountainhead of prejudice," and they analyze America as "the Prejudiced *Society*" (1962: 48; emphasis in original). Dietrich Reitzes states the relationship between structure and attitudes nicely. "The organizational structuring of the situation," he says, "mobilizes individuals in terms of their 'interests,' and provides the individual with well formulated statements and reasons which can be used to justify his activity" (1964: 484).

Herbert Blumer has been among the foremost critics of what he calls "the prejudice-discrimination axis" (1958a). His statement of "Race Prejudice as a Sense of Group Position" is perhaps the most important perspective on racial beliefs to appear in this context (1958b). In contrast to the dominant view of prejudice as a set of feelings lodged in individuals, Blumer suggests that "race prejudice exists basically in a sense of group position rather than in a set of feelings which members of one racial group have toward the members of another racial group" (1958b: 3). Prejudice, he argues, is best understood as a relationship between racial groups, a relationship which is defined in "the process by which racial groups form images of themselves and of others" (1958b: 3). In his estimation the feelings which emerge in this process refer to the positional arrangement of racial groups in America; they reflect real concerns of people in superordinate racial positions. "The dominant group," he tells us, "is not concerned with the subordinate group as such, but it is deeply concerned with its position vis-à-vis the subordinate group. . . . The source of race prejudice lies in a felt challenge to this sense of group position" (1958b: 4–5). His conclusion: "Race prejudice becomes entrenched and tenacious to the extent the prevailing social order is rooted in the sense of group position" (1958b: 7).

Assumption: egalitarian ideals govern American attitudes

Since most people who study racist attitudes do not relate them to the structure of racial subordination, their analysis begins with ideals. They make the assumption that egalitarianism is a value that most Americans have internalized and thus it is reflected in their thinking. Attitudes toward people of color are then analyzed in terms of how closely they approximate the values contained in the American Creed. To the extent that attitudes reflect these values, they are evaluated as unprejudiced thinking. Prejudice, on the other hand, is a deviation from American ideals. As Schuman and Harding (1964) observe, it is often defined as a departure from American norms of justice.

This strategy for conceptualizing attitudes concerned with racial issues is often reflected in the kinds of questions sociologists use to measure prejudiced or unprejudiced beliefs. Consider, for example, some of the questions used in a National Opinion Research Center (NORC) survey. The questions were the basis for a Guttman scale of "prointegration sentiments" (Sheatsley, 1966: 301).

> Do you think Negroes should have as good a chance as white people to get any kind of job, or do you think white people should have the first chance at any kind of job? (Prointegration response: "As good a chance.")

> Generally speaking, do you think there should be separate sections for Negroes in street cars and buses? ("No")

> Do you think white students and Negro students should go to the same schools, or to separate schools? ("Same schools")

> White people have a right to keep Negroes out of their neighborhoods if they want to, and Negroes should respect that right. ("Disagree slightly" or "disagree strongly")

> Do you think there should be laws against marriage between Negroes and whites? ("No")

Presumably a person ranking highly on this scale is not

prejudiced. The scale then gives us some indication of what sociologists mean when they evaluate someone as being unprejudiced. Prointegration sentiments on this scale are measured essentially in terms of how closely the attitudes conform to the American Creed. The questions are really only capable of assessing the following: whether or not people verbally subscribe to certain ideals of American society; whether they feel that Supreme Court decisions are legitimate: and whether people are tolerant of the rights of minorities. Prejudice, then, is essentially sentiments that depart from American ideals as stated in the Constitution. Prointegration sentiments are synonymous with those ideals. And as we shall see, when attitudes are evaluated in terms of their closeness to ideals, the people subscribing to them are limited to certain groups — people who can afford to subscribe to them and for whom the ideals thus have some meaning.

Another assumption is evident at this point. All Americans are affected equally by racial issues. The logic runs something like the following: American ideals speak of racial equality. The ideals, moreover, are an important influence on the beliefs of Americans. As a consequence, the existence of racism (that is, attitudes expressing racial superiority) presents a challenge to the thinking of all Americans. Note that the challenge is to their belief systems, not to their socioeconomic situation. Note also that all Americans are affected in the same way by the challenge since it operates on ideological rather than structural levels. Thus the conflict set in motion by racism is ideological, not structural. The struggle over racial issues in America is not a conflict over scarce resources that affect different groups in varying ways: material interests are not what is at issue. Instead, when people disagree on racial questions they are in disagreement over ideals.

Given this logic, people who express beliefs that are not

consistent with the American Creed are evaluated as deviants. Their "deviant" attitudes, however, are not analyzed in relation to the realities of their existence. Instead they are explained in psychological terms. The assumption is that if racial issues are not a function of social arrangements, they must be the result of psychological problems. Thus the typical way of explaining racist beliefs is to look for indications that people expressing racist attitudes have psychological troubles which lead to "intolerant," "prejudiced" or "authoritatian" frames of reference. The implied assumption is that tolerant, unprejudiced, democratic world views are characteristically American.

These kinds of assumptions operate, for example, in a scale constructed by Frenkel-Brunswick for the purpose of measuring prejudice among children (1948: 295—6). Children endorsing the following kinds of beliefs were evaluated as being prejudiced.

> "There is only one right way to do anything."
>
> "If a person does not watch out somebody will make a sucker of him."
>
> "Girls should learn only things that are useful around the house."
>
> "There will always be war; it is part of human nature."

The questions used by Allport and Kramer (1946: 10--12) to measure prejudice among adults are also guided by these assumptions.

> "The world is a hazardous place in which men are basically evil and dangerous."
>
> "On the whole I am more afraid of swindlers than I am of gangsters."

Endorsements of these sentiments presumably indicate intolerant, rigid, or categorical thinking. People who subscribe to these beliefs are assumed to have weak or crip-

pled egos. Since such people also express explicitly prejudiced sentiments, there is obviously a correlation between
intolerant thinking and prejudice. This relationship is explained in the following manner: People with weak egos or
insecure personalities need to repress the complexities of
life. A crucial way in which they repress complexity is to
externalize their personal failures onto members of minority
groups.[2] Prejudice is the most obvious form that this ex-
ternalization takes.

Assumption: racism serves no rational interests

Any definition of racism based on these assumptions will
be exceedingly limited. The only kinds of beliefs that can
be considered racist are misconceived, rigid, stereotyped
kinds of thought. Racism, in other words, will be limited
to prejudice: antipathy or hostility, based on rigid and
faulty generalization about racial groups. So conceived, racism refers exclusively to imaginary conflicts, irrational
hostilities, unrealistic fears, and obsessions with racial purity. In Schuman and Harding's terms, it is measured as a
"failure of rationality" (1964: 354). The defining characteristics of racism in this conception are the same as prejudice: crude expressions of racial hostility – explicitly intolerant, hostile, ethnocentric, or authoritarian beliefs.
Viewed in this manner, racism is also evaluated like prejudice: It is neither rational nor realistic; is contrary to American values; and stands in the way of industrial-political development. In short, it is a psychological problem reflecting the individual needs of racists.[3]

For Thomas and Park, prejudice is instinctual: It reflects

[2] For other examples of this approach see: Allport, 1958: Chapters 21–25;
Lipset, 1959; Cohen and Hodges, 1963; Vander Zanden, 1965.

[3] For example, see the "sociological" account of racism presented by Kitano and Daniels, *American Racism: Exploration of the Nature of Prejudice*,
1970.

a fear of the unknown and an unwillingness to compete with people of other races. To Myrdal, it is a device that defends Americans from having to live up to their national ideals: It allows individuals to appear rational in a situation that is morally, politically, and economically irrational. It is a mechanism that psychologically papers over the "American dilemma." For personality theorists, prejudice serves to bolster the weak egos of individuals unable or unwilling to confront the real source of their frustration. As a weapon in the hands of lower-class people, prejudice simplifies a world they cannot cope with. It divides the world in terms of ascribed traits, allowing people who fear they may be judged as inferior to feel superior.

Psychological conceptions of prejudice have attracted some unlikely adherents among students of race relations. "In our sense prejudice is always irrational," wrote John Dollard, author of a study that relies heavily on the sociological variables caste and class to analyze southern race relations. "[I] f antagonism can be sufficiently explained by real, personal, or social rivalry we do not talk of 'prejudice'"(1957: 446). Even the "dean of black letters" in America, W. E. B. DuBois, a man usually associated with a distinctively sociological view of race relations, for many years felt that prejudice was essentially a psychological issue. As he tells us in his autobiography, *Dusk of Dawn*,

> My basic theory has been that race prejudice was
> primarily a matter of ignorance on the part of
> the mass of men, giving the evil and anti-social a
> chance to work their way, that when the truth was
> properly presented, the monstrous wrong of race
> hate must melt and melt quickly before it [1940:
> 282].

Not until he had observed the Russian revolution firsthand did he begin to feel that,

beyond my conception of ignorance and de-
liberate illwill as causes of race prejudice, there
must be other and stronger and more threatening
forces, forming the founding stones of race antagonisms, which we had only begun to attack or
perhaps in reality had not attacked at all [1940:
284].

DuBois was not the only sociologist to challenge psychological conceptions of prejudice. As noted above, a
number of sociologists have consistently attacked this notion. They have countered that prejudice results from community practices and reflects a sense of group position. Still
other sociologists (e.g., Roucek, 1956: 24–31; Schermerhorn, 1956: 53–6) have argued that any analysis of race
relations that ignores the question of power is incomplete.

Discussion

By and large the sociological community has disregarded
these warnings and counter-conceptualizations, with the
result that we have failed to explain the persistent, widespread nature and content of modern racism in America.
Taken together, the assumptions used by sociologists reflect a distinctly middle-class, liberal view of race relations:
Racism is not a structural characteristic, it exists mainly in
the minds of people; it is the exception, not the rule; it is a
problem that can be solved without basic institutional al-
teration of society — people's thinking can be changed,
their consciousness "raised," or we can benignly neglect
the problem.

Through these lenses the sociological portrait of racism
is photographed. These lenses - assumptions — limit our
focus. They insure that sociologists will photograph only
certain actions and actors. Many sociological conclusions

concerning racism are built into the assumptions with which we begin. Therefore, if the conclusions do not adequately or accurately depict the realities of American racism it is imperative to reexamine the assumptions in light of how they affect our vision. Let us see how these conceptual difficulties show up in the conclusions sociologists have reached about racism.

• If racism is incorrect or irrational thinking, then it must be explained in terms of the psychological traits of the people expressing it. Research based on these assumptions therefore focuses on the personality differences between prejudiced and unprejudiced people. Tolerance, for example, is assumed to be associated with certain types of personalities and social classes (Adorno et al., 1950; Allport, 1958). The proposition is advanced that there is a relationship between intolerance and prejudice. There are, however, serious limitations involved with the concept of tolerance. First, certain untested assumptions about human relations are built into it. It assumes that a rigid or harsh view of the world is unwarranted. If people hold such views this is taken to reflect more about their personalities than about the world in which they live. Their *personalities* are considered intolerant or "authoritarian." The indicators that sociologists use to measure this, however, are heavily biased by their own liberal, middle-class world view. The sociologists' point of view is imposed on social reality as if it were *the* objective reality. Deviations from this perspective are evaluated as intolerant or authoritarian. The research does not entertain the possibility that so-called authoritarian viewpoints may reflect an accurate assessment of a hostile environment rather than a hostile individual. Instead, it is presumed that such a perspective reflects intolerant personalities. In this way conclusions about intolerance and prejudice are built into research instruments.

Second, equating tolerance with the endorsement of liberal middle-class beliefs nearly precludes that   poor or working-class whites will appear "tolerant." People denied the opportunity of a liberal education will almost always, by definition, be "intolerant" or "prejudiced." It is not surprising, then, that many studies find prejudice disproportionately among poor and working-class people even though indications abound that racism is hardly so restricted. Middle-class whites are *trained* to subscribe to American ideals and to verbalize tolerance. Thus, the conclusion that unprejudiced attitudes are found mainly among middle-class Americans is inherent in the assumptions on which this research is based.[4]

Third, recent studies seriously challenge the empirical underpinnings of the alleged association between class and tolerance. Richard Hamilton (1972: 399–507) shows quite conclusively that when one separates out southerners, tolerance is not significantly related to social class; it is not the exclusive property of certain groups. The differences he finds between classes with respect to tolerance are minimal. And in five of eight comparisons he finds that nonsouthern lower-middle-class people are *more* tolerant than the upper middle class. Hamilton's findings suggest another difficulty with the concept of tolerance. On most of the items he explores, a majority or near majority of white Americans are personally "tolerant." Yet despite this tolerance, racial division stubbornly persists in America. Thus the concept does not shed much light on American race relations. Hamilton's study shows that people are not simply tolerant or intolerant; they are both, and often at the same time.

[4]The ability of middle-class people to disguise their prejudice is discussed in depth by L. A. Kahn, 1951: 1–39.

Finally, tolerance is not simply an attribute middle-class people learn; it is also a luxury they can afford. Sociological questions designed to test "ethnocentrism," "intolerance" or "prejudice" may be answered in a "tolerant" or "correct" manner because the questions are so posed that the issues raised have no direct meaning for these people. Until recently, the social rearrangements necessary to facilitate racial equality hardly affected middle-class whites. School integration, as long as busing was not involved, was a relatively costless principle to uphold. Residential desegregation was also a worthy — if unattainable — principle. On-the-job equality had an "All-American" sound to it — especially if there were very few blacks in one's occupation. Upgrading blacks from unskilled to skilled work was a fine goal if one's own work was neither unskilled nor skilled but rather white collar or professional. But as recent events indicate, when the demands of black people hit closer to home and begin to affect middle-class whites in direct ways — ways in which poor whites have always been affected — middle-class whites start sounding less tolerant and acting more like the lower-class whites who have traditionally been defined as the "source" of racism.

• Survey questions devised to assess prejudice probably measure people's distance from racial problems (Sheatsley, 1966). People who disagree with the ostensibly prejudiced statements found in questionnaires are not necessarily less ethnocentric or prejudiced or more tolerant than the people endorsing them. The case rather seems to be that they are less affected by racial issues than the others. In fact, the people scoring highest on scales purporting to measure "prointegration" sentiments are economically the most secure; they are the people least affected by policies directed at minimizing racial inequality. Thus the highest scorers on Sheatsley's prointegration scale held three features in common: They had attended college, earned $10,000 or more per year, and were professionals (1966: 312). Needless to say, these are characteristics of people who traditionally have had little at stake in racial controversies.

Black people have recently begun to make demands that directly affect this class of Americans. As a result, middle-class sentiments about such issues as busing conflict with their tolerant world view. Their commitment to tolerance and equality does not change, however. Indeed, they will still rank high on tolerance scales. However, while they may still be tolerant, they are affected as they have never been before by the demands made by black people. Consequently, liberal ideals no longer have an abstract, theoretical meaning and middle-class whites are put to a "test." They do not become "prejudiced" when they resolve the contradiction between their ideals and their realities, however. Instead, they develop ways of explaining their opposition to change *that do not explicitly contradict egalitarian ideals*. Some people say, for example, "I'm not opposed to busing; I'm opposed to the time it involves." Other people don't object much to blacks *like themselves* living "next door." By asserting egalitarianism with respect to race, they endorse inegalitarianism with respect to class and class cultures.

The significance and meaning of these kinds of expressions cannot be adequately understood as long as racism is interpreted as prejudice. Even though they may oppose busing or integrated housing they will not be prejudiced since they are not explicitly "anti-black." The consequences of their opposition, however, regardless of the justification, are the same as if the opposition was the result of prejudice. Thus the distinction between prejudiced and unprejudiced people hardly helps explain racism in America. Moreover, if elements of racism are recognized in sentiments that are strictly speaking not prejudiced, they cannot be explained by current theories. Such sentiments are not intolerant, do not depart from American ideals, and do not reflect personality problems. Many of the inconsistent and contradictory findings in research on prejudice stem from this conceptual difficulty.

• The assumption that racism is a departure from American ideals leads to another inadequacy in studies of prejudice. Some sociologists attribute prejudice to ethnocentric beliefs and stereotyped thinking (Adorno et al., 1950; Caton, 1960–1961; Swartz, 1961). This presumably explains why some people are prejudiced in a society that professes to be egalitarian. To document this approach, sociologists test people's willingness to agree with stereotyped or ethnocentric statements: If they agree, they are considered "prejudiced." The only thing this research really tells us is whether or not stereotypes exist. Stereotypic thinking is assumed to be characteristic of racist thinking, but the assumption is never tested. Thus a conclusion is built into the premises of the research: Racist thinking is stereotyped thinking. Those whites who *do not* think of blacks in these terms are considered unprejudiced regardless of the content of their beliefs. Racism expressed in nonstereotypic terms goes undetected.

• The assumption that racial divisions are based on either misperceptions or prejudgments accounts for the most serious limitations in the analysis of racism as prejudice. This assumption views the problem as psychological rather than social. It does not consider that racial groups may have different *interests* rooted in the racial organization of American society and that these interests may be reflected in people's thinking about racial issues. If "correct" perceptions are expressed in racist terms, research based on the assumption that racism is a psychological problem will be unable to detect them.

The past decade has discredited many sociological studies of prejudice. People expressing intolerant attitudes are not the only racists and their racism is not abnormal. My argument is that racism is quite characteristically American and that it can be found in different forms throughout the class structure. When racism is viewed as prejudice — as misperception — sociologists are unable either to explain its widespread character or to anticipate its persistence. Careful research may be confounded with inconsistent findings, and researchers may continue to make distinctions that have little explanatory value in modern society.

Toward an alternative perspective

There is another approach to white racism. If we view it as a culturally sanctioned, rational response to struggles over scarce resources, we can account for its widespread character and avoid the inconsistencies and meaningless distinctions that arise when it is viewed as prejudice. But to do so means dropping certain assumptions and adding others.

I view racial stratification as part of the structure of American society, much like class division.[5] Instead of being a remnant from the past, the social hierarchy based on race is a critical component in the organization of modern American society. The subordination of people of color is functional to the operation of American society as we know it and the color of one's skin is a primary determinant of people's position in the social structure. Racism is a structural relationship based on the subordination of one racial group by another. Given this perspective, the deter-

[5] This perspective is based on the writings of Robert Blauner, (1972a, b, c), as well as a body of theory beginning at least with W. E. B. DuBois and extending to Harold Cruse (1969), and Stokely Carmichael and Charles Hamilton (1967). There is also an emerging body of research that lends evidence to the perspective. See especially Baron (1969, 1971), Reich (1972), Tabb (1970), and Bloch (1969).

mining feature of race relations is not prejudice toward blacks, but rather the superior position of whites and the institutions — ideological as well as structural — which maintain it.

This is a perspective that is argued for by a growing number of sociologists who contend that racism must be studied within the context of social stratification and social conflict. While there are important differences between these scholars, each anchors race relations in social structure. Shibutani and Kwan (1965), for example, contend that majority—minority relationships need to be located in systems of social stratification. Taking his cue from them, Newman begins his examination of this relationship with "the process of ranking between groups, as well as the distribution of social resources between groups . . . " (1973: 4). Schermerhorn (1970) and van den Berghe (1967) explore how different kinds of stratification systems relate to varying group relationships. Van den Berghe analyzes the effect of social structure on social-psychological issues such as prejudice and discrimination. In contrast, Schermerhorn contends that historical variables are causally prior; that they produce different types of societies which in turn create varying group relationships. But as Newman points out: " . . . regardless of the social-psychological aspects of group interactions, these interactions are themselves a structural phenonenon. Moreover, the structural relationships . . . are dependent upon other structural characteristics of societies" (1973: 26). Still other sociologists relate racial conflict to structural issues. Blalock (1967: 109), for example, develops a theory of power and discrimination in which race relations are seen as intergroup "power contests." In a comparative study of South Africa and the United States, Wilson argues two points:

(1) that a comprehensive account of the nature of

race relations in these two societies must deal with dimensions of power and their relation to dominant- and minority-group contact and (2) that the dimensions of power cannot be completely understood if treated independently of the phenomenon of racism (1973: 5).

From this vantage point, racism can be seen to systematically provide economic, political, psychological, and social advantages for whites at the expense of blacks and other people of color.[6] In Blauner's terms racism generates unfair advantage, or privilege, to whites (1972a: 22). Given the organization of society, there are only so many resources to go around. If race is one of the basic divisions around which access to resources is determined and if institutional changes demanded by blacks are accommodated, then some groups of whites stand to lose certain advantages. The analogy of a zero-sum game is appropriate. For blacks to gain may mean whites will lose. White people thus have an interest in maintaining their position of racial advantage. The issues that divide black and white people, then, are grounded in real and material conditions. The justifications for this division, moreover, have an element of rationality to them; they are not simply manufactured reasons, misperceptions, or defenses for personality defects. In crucial ways they are ideological defenses of the interests and privileges that stem from white people's position in a structure based in part on racial inequality.

Unlike other forms of inequality, which do not necessarily deny American ideals, racial inequality needs to be justified since it contradicts publicly espoused ideals and orientations. It is an ascribed rather than "achieved" inequality. How people *explain* this situation is the heart of racist thinking.

[6]Cf. Glenn (1963, 1966), Cutright (1965), Heer (1959), Becker (1957), Thurow (1969), Blau and Duncan (1967), Siegel (1965).

Racist thinking is also dynamic, and this is reflected in its changing content. As political and economic forces move subordinate groups into new or different social positions, or if racial hegemony is challenged, the racial thinking of whites changes to accommodate these new realities. So, for example, as blacks were transformed from indentured servants into slaves, the justification for their position changed: instead of just being "different," they became somehow innately inferior. In turn, biological justifications gave way to historical ones, which later became physiological reasons (Vander Zanden, 1959). Moreover, as the Civil War dealt politically with the slavery issue, new kinds of justifications for the continued subordinate position of blacks had to be developed. In the modern context, when the civil rights movement made it apparent that legal restrictions in the South did not explain the subordinate position of black people throughout the United States, new kinds of reasons were offered. It has become commonplace for enlightened Americans to attribute the persistence of racial inequality to shortcomings in the *culture* of people of color.

Two points follow from these obervations. First, justifications for inequality change as new realities and issues emerge. An appropriate justification ten years ago may not suffice today. The issues posed by black people today are different than they were before. Thus the kinds of indicators that sociologists use to measure racism in the 1960s and '70s must reflect the issues of this period and the spirit of the times. In large part this has not happened. Sociologists who attribute racism to prejudice are often still using questions developed thirty years ago as indicators of prejudice.

The changes that have occurred in justifications of racial inequality also provide a clue to how racism might be approached. Analytically speaking, at the heart of each justification is an explanation of racial inequality, regardless of the period in which it is expressed. In each instance, the belief represents an attempt to explain or understand why black people are in a subordinate position in a society that professes egalitarianism. Many of the "explanations" place the reason for inequality with the oppressed themselves — their biology, their psyche, their culture. In most instances the responsibility for inequality is attributed to the victim. If there is a consistent theme in American racist thinking, it is this.

A word is in order about the definition of "racism" used in this book. Racism has various faces; it manifests itself to the world in different guises. Sometimes it appears as "personal prejudice" which, it is argued here, is really a disguised way to defend privilege. Other times racism is manifested ideologically. Cultural and biological reasons are used as rationalizations and justifications for the superior position of whites. Racism is also expressed institutionally in the form of systematic practices that deny and exclude blacks from access to social resources. Recognizing that racism has at least three faces, or meanings, some social scientists argue that the three need to be clearly distinguished and separately analyzed. Fredrickson (1971) and Noel (1972) contend that if we are to understand the causal relationship between racism and slavery, we must be able to distinguish between discrimination, racist ideology, and prejudice. The distinction is useful for assessing causal priorities in historical sequences. However, the everyday workings of racism are not so neatly divided. People living in a racially stratified society manifest racism in each of its guises. Sometimes we can distinguish between them; usually we cannot. The ways in which racism is manifested are so intertwined, so much a part of each other, that they are often inseparable. Each is generated by and fundamentally interrelated to the structural issue of privilege. Thus, to see how white people "do" racism in America we cannot compartmentalize their thoughts and actions; to see the full picture, the three distinct concepts need to be combined.

This book suggests that racist beliefs simultaneously include and reflect many facets of life in a racially divided society: ideological, institutional, and personal. They are ways of coping with the presence of people of color as well as explanations of shifting patterns of racial inequality. Viewed this way, we can see the dynamics of racial thinking. Racism can be seen as a changing phenomenon, reflecting the sociopolitical exigencies of race relations in specific historic periods.

White racism as a strategy for maintaining privilege

Sociologists studying racial attitudes in the twentieth century have not been completely unaware of the structural basis of racial inequality. When they have located it, however, they do so almost exclusively in southern institutions. As I have pointed out, black migration to the industrial North along with industrialization in the South were expected to eliminate the structural bases of racial inequality. Given this perspective, it was reasonable to assume that once the roots of racism were eliminated, those racist ideas that persisted would be prejudice or bigotry. Since racist ideas did not stem from structural arrangements they could not be based on "real interests." They had to be the result of misperceptions or irrationalities on the part of prejudiced people.

In fact blacks have migrated in considerable numbers to the North, and the South has to a large extent been industrialized; and yet racism, in both objective and subjective terms, persists. Sociologists who continue to interpret racist beliefs as prejudice are wedded to a nonstructural account of their persistence.

In contrast, a more structural interpretation has greater explanatory power. On the simplest level, racist attitudes persist because racial inequality persists and the beliefs reflect it. If we extend the definition of racism beyond prejudice to include sentiments that in their consequence, if not their intent, support the racial status quo, racist beliefs will not be found predominantly among America's lower classes. Rather they will be found among all Americans. From this perspective, the surprising rise of "intolerant" attitudes among previously "liberal" and middle-class whites can be seen as the result of a decrease in the number of alternatives available to them for coping with the presence and demands of black people. The historic debt has come due. White people in America can no longer ignore the problem, deny it, run away from it, or revert to old forms of suppression. At the same time, however, many demands made by black people, if implemented, could potentially involve losses of privilege to whites. How then, do white people currently explain the subordinate position of blacks and justify the advantaged position of whites?

Their alternatives for explaining the racial order are limited. It is no longer publicly acceptable to explain the racial situation in crude terms that refer to biological differences. Alternatively, to explain racial inequality in structural terms, and open the possibility that blacks are in subordinate positions through no fault of their own, implicates white people in the system of racial injustice. The issue is thus framed: what do people do when their interests are threatened and there are few acceptable and publicly legitimate ways of articulating their interests and their fears?

The concrete problem facing white people is how to come to grips with the demands made by blacks while at the same time *avoiding* the possibility of institutional change and reorganizaton that might affect them. Put another way, they must be able to explain racial inequality *without* implicating themselves. In various ways every white American must deal with the contradiction. If we view racist thinking as a way of coping with a structurally generated contradiction that is faced by all Americans, we avoid a major limitation in current perspectives: We do not build into our analysis the self-aggrandizing conclusion that racism is restricted to poor and working-class whites.

Despite some variety of formulation, most racist thinking shares a common thrust: It is an ideological stance that removes the white person as complicitor in the problem and at the same time places the responsibility for alleviating oppression with the oppressed. A classic example of contemporary racist thinking is the contention that blacks are in subordinate social positions because they lack the initiative to advance themselves. Since this kind of thinking does not call into question the system of racial priviliege, it thereby insures that it will continue. One of the consequences of this reasoning is that white racial privilege is maintained. I am arguing that racism is more effectively analyzed as a strategy for the maintenance of privilege than as prejudice. This allows what would ordinarily be considered unprejudiced thinking to be seen as an ideological justification for the continuation of racial inequality.

When racism is analyzed in this way, the demands and challenges that black people impose on the American racial order figure prominantly. White racism is often a response to and a reflection of the issues generated by black people. The focus on issues that blacks raise in white thinking also makes it possible to assess the various privileges that whites are defending and the ideological ways in which this is accomplished.

The emphasis on issues raised by blacks, rather than stereotyped attitudes toward them, makes it possible to get around the "correct profiles" or "liberal" stances that some white people have developed toward racial problems. The approach is capable of detecting racism of all kinds and forms, not just that which is expressed by people untrained in the etiquette of liberal education. It becomes possible to analyze "modern" or subtle manifestations of racism, since it avoids the built-in class bias that limits the scope of analyses that see racism as prejudice. Most white Americans experience some sort of privilege at the expense of black people; racial privilege is not restricted to the poor. Thus, in varying ways, all white Americans have formulated strategies for justifying their privileged position. Analyzing racism as a defense of privilege permits detection of it among all, not just a few, Americans.

There are undoubtedly differences in the ways in which white people cope with issues raised by blacks. The variation in their expressions is critical to the approach I am proposing. I assume that racial beliefs vary by the class position of the people expressing them; different classes experience different kinds of privileges and have different relationships to racial problems. The overall focus, however, is on what is being defended in white explanations of racial issues.

This approach converges at critical junctures with Blumer's (1958b) characterization of prejudice as a sense of group position.[7] Both perspectives suggest that racial beliefs reflect those concerns of white people that stem from their position in society. Both reject the notion that racial

[7]With Wilson (1973: 38–9), I would contend that Blumer is in fact analyzing racism rather than prejudice.

sentiments are lodged in the individual. Along with Blumer, I locate racial thinking in historical variables, in positional factors, in the process of interaction that occurs between racial groups, and in the struggles between races that shift the bases of racial identification. Each approach attempts to capture the dynamic, changing quality of race relations. However, there is an important difference. Blumer's purpose is to show that prejudice is a "collective process," a group phenomenon. He does not relate the process to a structure of reward and advantage based on race. The notion that racism is a defense of privilege highlights the relationship between the structure of race relations and the sentiments generated within its context. The concept of racial stratification is critical in my analysis. For Blumer's purposes it is not.

Translating this perspective into researchable propositions is difficult. If we are to understand white racism as a way of defending racial advantage, then we need answers to the following questions. (1) Do white people recognize the existence of racial inequality? (2) If they do, how do they cope with it? How do they explain it? (3) How do they deal with challenges to the racial order? Do the ways in which they handle challenges indicate any consciousness of interests or privileges in the system of racial stratification? In other words, what, if anything, do their explanations of the situation defend? Finally, it is crucial to know (4) if and how they justify their racial interests. The last question gets to the heart of racist thinking in the current period of American race relations.

2 From theory to research and back again – a methodological discussion

Introduction

Discussions of research methodology follow theoretical presentations with nearly the same inevitability as night follows day. One can assume with a good deal of accuracy that a sociologist will immediately turn to a methodological discussion once his or her theoretical claims have been staked. The format is standard in any "scientific" presentation. The idea is that one begins with a theory and "tests" it against the "real" world. Methodological discussions supposedly link theories to findings; they tell readers how sociologists arrived at their conclusions.

Stripped of pretense, talk about research methods is a claim to credibility. Essentially it is an attempt to persuade an audience that what a researcher says is "true." Believability is established by suggesting that if the audience does what the researcher did they will reach the same conclusions. Understandably, then, a discussion of research methods is an important one. If a researcher's methods are suspect so are the findings.

The traditional method for establishing believability in the social and behavioral sciences takes a sequential, narrative form. In the words of Schatzman and Strauss, it is a "linear series of thoughts, operations, and outcomes – beginning with a statement of the problem, followed by a description of procedural design as intention, then by a description of actual operations, and ending with an itemization and discussion of findings" (1973: 142). Descriptions of the research process are also linear or sequential. Theory is described first, hypothesis formulation next, after that sampling, then data gathering, and finally the analysis of data is presented. The idea is that if an audience follows these steps, in this order, their conclusions about some evidence will mirror the researcher's. Thus the researcher is believable.

Establishing credibility in this manner rests on a number of assumptions. (1) Theory always precedes research; research merely tests the ideas with which one begins. (2) The research act is a linear one — moving sequentially from the general to the specific, from theoretical propositions to empirically tested findings. (3) The doing of research and the writing of it are indistinguishable; they are two sides of the same coin. The research act supposedly duplicates the linear, sequential form in which findings are communicated.

Sometimes these assumptions are valid and sometimes they are not. But an audience rarely knows for sure which is true because, regardless of the actual sequence, sociologists traditionally present studies *as if* these assumptions were valid; as if this was the actual sequence of events.

Were I to stake a claim on truth in this way I would probably make the following points. I would start with a statement about how the ideas in the preceding chapter were transformed into testable hypotheses. Then I would describe how the hypotheses were operationalized. Next I would discuss the basis on which a representative sample was drawn in order to test the hypotheses. After that I would detail the data-gathering process. And finally I would outline the way in which the data were analyzed.

The remainder of the study would hopefully show that the ideas presented in Chapter 1 were not contradicted by the data; having been empirically tested, they proved tenable. My claim that they were valid would be believable since anyone could duplicate the process I went through to test the ideas.

Few people would reach my conclusions if they repeated these procedures, however. That is not what happened.

As most researchers know, but seldom state publicly, the linear, narrative way in which research is presented is very rarely matched by the research act itself. Writing up research and doing it are two essentially dissimilar activities with differing forms of organization and sequence.[1]

The research act occurs mainly in the process of *inquiry*. Sometimes the process is straightforward and linear. I suspect, however, that often it is not. Thoroughgoing inquiry moves in many directions, backward as well as forward, often at the same time. Important discoveries are sometimes chanced upon through unanticipated, nonlinear kinds of probes.[2]

Research writing, on the other hand, is mainly a process of *communication*. The linear narrative form is useful in this process because, as Schatzman and Strauss point out, "it provides order and parsimony: it identifies problem, method and findings conveniently and provides a form for creating the credibility of a linear, logical, and causal relation among them" (1973: 143).

Potentially, then, there is a discrepancy between the actual process of inquiry and the traditional formats for presenting it. The "context of discovery" differs greatly from the "context of justification" (Hammond, 1964: 3). Com-

---

[1] My argument is similar to the one made by A. Kaplan (1964) regarding "reconstructed logic."

[2] For example, see Merton's discussion of the serendipity pattern (1961: 103–8).

municating the research process takes a linear form, but the research process itself does not always proceed in this manner. Yet to receive the designation "scientific," research usually is presented as though it occurred in a linear fashion — this being a major dictate of the natural science model that many sociologists currently subscribe to for establishing proof and predictability. This accounts for the potential conflict between acts of inquiry and acts of writing in sociological research. Traditionally sociologists have ignored this conflict or have collapsed the two acts into one, proceeding as if they were the same.[3]

I shall follow a different strategy. In this chapter I will reconstruct the process of inquiry as I remember it — not as selected events ordered sequentially, as if they fit a linear model for scientific proof, but as I recall the process. My claims for validity and believability will then have to be made on grounds other than purely scientific ones.

This chapter sets the stage for subsequent ones, linking them with the theoretical issues raised in Chapter 1. The sequence in which these chapters appear is misleading, however. It looks as though I began with the issues raised in Chapter 1 and moved into the field to "test" them. But things did not work out so simply. In effect, the chronology of chapters testifies more to the power of tradition than the actual sequence of events. The ideas contained in this study are the result of interaction between theory and research. The interaction, moreover, was not linear from theory to research, as is suggested by the order of these chapters. In fact, a more accurate representation of this study might *start* with the research process and then move

---

[3] An important exception to this tradition is Phillip Hammond's collection of essays by prominent American sociologists, *Sociologists at Work*. In these essays the actual process of doing research is detailed. Interestingly enough, these accounts were written *after* the research had already been published and under separate cover.

to the theoretical issues. That was the actual chronology. But that gets me ahead of the story.

Organizing a research project: original
interests and intentions

People make decisions to participate in research projects for all sorts of reasons: some intellectual, some not. In the spring of 1967 Professor Robert Blauner asked me to be research coordinator for a project funded by the National Institute for Mental Health (NIMH). He had been given a grant to study manhood orientations in ethnic communities with a special concern for black men, and he needed someone to facilitate and oversee the fieldwork.

The decision to accept was easy. I had taken courses with him and was excited by his work; I also had a strong interest in race relations, having written a master's thesis on black leadership in San Francisco. During the previous two years we had worked together on projects preparatory to the grant and had established a rather close intellectual as well as personal relationship.

The future was also decisive in my decision. While I was about to take my Ph.D. qualifying examinations, I had no specific thesis topic. Blauner pointed out that a topic would likely evolve from the research and assured me a free hand in the use of data. He was flexible about the research and expected me to contribute to its direction. The position was also attractive because it provided a full-time salary that was well above my graduate student subsistence level at that time.

The project was titled, "Manhood Orientations and the American Race Problem." The title reflected Blauner's original research objectives. At the time he was impressed by the importance of what he termed "manhood issues" for understanding racism and the social position of blacks in American society. Initially his theoretical approach to the low status of black people focused on cultural and social determinants within the group. His ideas paralleled other sociologists' attempts to explain the relative mobility of various ethnic groups in terms of their distinctive group characteristics. He was struck by indications of strong tensions between men and women in the black community and by a variety of data that suggested that the women tended to be relatively more resourceful, assertive, and perhaps "less damaged" by the legacies of slavery and discrimination. One of his early hypotheses was that black lower-class society had innovated a concept of manhood — a street or hustling ideal —which, while viable as a survival technique, actually functioned to impede the integration and success of individuals and — by aggregation — the group as a whole into the larger society. The research design called mainly for interviews with black men. Some black women and white people were also to be interviewed, but basically for purposes of "control" or comparison.

My tasks as research coordinator were diverse. Our first priority was to select a research staff. Because we wanted our data to capture the lived experience of ordinary people, we had to deviate from conventional notions of an appropriate research staff. Science is usually restricted to "experts" who are traditionally selected by "objective" criteria: formal education, degrees, research experience. These criteria often effectively exclude people of color from actively participating in studies of their own communities.

We decided to consider as "experts" those who had lived the lives we wanted to understand. Thus in selecting the original staff, degrees and research experience were hardly considered. Of the five black research assistants in a group of seven, only one had a university degree, and three had no association with any college or university. More pertinent to us were their ties to diverse segments of the black community. The five field-workers and interviewers included a working longshoreman, a community worker in the schools, a Bohemian-oriented part-time musician, a southern-born civil rights veteran, and a graduate student from a middle-class Berkeley background, the one woman in the group. Their informal education had included such schools as street hustling, new careers programs, other poverty programs, civil rights activism, and nationalist movements. What impressed us about this original staff was their ability to talk about sensitive issues, to draw people out, and to understand the feelings of a variety of sectors of the black community. The one white research assistant, a graduate student, had similar capabilities.

My next task was to train the staff in the art of sociological research. Training a conventional research team is not easy. The problems are magnified in a group with minimal exposure to sociological thinking. The problem was compounded by a commitment to use the assistants in conceptualizing problems as well as for data collection. I organized weekly seminars which were also attended by other social scientists interested in race relations. These seminars provided a structure both for training and for generating intellectual contributions from the staff.

The seminars began with discussions on the aims and ideas of the project, and served a number of purposes. They allowed the staff to participate actively in the ongoing development of the study and they dealt with specific issues of data collection — staff members shared with each other the various problems faced in their work. We also related current issues to our emerging framework. Although time-consuming, and often frustrating, the weekly seminars were successful. Besides developing a certain collective spirit, they served to formulate and reformulate the basic assumptions and concepts underlying our research.

They gave all of us a better grasp of the complexities surrounding race in America.[4]

Research strategy

Once people were in the field, my responsibilities shifted, ranging from straw boss, administrator, and quality controller to confidant, interviewer, and mediator. I also began trying to make sense of the three kinds of data we were collecting. We were observing institutional situations which we thought shaped the character of life in the black community — courts, welfare agencies, occupational experiences. We were also conducting in-depth, relatively unstructured interviews and group discussions involving from three to five people. There were two stages to our research strategy: first we led group discussions, and then we conducted individual interviews with the people participating in the group sessions. We hoped the observations would enrich our interviews as well as provide new insights.

Group discussions

Our goal was to hold approximately seventy meetings of informal and formal groups at which discussions would be directed toward the meaning of manhood and racial conflict in the current period. The groups were selected to represent a range of ethnic, sex, age, class, and political-religious orientations. The groups included members of Kiwanis Clubs, labor unions, church organizations, political organizations, student groups, and youthful countercommunities. In order to maximize rapport, we suggested that the staff establish contact with leaders of these groups — or with trusted figures in them — and explain the aims of

---

[4] For a more detailed discussion of this aspect of the research project see Blauner and Wellman, 1973.

the study in general terms. We then asked these people to arrange group discussions for us.

The format for the group discussions was a rather loose one. We wanted the direction of the meeting to be influenced by the special concerns of its members, by the natural climate of the group, and by the rapport developed between the group and the researcher-discussion leader. The meetings were to begin with a frank and thorough explanation of the study. To insure a basis for comparison between the groups, some standard opening questions were prepared. The form of discussion "openers" varied according to the composition of the group, but all began with a question designed to elicit people's feelings about which racial issues were crucial and what might be their causes. A number of questions were also formulated to facilitate shifts in focus.

Group discussions were selected as an important data-gathering technique because of their potential to stimulate spontaneously frank and heated talk about the problems of manhood and race relations. The group meetings were to serve a number of functions. They would act first of all as "icebreakers." We felt that touchy questions could best be raised in a group context — that the collective support of a group would give its members a greater sense of confidence than if they were facing an interviewer alone. We were aware of the possibility that in the highly charged racial climate of the late 1960s, group meetings might encourage hostile, and even demagogic responses rather than the kind of critical soul searching that we sought. We felt, however, that the exposure of these views would clear the way for participants to move to other aspects of the problem. The heated airing of opinions could provide other advantages as well. The format would encourage a variety of responses to issues. Group members would be forced to confront and disagree with each other and be able to ap-

proach issues without being overly concerned with researcher reactions.

We also felt that group discussions would provide our
researchers with an opportunity to establish trust with
group members and an identity as someone who could be
spoken to in a frank manner. The discussion leader would
then be able to ask members of the group for individual interviews in which the issues raised during the discussion
could be pursued in greater depth and in a more private
setting.

In-depth interviews

We intended to collect most of the data from in-depth interviews; our goal was to obtain 200 of them. Since we
wanted to capture the dynamics and subtleties as well as
the meaning of racial experiences and manhood orientations, we designed the interviews to be as open-ended as
possible. We developed an interview guide rather than an
interview schedule and organized the guide around people's
life histories.[5]

In-depth interviews were chosen because they seemed
best suited to the exploratory character of the research
and the sensitive nature of its content. We felt that such
variables as "manhood orientation" were not sufficiently
developed to permit the use of precision instruments normally associated with the multivariate analysis of survey
designs. We wanted a different kind of research situation:
one which allowed us to explore the meanings of people's
ideas. We felt that in-depth interviews that were open-ended
and spontaneous would facilitate our purpose.

To encourage spontaneity and looseness we conducted
the interviews with tape recorders and transcribed them later. The tape recorders permitted interviewers to participate — to exchange ideas with the respondents. The inter-

[5] A duplicate of the guide is contained in an appendix.

views themselves were also set up to promote looseness. They were organized around people's life histories — their experiences with such major institutions in American society as family, school, work, police, politics, and welfare. We hoped to be flexible — to get inside the person and come out with a sociological portrait in his or her own words. Our idea was that ultimately the portrait would explicate the person's life — their racial experiences and attitudes, their manhood orientations.

Sample

A word is in order concerning the manner in which we selected a sample. One may wonder why we did not use a traditional household survey, based on a systematic random-sampling design. We felt the area of manhood as cultural orientation and as social variable was not sufficiently developed for a highly systematic research design. We were not ready for precision instruments or precise questions. We felt that what was needed was preliminary knowledge about the broad contours of the problem. We were comfortable with the fact that the study's generalizations and comparisons would be suggestive rather than final or definitive.

We were satisfied with a nonprobability sample for other reasons as well. A probability sample insures that each person in a given population has a specified chance to be interviewed. Random procedures guard against the introduction of a systematic bias into the research design. Our interviews were based on a purposive sample. While not random, the sample was stratified to represent diversity in class, age, sex, and religion. Although each person in the population obviously did not have a specified chance to be interviewed, the stratified sample did prevent us from speaking with only one type of person.

There was still another reason for not employing a systematic survey-sampling procedure. The issues with which we were concerned were personally sensitive. We felt it was unrealistic to expect people to discuss these issues frankly when confronted "cold" through door-to-door canvassing. This is why the initial setting for data collection was organized on the basis of personal contacts in specific organizations. We also felt that the growing gap between academic researchers and the people whom they research could be narrowed if the research process was designed not as disinterested social census-taking but rather to facilitate humanly meaningful encounters between university intellectuals and nonacademic communities. The group situation and in-depth interviews permitted a more reciprocal exchange in the research process as contrasted with the more one-sided interaction of conventional polling.

The data "talk back"

Our initial experiences in the field forced us immediately to come to grips with the theoretical orientation guiding the research. Manhood issues in the black community were not nearly so salient as we had anticipated. Respondents were willing to talk about these issues but they sometimes had to be prodded. The topic did not arise spontaneously as we had expected it would. People seemed more concerned with racism, power, and privilege. Some of our staff members had argued that this would be the case, and the situation seemed to validate their claims. As people who knew racial oppression from firsthand experience, they had been insisting that we look more closely at the realities of race rather than manhood. It became imperative that we revise and clarify our theoretical position.

The controversy surrounding the "Moynihan Report" (Moynihan, 1965) was still raging at this time. His perspective overlapped with our own in many ways, though there were significant differences. The critical responses to this report from the black community and its scholars, as well as from white social scientists, were important "inputs" for the clarification of our theoretical position. The emergence of the black power perspective, as well as our continuous involvement with groups and individuals in the ghetto, also helped sharpen our awareness of the complex theoretical and political issues of contemporary racism.

We decided that such questions as manhood and male—female relations could not be isolated from the larger structural pattern of racial domination. To pursue the problem from our initial perspective, no matter how sophisticated and sensitive our research, would have clear theoretical and political consequences. As Moynihan must now know, *emphasis* is not just a matter of style; it has substantive implications. Our original research emphasis had implied a denial of the historical and contemporary power of racism, power, and privilege as first causes of our racial arrangements.

We therefore shifted our project's focus, giving primary consideration to racism and institutional conflict, and reformulating within this larger context our concerns with manhood and culture. We enlarged our concerns to deal with the interaction between minority individuals and the social institutions that shape their views of themselves and their possibilities in the larger society. We sought to uncover subcultural and social-psychological mechanisms developed by minority group members to protect their self-dignity and manhood.

We decided to retain our techniques for collecting data, and continued to conduct group discussions and in-depth interviews. White respondents, however, acquired a new significance for the study: They were no longer a "control" group; instead they were key participants in the racial mosaic we wanted to piece together. The interaction between black people and American institutions involves white people, and we needed to understand how whites felt they fit into the picture.

We now had a dual purpose in interviewing white people. First, we needed to know about the white person's life, experience, and attitudes toward the world, because these are the majority Americans who live in and maintain the culture and the social system in which racial conflict and change takes place. We needed to know about their experiences with institutions, their attitudes toward work, and their conceptions of manhood and self in order to have a reference point for ethnic comparisons.

The second purpose in interviewing white people was to study racism from the perspective of the dominant racial group. We wanted to know how whites viewed the racial conflict of our times; how they saw black people and other minorities as relevant or irrelevant to their lives and concerns; on what issues they were prepared to move and change, and on what issues to resist. We wanted to find out about both the objective ways in which various whites were implicated in racism and the black presence, and their subjective perceptions of these realities. We wanted to know whether the old stereotypes that made up the ideological content of racism in the past remained and with whom, or whether they were being replaced by new and more sophisticated rationalizations, or perhaps even by a willingness to reconsider basic assumptions.

The project was modified. We added new questions to the interview guide, we hired additional white research assistants, and we sought more interviews with white people.

What does it all mean?

Developing interpretations

We conducted interviews and group discussions intensively for almost two years. The majority of interviews (200)

were done with black people; but we also had 100 interviews with whites. We completed 70 group discussions — 50
with black groups and 20 with whites. The process of making sense of the data occurred continuously throughout
the field experience, but at the end of two years the time
had come to determine just what we were finding — to
consolidate our thoughts and communicate them in some
systematic fashion.

The idea of single-handedly tackling all the material we
had collected seemed impossible. I had neither the compe-
tence nor the desire. It was a task for more than one person, ideally involving a black as well as a white sociological
perspective. I decided to limit my analytical energies to the
white respondents.

I approached the white interviews with notions that
were rather traditional, somewhat vague, and perhaps un-
sophisticated. I wanted to explore some of the ways white
Americans contribute to and perpetuate racist relationships. I was especially interested in how they might be "in-
voluntarily" implicated in the racial system. I wanted to
know how salient racial issues were for white people, what
were their interpretations of racial conflict, and what was
their racial world view. I assumed white people differed
among themselves on these questions and that the differences were probably attributable to various kinds and degrees of prejudice or authoritarianism. I did not have very
high hopes about the theoretical contribution my study
would make — it seemed rather standard. If it had a
unique contribution to offer, it would probably come
from the data. I felt the in-depth interviews would put
some flesh on what I considered analytical bones.

The interviews provided plenty of flesh, but I had to
create the bones. Try though I might, I was unable to
make sense of them using explanations involving the notion of prejudice. This realization became more apparent
each time I reread the interviews. The respondents simply

refused to fall into categories based on theories of prejudice; people did not think the way one would expect based on the research about prejudice. Many working-class people expressed a sophisticated understanding of racial problems. Others appeared quite "prejudiced" on some matters but promptly contradicted that label when confronted with different issues. Many middle-class people appeared to be amazingly "prejudiced," albeit in socially acceptable terms. Young people, college students as well as counterculture participants, hardly seemed to be the vanguard of an unprejudiced society.

If just a few people had presented themselves in this way, I could have written them off as anomalies and continued to work within the prejudice framework. But the phenomenon was too widespread for that strategy. Refining the concept of prejudice did not make sense either. Prejudice simply did not capture what these people were about. Their thinking did not characteristically seem to result from preconceived ideas, prejudgments, or systematic misrepresentations of facts. It was more rational than that. The majority of people were consistently open to certain kinds of behavior from black people and closed to others. Their "openness" or "closedness," moreover, seemed to be related to interests they were defending rather than prejudice.

Blauner was refining his ideas about colonialism while I mulled over the white interviews. The notion that colonial systems generate privilege — unfair advantage or a systematic head start — for colonizing groups was emerging as a central theme in his thinking. He argued that white people benefit from the racial organization of colonial societies; wittingly or unwittingly they benefit from racial privilege. Without realizing it, Blauner provided me with a clue for decoding the interviews. Maybe the respondents were defending privileges, I thought. Perhaps their positions on racial issues could be explained in terms of the privileges they thought were involved. I wondered if they were open on certain issues because they saw no challenge to privilege and closed on others because they did. I reread the interviews again, now with this idea in mind.

The new approach fit well. It helped me understand why people I thought would be "prejudiced" were not, and why people I expected to be "tolerant" were barely so. I was also beginning to understand why I found contradictory sentiments within the same person. The perspective made sense: It seemed to accurately reflect what our respondents were feeling and it clarified issues that previously appeared inexplicable. I became convinced that what I heard in the interviews could not be analyzed as prejudice; it made more sense to analyze it as strategies for maintaining privilege.

Why, I wondered, had sociologists always analyzed racial thinking as prejudice? What kinds of assumptions pushed them in this direction? Had they always analyzed racial thinking in this manner? My wondering led me away from the interviews and into the library. During the next six months, I found that with a few notable exceptions they had — all the way back to the so-called founding fathers of American sociology. In 250 pages I described how, regardless of their political or sociological orientations, sociologists typically analyzed racial beliefs as prejudice. That is how Chapter 1 came to be; it is an extremely condensed version of that intellectual voyage.

Important as that inquiry was, however, it did not interpret the interviews. It did give me insights into why most sociologists had not and could not interpret racial beliefs as defenses of privilege. It also helped me develop a number of dimensions for figuring out the ways privilege is defended — some of which also appear in Chapter 1 — but it did not automatically suggest a way to present evidence bearing on the issues raised in the chapter. That had to be worked out separately.

Bringing evidence to bear . . .

My original analysis of the interviews was very traditional, mechanical, and had all the trappings of "science." It proceeded in four stages. Since I wanted to explore how racial beliefs varied throughout the class structure, I first sorted the interviews into three rough categories: working class, middle class, and young people. Next I had to show that people were aware of racial inequality. I could not very well argue that racial beliefs were rational unless I could first show that people were conscious of the social arrangements that generated the privileges I assumed they were defending. So I separated those respondents who indicated that they recognized or were aware of racial inequality from those who did not. Better than 80 percent of them did. I distinguished between the various ways in which people recognized racial inequality, counted them up, and pointed out how they were grouped within each social class. My third task was to show how the people who recognized racial inequality explained it; the assumption being that in America if someone recognized inequality they would be forced to explain or come to grips with it since the situation departed so radically from publicly espoused ideals. I counted the different kinds of explanations people offered and showed how they were related to class position. I also indicated that the ways in which people recognized racial inequality were related to their explanations of it. The final operation was to show that people who recognized inequality not only explained it but justified it as well — and justified it in rational, culturally sanctioned ways. I argued that the justifications were essentially defenses of privilege, not prejudice, and were related to specific racial interests stemming from their class situation. I demonstrated this by counting the various justifications, relating them to explanations of inequality, and indicating that the justifications tended to vary by social class.

The outcome was 200 pages of boring, alienating analysis. It sounded flat and it was flat. It sounded uninteresting and it was. But there was a more serious limitation: While it paid lip service to what Herbert Blumer calls "scientific protocol" (1969: Chapter 1), it was dishonest. The data were not collected for a semiquantitative analysis, and the qualitative nature of those data seemed to resist that kind of treatment. Perhaps that is why I felt so alienated and why my writing reflected that estrangement.

There was yet another drawback to the analysis: It did not do justice to the sources of the data — the people with whom we had worked. It flattened them out and forced them into categories that were part of my vocabulary, not theirs. We had collected qualitative data to allow people to speak for themselves, rather than to respond to our preconceived ideas. My analysis subverted that potentiality. Treating qualitative data as if they were quantitative did not work. The respondents' ideas and my interpretations of them came across as trivial, obvious.

The analysis was a failure. I could "prove" my points — the only problem was they did not ring true. They did not resonate with what I was hearing from the respondents and what I wanted to say about them. What I was writing did not accurately represent what I had encountered in the interviews.

If at first you don't succeed . . .

The question of how sociologists accurately represent the data with which they work runs up against the problem of establishing validity or believability. Scientific protocol suggests that believability is established through adherence to specific "methods" for manipulating data; however, the issue of whether or not these methods lend themselves to an accurate picture of the phenomenon is sometimes ignored. Sociologists sometimes seem more concerned about the elegance of their methods than the accuracy of the sociological portraits they paint. On the other hand, one ignores methodological rigor only at considerable peril. The price people sometimes pay is the validity and generalizability of their study.

The dialectic between methodological respectability and sociological accuracy weighed heavily on me as I grappled with new ways to present evidence bearing on the theoretical issues I wanted to raise. Try as I might, approaches that leaned toward methodological orthodoxy continually got in the way of accurately depicting both the people we had spoken with and the genesis of my ideas. I decided, with great encouragement from Robert Blauner, to give up any pretenses at maintaining scientific protocol and be as faithful as possible to the interviews, which after all were the source of my ideas in the first place.

Character portraits

I felt that if respondents could speak for themselves as much as possible, this would be an effective way to present the idea that racial beliefs are rational explanations of inequality. It would accurately depict the data upon which my ideas were based, and it would be much more interesting than the semiquantitative approach I had tried. There was some precedent for this procedure. I was encouraged and impressed with the works of Robert Coles (1971) and Richard Sennett and Jonathan Cobb (1972). These authors presented their ideas through the words of the people they studied; to a great extent respondents spoke for themselves. My adopting this approach was not without problems. Coles and Sennett and Cobb had conducted extended interviews; mine were one-shot affairs. The only way I could allow 107 people to speak for themselves was to develop categories and have people speak through them. This strategy, of course, would generate the very problems I wanted to avoid. I, therefore, chose to work with only a portion of the sample and to develop those interviews in depth: these would be "sociohistories" or "character portraits."

The point of this approach is to project holistic and faithful pictures of respondents, to permit the reader to see whole, complex persons. The complex life-fabrics that create these pictures contain respondents' histories; the important experiences that have affected them; their ambivalences and contradictions; their hopes and joys; their concerns — in short, the forces working in their lives. The assumption behind this approach is that if the reader can see the totality within which people operate — which of course *is* the person — the reader can then understand the rationale or logic that is reflected in their racial beliefs.

This approach, quite obviously, does not completely allow respondents to speak for themselves. The respondents did not write the character portraits; I did. They did not organize the writing, or highlight certain issues; I did. They did not ask the questions on which the portraits are based; the study did. And to insure the anonymity we promised, I have changed people's names. Thus there is a great deal of me in each of the portraits. I have, however, tried to make explicit in each where the respondent ends and I begin. I clearly demarcate their ideas from mine as well as the ideas they spoke of spontaneously from those that we provoked. Each portrait begins with a "prologue" which introduces the interviewer, the respondent, and the situation; each ends with an "epilogue" in which I discuss what I consider important about the person. In between is the most complete picture I am able to construct of the respondent as a dynamic, whole, real person.

The interviews on which I decided to base the portraits were chosen according to certain criteria. I wanted interviews that lent themselves to this kind of presentation. I looked for more complete interviews — some had been done rather sketchily and did not contain enough material to fully develop the person. I looked for interviews that reflected the variability of racial beliefs along class, age, and sex lines. But primarily I looked for interviews that reflected the range of racial beliefs expressed by our respondents. The following chapters represent five different ways in which white people defend racial privilege: they are not the only defenses possible, they are simply some of the more obvious ones.

A note on methodological orthodoxy

Some people may quarrel with this approach to data. There are those who will say it is neither scientific nor sociological; valid nor reliable. This approach does have its limitations and so do the data. I am painfully aware of the problems. The sample is not a random one. The people with whom we spoke all reside in California. I did not do all the interviews myself. We only interviewed respondents once. Thus there is the possibility that the views they expressed were colored by where they were in their thinking that day, or by the particular events of that week.

There is another problem. While these were some of our best interviews and most interesting people, every interview had some unfortunate aspect. Some interviewers asked only certain questions; others did not follow up on ambiguities; still others left out entire areas for questioning. This makes it difficult to compare the five people with one another. I do not know how much the flow of an interview was determined by the direction in which it began, the interests of the interviewer, or what. These are real restraints on my conclusions; generalizations will have to be offered cautiously.

The period in which the study took place was unique, which undoubtedly affected people's sentiments. The years between 1967 and 1970 were supercharged times. Dramatic events occurred with surprising regularity. It was an intense, exciting period in American history. Race relations were hardly normal. I do not consider this a liability; in fact, the uniqueness of the period may have been an asset. People were talking quite openly about their feelings. Racial issues figured rather prominently among people's concerns. Sentiments which in the past may have been discussed only in private were open to public debate. Thus we could hear some rather frank and candid assessments of the situation as well as people's feelings about them.

Some people will question the validity of a study based on five interviews. They will ask, how can you say anything meaningful on that basis? My answer is that this study is not based on five interviews, it is based on 107. My ability to make sense of the five interviews, to bring them alive, absolutely depended on absorbing the other 102 interviews, thinking about them, and analyzing them. The five people in this study are both unique and representative. They were neither chosen nor analyzed in a vacuum. My decision to choose these five people could not have been made had I not interacted with the other people in the sample. I would not have known what made them unique or representative. The issues these five people raise and the ways in which they raise them would have fallen on deaf ears had I not read the other interviews. As I read all of them over and over and over again I began to hear certain themes. Once I heard them and they began to ring true, I looked for interviews that best captured them. This is why I say the study is based on a sample of 107 interviews. The five people I have chosen to write about are the medium through which I can most effectively convey the feelings, concerns, and beliefs of all the white people with whom we spoke.

Nevertheless, many people will challenge this approach on the grounds that it is not scientific. They will say there is little basis for assessing either its validity or reliability. As I have argued above, the scientific model is essentially a method for establishing proof, predictability, and believability.

First a disclaimer. I do not think proof is established by a particular method or set of data. Whether or not proof is established — or someone is convinced about the correctness of a theory — depends more on whether people accept the assumptions underlying a theory than on the data used to document it. If someone rejects the assumptions upon which a theory is based, no amount of scientific manipulation of data will convince them that the theory is correct. My assumptions are stated in Chapter 1. If I have argued them convincingly and if the following character portraits ring "true" or resonate with the reader, I will feel that my points are proven. Robert Coles captures my sentiments nicely. He says about his own work:

> Once upon a time . . . I desperately wanted to make
> sure that I was doing the respectable and approved
> thing, the most "scientific" thing possible; and
> now I have learned, chiefly I believe from these
> people in this book, that it is enough of a challenge
> to spend some years with them and come out of it
> all with some observations and considerations that
> keep coming up, over and over again — until, I
> swear, they seem to have the ring of truth to them.
> I do not know how that ring will sound to others,

but its sound after a while gets to be distinct and unforgettable to me [1971, vol. 2: 42].

Another disclaimer. I am not interested in being able to predict human behavior. Achieving that goal rests on certain assumptions about human beings to which I do not subscribe. Therefore I do not intend to make predictions about human group life. My task is different; it is one that Coles describes when he introduces his work. It is " . . . to convey not only *what is* (itself rather a daunting task) but how men and women and children, *who are*, deal with the things of this world, the 'reality' or 'environment' one hears so many psychiatrists talk about" (1971, vol. 2: 25).

Enough disclaimers and defensiveness; there is sociological precedent for the task. It is found within the "sociological imagination" described by C. Wright Mills. The task for people guided by this quality of mind is to "grasp the interplay of man and society, of biography and history, of self and world" (Mills, 1961: 4). Their purpose is to understand the meaning of historical issues for the "inner life" of individuals; to account for the ways in which people become aware of their social position; to seek within these forces the framework of society. Recognizing a promise within the task, Mills felt that individuals could understand personal experience only through awareness of people located in similar historical and sociological circumstances. The task and promise of the sociological imagination, then, is to "grasp history and biography and the relations between the two within society" (1961: 6).

The character portraits or sociohistories that comprise this study accomplish the union of sociology and lived history that Mills insisted was necessary to locate "the intersections of biography and history within society" (1961: 7). This approach has been used quite successfully in certain research traditions. What I am calling "sociohistory" is a variant of the case study or life history approach; a method with a long tradition in American sociology. As far back as the 1930s, sociologists influenced by Robert Park and Ernest Burgess at the University of Chicago have relied heavily on this approach. Using archival records, autobiographies, diaries, letters, and extended interviews, these sociologists presented "the experiences and definitions held by one person, one group, or one organization as this person, group, or organization interprets those experiences" (Denzin, 1970: 228). People involved with this method have generated theory on topics ranging from criminal behavior (Lemert, 1958; Shaw, 1966; Sutherland, 1937) to immigrant life (Thomas and Znaniecki, 1927), religious cults (Garfinkel, 1967; Lofland, 1966) to suicide (Douglas, 1967; Jacobs, 1967).

The character portraits on which this study is based are also in the same family as the biographical approach in history and psychology. The union of history and sociology is duplicated in psychology. Sometimes called "psychohistory," this approach begins with the recognition that "psychological man lives in a history extending beyond himself, and that history is bound up with conflicts and struggles within the minds of men" (Lifton, 1974: 24). In some instances the focus is on individuals, or "great men in history"; notable examples are Erikson's studies of Luther and Gandhi and Freud's study of Moses. Other times the focus is on collective psychological struggles which Lifton calls "shared psychohistorical themes" (1974). The work of Keniston (1965, 1968), Coles (1971) and Lifton (1967, 1961) are exemplary in this tradition. Regardless of the focus, people doing psychohistory are engaged in a common project: By studying individuals and groups of individuals who share, in Erikson's words, "a grim willingness to do the dirty work of their ages" (Lifton, 1974: 28), they are trying to discern the meaning of historical epochs.

While I do not share the theoretical orientation of psychohistory, the research techniques employed by psychohistorians often overlap with my own. Like the character portraits or sociohistories in this study, in-depth interviews, life histories, and group discussions that approach a dialogue between the researchers and the researched are critical aspects of psychohistorical research. Lifton describes his method in terms that are appropriate for mine: It is, he says, partly empirical, partly phenomenological, and partly speculative (Lifton, 1974: 32).

A number of methodological observations arise from psychohistorical and case-study research. They have bearing on the legitimacy of my approach. Neither approach is particularly concerned with sample size. In some instances the sample is relatively large, often it is small, and occasionally it is a single case. At some points the sample is random, in other situations it is not. The adequacy of a sample is a function of the questions being researched rather than predetermined criteria. Both approaches are capable of generating theory. Research done within these traditions need not be restricted to the exploratory or descriptive type. The works of Lemert, Shaw, and Sutherland in sociology and Erikson, Lifton, and Keniston in psychology are testimony to this proposition. Not only does this kind of research lend itself to theorizing, but according to some people life-history data are "at least as valid and reliable as structured survey data" (Denzin, 1970: 256). This also was the conclusion of Cavan et al. (1930), following their review of twenty-two studies based on life-history material. Research conducted in these traditions suggests that it is possible to understand social issues by focusing on individuals and finding the general in the particular. These methods also suggest that, as Denzin points out, "it is possible to discover propositions that pertain to a total population by the use of a single or small set of life histories" (1970: 239).

These then are some of the grounds upon which my approach can be defended. They suggest that there are reasonable rationales and traditions for the methods I employ.

The approach can be defended on other grounds as well. It contains an element of sociological "reliability." We did ask clusters of standard questions and if there are people who wish to duplicate or replicate the study their purposes will be served by these questions. I must point out, however, that simply re-asking these questions will neither prove nor disprove my conclusions; replication will not make me any more or any less believable. None of these issues can be settled outside the context of my theory.

Despite these arguments, some people will find my approach "unsociological." It may be "legitimate," they will argue, but it is more appropriate for psychology than sociology. Whether or not one accepts this approach as sociological, of course, depends on one's assumptions about the nature of sociology. There are three sociological premises upon which my approach is based; they are stated succinctly by Herbert Blumer. (1) " . . . human beings act toward things on the basis of the meanings that the things have for them"; (2) " . . . the meaning of such things is derived from, or arises out of, the social interaction one has with one's fellows"; (3) " . . . these meanings are handled in, and modified through, an interpretative process used by the person in dealing with the things he encounters" (Blumer, 1969: 2). The approach I am using is quite compatible with these sociological premises. It highlights the meanings that racial inequality has for white people. It shows how these meanings are developed, the contexts within which they operate, and how they are played out in people's lives. If sociological knowledge is based in the first instance on the meaning systems people use to interpret and act on the world in which they find themselves, then my approach fits comfortably under the rubric of sociology.

It may be sociological in that respect, but the question remains: Are the findings generalizable? After all, generalizability is one of the features that distinguishes sociology from good journalism. I find it difficult to develop a totally satisfactory answer to this query. On the basis of the following five portraits I obviously cannot talk about what is representative of white people in general. Sennett and Cobb faced a similar dilemma and came up with what I feel is the most reasonable resolution for this issue. "The only way we can generalize," they say,

> is to turn the matter around and ask what is representative or characteristic of American society in its impact on the people interviewed. It is not so much as a replication of other workers that their lives ought to bear a larger witness, but as focused points of human experience that can teach something about a more general problem of denial and frustration built into the social order [1972: 45].

If one substitutes the words "white people" for "workers," and "racial inequality" for "denial and frustration," their formulation captures my sentiments.

Ultimately most of these questions boil down to the issue of whether the approach is believable. Is it "true"? No methodological treatise will settle that question. What I have done in this chapter is chart for the reader a trial-and-error map of my inquiry — the stops and starts that led to the approach contained in this study. That is my claim for believability. The following chapters describe some of our respondents — who they are and why they are; how they explain racial inequality and how they justify it. Does it all ring true?

That I leave for the reader to decide.

3 "I favor anything that doesn't affect me personally." Gene Danich

Prologue

Most sociologists would not recommend that black people interview whites. Common sense says as much. The barriers separating racial groups are immense. Black and white people often relate to each other with fear and suspicion. Hostility is commonplace. Who would think that a white person could open up to a black and honestly express his or her fears, emotions — or talk about deeply troubling racial controversies? And so when Alex Papillon, a black man on our research team, asked me if he should interview white people, I was hesitant.

I hesitated for all the obvious reasons. But I had other reservations about the idea as well. Alex was not a "typical" black research assistant; along with Huey Newton and Bobby Seale he was one of the founders of the Black Panther party. He was active in the party when he was working with us. How many white people would be willing to talk with a known Black Panther?

Alex also looks imposing and asserts himself aggressively. He is handsome, at least six feet two inches tall, and must weigh well over 200 pounds. He speaks his mind in a rather loud tone of voice and minces words with no one. I was concerned that white people might be put off by him

74

and clam up even if they were willing to be interviewed.

Alex is also intensely opinionated. He never hesitated to lecture the people he interviewed about how they should conduct their lives. This was a problem with some of his interviews with black people. We had many discussions about this. I knew what Alex's opinions were; I wanted to find out what other people thought. So I had visions of Alex coming back with an hour or two of barely disguised monologue directed at a white "respondent."

Yet I found something intriguing about the idea. Alex was not only a research assistant, he was also a working longshoreman. He would be on the docks in the morning and interview for us in the afternoons and evenings. Many of his respondents were fellow longshoremen who seemed quite willing to be interviewed by a coworker in whom they had some trust. I knew that a small percentage of the longshoremen Alex worked with were white. And I thought there was a chance that a white person with whom Alex had worked might be willing to be interviewed by him. Perhaps when people worked in integrated situations all the "obvious" reasons for not having blacks interview whites would not hold. We also needed interviews with working-class whites and they were not as easy to get as I had hoped.

Why not try it, I thought? What could we lose? It might not work out, but if it succeeded we would be that much further along.

It worked.

Some of the interviews Alex conducted with white people were the finest in our sample. He tended to interview people who were strong, sure of themselves, and not easily put off by his demanding style. This is to be expected, because his sample was self-selected. Alex's opinionated nature did not inhibit interviews; it stimulated them. Respondents reacted to his frankness and candor with an openness that equaled his. People assumed that they would not easily be allowed off any hooks by a militant black interviewer, and they were right. Alex pushed and probed people masterfully, with sensitivity as well as determination. As a result he came back with a number of first-rate interviews which were both penetrating and fascinating.

Alex had been working with Gene Danich for almost a year when the two got together to tape an interview. While never really friends, they more than tolerated each other; there was respect between them. They both took their work seriously. They impressed each other as hard workers. If they worked in the hold of the same ship they struck up some good conversations. When I gave Alex the green light to interview white people he was excited about talking with Gene. Gene was not sure how much he would contribute to a sociological study but he was certainly willing to be interviewed by Alex. He suggested that Alex come by his house one evening after work with his tape recorder and they would see what happened.

Alex conducted an excellent interview. The two men were amazingly candid and frank about racial issues. They even shared laughs at incidents in which Gene was the recipient of black aggression. Why was this interview so successful? It certainly says something positive about the two men as individuals. Most likely it has something to do with the context in which they work and the racial atmosphere that has been created by their union — the International Longshoremen's and Warehousemen's Union (ILWU).

The interview was not an easy one to conduct. Gene was difficult to pin down. He was not evasive, but he was complex. He had not thought through certain issues and he refused to pretend otherwise. He resisted closure on questions that were still open for him. Where Alex detected contradictions, Gene saw consistencies. Gene was also uncomfortable and restless about some of the questions Alex asked. Not that he was threatened by them; they were just too abstract or sociological. And Gene is a man of action, not words. He would answer tough questions but he seemed ill at ease when speaking about some things that might have been unfamiliar. Despite his reluctance, however, Gene proved remarkably articulate and sometimes, perhaps, even eloquent. But decide that for yourself.

"I've got the last job I'm ever gonna have."

Gene Danich figures that when the longshoremen's hiring hall caves in from old age, he will be standing in it. He has the last job he is ever going to have. As far as Gene is concerned, a man likes to be right, hates to be wrong, and when he is right likes to have other men say, "That guy's right; he did the right thing." The way Gene figures it, all men like to be praised; everybody is vain. Of all the jobs he has had, the waterfront allows him more of a possibility to be right; to be part of his work; to have some degree of "control" over his situation.

Gene likes working on the docks. It allows him to feel responsible. For eight hours a day he is down in the hold of a ship with four other guys. They decide how to store cargo and how to remove it. Except for some periodic interference from ignorant walking bosses, how they do the work is up to them. They can use their initiative; they have responsibilities.

Gene enjoys longshore work for yet another reason. He is an avid outdoorsman. When he wants to go hunting or fishing, he simply does not go down to the hiring hall that day. Not too many jobs permit this; but a longshoreman can take off as many days as he pleases without jeopardizing his job.

Gene also likes to be "physical"; he wants to deal with the world directly, one to one. "Meekness" is a quality he dislikes in people. As a longshoreman, Gene can be physical when he lifts heavy cargo or survives another backbreaking eight-hour shift. He derives great satisfaction from that.

Gene wants to be "self-sufficient"; he wants to be able to "survive" where he is. He does not measure people by their occupation: A janitor is just as good as a banker in his eyes. A "successful" person to Gene is someone who decides for himself what kind of work he wants to do. As he figures it, people cannot do a job they are not happy doing and they cannot be happy doing a job they know nothing about. So the best job people can have is one they know something about and are happy doing. The waterfront meets these needs for Gene.

Gene has not always been able to live his life the way he wanted, and his refusal to mask true feelings through either subtlety or propriety has often had tempestuous consequences. His father was not Gene's "kind" of person. Gene defined himself — the kind of person he wanted to be — in direct opposition to his father.

By most standards his father is a success. A self-made man, he started out as an apprentice machinist with only an eighth-grade education and has done well. He is now a plant manager for a large company that builds heavy construction equipment. He troubleshoots for the company; when they build a new factory Gene's father is there to open it and work with it until the plant is on its feet. He travels throughout the world and makes good money — between $75,000 and $80,000 a year, Gene estimates. He is also a "pretty powerful" man around town. He is a member of the chamber of commerce and sits on the school board of the East Oakland community where Gene was raised. Gene is pretty impressed with his father's "success," but he never wanted to follow in his footsteps. "It's just too much responsibility to be that successful in management," Gene says. It also takes up too much energy; and

when he gets "right down to it," Gene is a "lazy bastard."
Gene also feels that his father's life is incomplete. The "old
man's" interests are almost indistinguishable from his work;
one of his main hobbies is working on machinery.

His father never tried outdoor sports until Gene and his
younger brother conned him into taking them hunting and
fishing. Soon he picked it up and now he is a good outdoorsman. Even so, his outdoor activities are rather limited
because of a childhood accident that crippled him for life.
He fell out of a window and broke a leg that never healed
properly. He has a short left leg as a result.

Gene sees his father as a "meek" person and attributes
this to his crippled leg. When Gene was a child, he was
frustrated when his father would get angry about something but not do anything "physical" about it. One Fourth
of July evening when Gene was between ten and twelve,
some older kids threw cherry bombs into his backyard,
where the family was celebrating the holiday. One of the
incendiary devices exploded close to Gene's brother, burning his leg. Gene immediately grabbed a board; he intended
to administer some sidewalk justice. When his father inter-
vened, saying, "No, we'll call the police," Gene resented
the suggestion; in his estimation the local cops weren't up
to the assignment. "Hell, those cops can't catch their own
shadow," he says. "Them guys would have been gone." So
when his father went into the house to call the police,
Gene hit the teenagers over the head with the board.

Gene was bothered by his father's failure to deal with
the situation directly, without the aid of outside forces. It
reflected on his father as a man. Gene feels that a "complete man" should be self-sufficient. If a situation developed where he had to take care of himself without the
support of a police department, grocery stores or clothing
stores, a complete man would be able to survive. Gene
feels that his father could not do that, and to Gene that is

"a considerable deficiency"; one that is not compensated for by prestige, money, or occupational status.

Gene may have been "disappointed" by his father; high school, on the other hand, was a complete "hang up." It was a four-year exercise in futility; a ritual of humiliation, authoritarianism, and pettiness. Gene resisted in the only way he knew how; he refused to do anything that contradicted his sense of decency. And he suffered the consequences.

Gene was a bright student and knew it. He got nothing less than "As" and "Bs" on tests. In spite of this, he rarely got a grade better than "D" in any of his classes. The reason for the discrepancy was simple: Gene refused to do homework. He knew that if he neglected to do his homework and turn in all that "bull shit" he would flunk regardless of the grades he received on tests. Nevertheless, when someone told him something and it was new to him he became excited. He then "had" that knowledge. But he felt that there just "ain't no reason you should have to turn around and write a fifty-page letter about the son of a bitch." Gene was not a radical trying to change things. He "just didn't care to go along with all the formal bull shit that went with high school." And it was that way all through school.

But Gene's real nemesis was a young history teacher named Shapiro. The two of them mixed like gasoline and fire. Shapiro was a small, dark-complexioned fellow with a very heavy beard and olive skin. From the moment they met, just by looking at him, Gene knew that he was "very thickly Jewish." He "knew" this without even knowing his name. After spending some time in his class, Gene became convinced that the history teacher was paranoid about being Jewish; he seemed to feel that "everybody looked down on him" because of it. At the time Gene did not really know much about "races or prejudice or anything of this." He simply interpreted Shapiro's behavior as defensiveness: "He thought everybody was putting him down." Gene felt Shapiro "put himself in a bad light." He became authoritarian toward anybody he thought was putting him down, and because he felt that way about everyone, his class was conducted in a very "strict and ridiculous" manner.

Gene was antagonized by Shapiro's classroom procedures. He had always been a "mess-up," going through high school with the attitude that "anything would go." It was Gene's senior year and he was just about at the end of his rope with school anyway. One day a minor incident in Shapiro's class quickly became a major one. Shapiro was just a trifle too authoritarian this time and Gene dug in his heels. One exchange led to another and Gene hit the teacher; "dropped him right in class." Three days before graduation he was thrown out of school.

Gene's father was quite upset by this. He was worried about how it would look if the son of a school board member, a local influential, did not graduate from high school. Gene "didn't give a fat rat's ass," but his father worked out a procedure that would allow Gene to participate in graduation ceremonies and he went through the motions of "graduating." Dressed in cap and gown just like his classmates, Gene walked across the stage and received the folder in which diplomas reside. Except that in Gene's case the folder was empty. He received a diploma through GED (General Equivalency High School Diploma) a few years later while in the Marine Corps.

Gene did four rather hard years in the Marines. His freewheeling spirit collided constantly against the regimented world of military life. He drank, fought, and "goofed off" throughout his tour of duty. Gene was happy to be discharged; there was "no kind of way" he would stay in the military — "not for nothing." However, finding a job that

suited his disposition without assaulting his sensibilities
was no easy task.

Gene's first job out of the Marines was packing auto
parts; $65 a week gross pay. He could not go "down" from
there — "you can't fall out of the basement," he quips.
For a while he bounced around between jobs. Whenever he
found a job he could "get along in" and which paid more
money than the previous one, he would take it. He loaded
planes at an air terminal; he sold auto parts; he even owned
a sports car shop for a while. For a couple of months he
worked for a company that manufactures calculators. The
pay was fine, but working on an assembly line "bugged"
him "no end." He sat on a little stool, took a calculator off
the line, put it on a bench, installed two or three little
springs and a couple levers in it, put the calculator back on
the line, and picked up another one to repeat the procedure. He performed that operation endlessly during an
eight-hour shift. The "simplicity" of it all was more than
Gene could swallow. It was a "nothing job" and had absolutely no room for expression. Gene felt like "a thing that
takes this thing from here and puts those things on there
and puts that thing back." That was all there was to it.

Gene found a reasonable job at a large farm machinery
manufacturer. He enjoyed working on heavy equipment
and was fairly successful at it. He became a temporary
foreman in a relatively short period of time. But Gene's
propensity to deal with the world in a straightforward, no-
nonsense, physical fashion got the best of him once
more. One day during lunch hour, some of the guys were
sitting in a circle downstairs eating their lunches. Gene and
another fellow were upstairs finishing some work. Gene's
coworker was throwing little quarter-inch nuts at one of
the people downstairs who was unable to tell which of the
two was the wise guy. But Gene was suspected and the victim turned to him and asked, "You do that at home?"

"I ain't throwing those nuts," Gene replied.

About a minute later another nut was thrown. This one found its mark; the fellow was hit right in the head.

"I'll bet you fuck your mother," he exploded at Gene. Without saying a word, Gene walked over and hit the guy "right upside the head." The man never had a chance to even get off his stool. Gene hit him repeatedly until the other guys pulled him off. He was fired immediately.

Gene was unemployed until he saw a notice in the newspaper announcing that the longshoremen's union was hiring people. He applied and was soon working on the docks. Gene realized very quickly that he had found his niche; longshore work was ideal for him. It allowed him some freedom, responsibility, independence, and autonomy. For the first time in his work career, Gene felt he had "some degree of control" over his life.

The job is not without problems, however. People with power, particularly those who abuse it, have always been a source of irritation for Gene. And there are a number of such people on the waterfront. The old "gang bosses," or "walking bosses," rub Gene the wrong way. No matter how much he talks to them, how much he points right at something and shows it to them — "black and white right there in front of them" — when they look at it, "it's still going to be green." He is unable to sway them one way or another. Once they open their mouths "that's got to be it." "That bugs me no end, man," Gene growls. And he feels a little hostile about it inside. He wants to say, "Dummy, come on! I'll rap you in the mouth. It fits! Put it in here! I *know* that's where it ought to be." But he never hits anyone because he knows that would get him fired. "You can't fight on the docks," he explains.

The only other job Gene would now consider taking is working in British Columbia in the woods, if he could make the same money he gets on the docks. That would be ideal, because everything he likes is up there. He could fish and hunt "without ever wearing it out." But he knows there is no money in the woods. "I've got the last job I'm ever gonna have," Gene concludes. "When that hiring hall falls in from old age I'll be standing in it."

"I never met a single colored person in conversation until I was over eighteen years old!"

Most of the men Gene works with on the waterfront are black; in fact between 70 and 80 percent of them are. Gene currently has more "general acquaintances" — people he says hello to, slaps on the back, talks to, and has coffee with — who are "colored" than are white. That was not always the case; it only happened when Gene became a long-shoreman. With the exception of work, Gene lives almost exclusively in a white world; he always has.

He was born and raised in a working-class suburb southeast of Oakland, California, that was mostly white. Some Puerto Rican people lived in the town, as did a lot of "Spanish people"; there were a few Orientals, and some Jews. All kinds of people lived there except "colored people." That was one group with whom Gene had no real contact. He knew there were differences between colored[1] and white people; they were not "one and the same." He is not sure how or why he knew that. When Alex pushed the question, Gene became a trifle defensive, although he was not hesitant about answering it. He just "knew" it, that's all. He also knew that white people "didn't like" colored people but he is not specifically sure how he knew it. Alex tried unsuccessfully to pin down how he knew. To Gene it was a fact; "it was just there, you knew it." He assured Alex, however, that he did not "pick it up" from his family. He "heard people talking; that's all."

One of the things they talked about was football games

---

[1]Throughout the book, "colored" and "Negro" are used when they were used by the person interviewed. Otherwise, "black" is used.

against predominantly black high schools. When Gene's team played one of these schools, "there were a lot of hassles between colored and white." People would say things like: "Be sure to get out of El Cerrito after the game right away when it's dark 'cause the niggers will get you." Gene claims he did not know what they were talking about. But he knew one thing: He wanted "no ass kicking." So he would get out with the rest of them.

Gene really did not know what to make of black people. He had never been introduced to one; they were never around in his life. When he described this period, his voice went up a couple of octaves and he spoke with conviction. When they *were* around, as at football games, "everybody was scared of them." He is not sure exactly why he was afraid of them. Gene paused nervously. He wondered if perhaps it was because "there were no people like that" around town and so he "never knew any" of them. He stopped speaking momentarily. But he remembers going to some football games where "there's hundreds of them"; and some would say things like "man, I'm'ona kick yo' ass." "I'll take your word for it," would be Gene's characteristic response.

Gene became frustrated when he tried to explain this period to Alex. In turn, Alex pushed him to try and figure out where he picked up his ideas about blacks. Gene was having trouble articulating his feelings. He finally blurted out in a frustrated tone of voice: "I never met a single colored person in conversation until I went in the service. And that's when I was eighteen years old! Does that help straighten out what I'm trying to tell you?" And then, sounding very intense, as if both explaining and apologizing, he repeated: "I never met, I never had a conversation of any kind with any colored person until I was over eighteen years old!"

The first Negroes Gene met were in boot camp, and all

of his fears about them were confirmed. Gene chuckled as he introduced the incident. He was eighteen; "knew nothing from nothing"; had never had a "piece of ass" in his life — he was "still a baby on the bottle." All kinds of people were in boot camp and they were from all over the United States. Among the recruits were three "colored guys" from Los Angeles who had joined the Marines together. Gene could tell by the way they acted that they had been raised in a "different environment." Unlike him, they were "hep" to the world.

The first night was traumatic. It was terribly cold, they were issued only one blanket, their mattresses were only half an inch thick, and there were no mattress covers. Gene felt "absolutely miserable"; he wanted to be back home. The drill instructor "panicked" Gene and when he walked in and said "lights out, get to sleep," Gene was all for that. He was tired and miserable and he thought, "Sleep, that's what I need to do; get away from all this." The DI left, closing the door and locking it to prevent young recruits like Gene from going over the hill their first night in the Marine Corps. Just as Gene was about to fall asleep, maybe fifteen minutes later, the three colored guys from Los Angeles turned on the barracks light and began to play cards.

"Hey man," Gene said, "shut that light off before that guy comes back in here and kills us all! Shut that goddamn light off!" One of the card players got down off his bunk bed and walked over to where Gene lay. He reached down and punched Gene in the mouth so hard he "didn't know what was happening."

Right then and there, Gene became "prejudiced." "I hate them people," he felt, "they're no good at all!" Alex and Gene burst out laughing at the story's conclusion. When they got back to the interview, Gene pointed out that the split-second interaction was a "very strong reaffirmation" of what he had always heard at home. The only thing he had "known" about black people was to "watch out for 'em; they'll get you." And that is exactly what he found out the first night he "met" one. It took four more years in the Marines and a good deal more association with black people for Gene to "grow up" and find out that not all colored people were like that.

He had to learn it in the Marines, because people in high school simply expressed fear and his folks seldom spoke about black people at home. Gene's dad had a couple of Negro friends at work. When he spoke of them, which was rare, he never did so in disparaging terms, but they never came over to the Daniches' house and Gene never saw them. This area was another uneasy one for Gene. He got somewhat irritated when Alex raised the obvious question — why? He had "no idea" why they never came over; as far as he could tell, his dad was not "prejudiced." Blacks "didn't bother dad one way or the other," Gene suggested evasively. Alex was not satisfied. "How come they didn't come over then?" Perhaps mom was the problem, Gene answered quickly. Then he remembered that she was a little bit prejudiced. He recalled that once while she was watching a television quiz show she became upset by an interracial couple on the program. "They should get a colored girl for him," she remarked. Gene stuck with his original formulation; black people were almost never discussed at home. They never came up as a topic, much less as an issue. "Why not?" Alex persisted. "I don't know," Gene sighed. And then, as if to please Alex, he added, "possibly they kept it out." Gene had the last word, however — "But really, I don't know."

The situation has not changed much with the Danich clan in two generations. While the people with whom Gene works are nearly all black, his close friends are "predominantly" white. Alex was rather surprised by this. "How could it be," he asked; especially since you have a fair-minded approach to people?" The question bothered Gene, "I don't know," he sighed, then added, "perhaps it's because that's just the way the balance of people fell." He certainly was not "prejudiced" — his closest friend in the Marines was an Indian.

Alex was not convinced. "I'm not sure I agree with you," he said. "I'll tell that right now." He allowed that maybe Gene could not answer the question, but also suggested that perhaps he was avoiding it. "I never tell a lie unless it benefits me," Gene shot back. "That's no bull shit. And how would it benefit me to lie about that?" Alex did not ask him his concept of benefit; whether it was strictly a material one, as he implied, or whether it might also be avoiding unpleasantness. Perhaps it did benefit him to lie in this situation. Gene is obviously not immune to self-deception, and may not always know when he is lying.

Alex pushed on, accepting Gene's terms for the moment, but asked if he still felt the only reason his friends were white was because of association. Gene thought about it a little more and then wondered out loud if maybe it was because he does not really have *any* close friends that come over to the house. He only has one truly close friend; a guy who used to come over all the time but is now over-seas; a civilian employee in Vietnam. And if he were black "it wouldn't be any different."

Regardless of the reasons for it, the fact remains that black people never visit Gene's home and he rarely talks about them with his children. His son is growing up much the same way he did, and with many of the same fears. Just the other day his son came home early from playing baseball.

"The coloreds were coming," he explained.

"So what?" Gene replied.

"Oh no, the colored are playing baseball down at the school so we had to leave."

"Won't they let you play ball?"

"I don't know. We had to leave."

Gene was upset over the exchange, but what could he do? "There it was all over again," he realized. "Twenty-five years later; the same thing as with me when I was a kid."

Like his parents before him, Gene lives in an all-white neighborhood. In fact, he lives in the same town, only a couple of miles away from them. The area is strictly segregated. If someone were to fly over it in a helicopter and look down they would see two apparently identical neighborhoods divided by a twenty-foot creek. Black people live on one side of the creek; whites on the other. Some people see the creek as a "natural border" between the two towns. But Gene is not sure how "natural" the border is; he has heard that over on "the elite side of town" there is a real estate "clique" that keeps out colored people. He does not know of any "specific instances" where that has happened, but he has heard about an association of real estate companies that get together and make sure blacks do not move in.

"How do you feel about that?" Alex inquired.

"It's wrong," Gene replied. "As long as a man can afford to live where he lives, I don't give a shit if he's green with purple spots." If a person "doesn't throw his garbage" over Gene's fence it makes no difference to him who lives next door. That being the case, had he taken any action against the real estate companies? Alex wanted to know. No, Gene never had any cause to deal with them. But if he opposed it, Alex wondered, why had he not done anything about it? Gene paused for a moment. "Because it doesn't affect me personally," he answered. "It never has. It's never come to me and my friends. If it comes to me, then I'll take care of it."

*"Equality means ain't nobody better than
anybody else."*

Gene may be isolated from black people; their problems
may not be his own. But he is certainly not insulated from
the issues they raise. He is regularly bombarded by radio,
television, and newspaper accounts of black power, riots,
busing, and Black Panthers. The black men he works with
talk about racial issues all the time. Gene relates to these
issues in a pragmatic sort of way. He does not really have a
distinct, integrated way of seeing the world. Thus he sorts
and sifts through issues and topics as they confront him
and takes a position based on what he thinks are his best
interests in each case.

Gene is no longer the frightened high school youth who
saw blacks only in fearful one-dimensional terms. Now he
is most impressed by the difficulty of their situation and
the unfairness of it all. He thinks blacks have a much
"rougher" life than white people. The majority of people
in the world are white and "they're all down on the colored
people." Not all whites, he points out. The majority of
whites are not down on colored people *outwardly*. But in-
wardly many of them say "don't let them marry my sister."
The problem is that a lot of people have "this prejudice inside them which they just keep in and won't let out."
People who let it out, in Gene's estimation, are "sons of
bitches," and he stays away from them because "I don't
like people who are that radical."

Prejudice is not the main problem facing black people,
in Gene's view. As he sees it "insufficient education opportunities" is a much more crucial issue; "all of their problems, as a race and as a group of people, would stem from
that." He knows that blacks do not have "as good a jobs"
as white people, but that is because they are not well educated. And because of that, they get a reputation for being

"crooks." But "what else can a man do?" he asked. "He's got to have some money." If a man has no education he cannot get a job; or if "because of his color" he cannot get a job, he has to get the money somehow. Sometimes he has to "hit somebody over the head" for it. "That's just the way it goes." But as far as Gene is concerned, "it ain't gonna make no difference if he's black or white." If a man has no education he is going to be "a crook." The way he figures it, "a man's got to have coins."

Gene is not sure how to solve the problem. He gets upset by some of the proposals he hears, and by some of the leaders he reads about or watches on television. He thinks Malcolm X's separatism is wrong. Gene breaks the world down in zero-sum terms; there is only so much to go around. The way he sees it there cannot be "two wholly separate communities and both communities have all the best advantages." As he calculates it, "there aren't that many best advantages available separately." If the "best advantages" are put together in a "lump," they might cover everybody. "But you can't make two lumps out of that and have them both be the same size lumps," he concluded.

The issue of separatism does not excite Gene. Stokely Carmichael[2] does. "Oh man," he exclaimed, "I'd shoot that son of a gun dead in the head if I had half a chance; Carmichael is nothing but a troublemaker. You can't name one single thing that Stokely Carmichael does, that *I* know about, that's constructive." The only thing Gene has seen him do is "get that shit stick and stir the pot"; "everything he does is to tear something down." Gene does not think that what Carmichael is tearing down is "right," however. He realizes that sometimes "you got to tear some things down to build some things up." But as far as he can tell,

[2]Chairman of the Southern-based Student Nonviolent Coordinating Committee, or "SNICK," the controversial Carmichael was considered by many people to have originated the "black power" slogan.

Carmichael "isn't building nothing; he ain't even *trying* to."

Gene does not claim to know much about Carmichael; just what he reads in the paper and sees on television. But what he knows he dislikes. All he sees is Carmichael making "big speeches," "going to Cuba," and "thumbing his nose" at the United States. He acts like a lot of other "big shots" who make his jaws tight. In his estimation, "that dude Stokely or Malcolm wants to be an all-powerful being, somebody that's better than me, and he ain't no more man than me in any way, shape, or form."

Gene is convinced that Carmichael wants to be the "all-powerful race messiah of the black people"; he wants to "run everything." Gene "can't go for that." "Nobody needs to have that kind of power," he declared. In his estimation, black people need money, not a messiah. Blacks have it hard because they have no money; they have no way to get out of trouble. If a man has money in the bank he can go to court and buy his way out. But what does Stokely Carmichael offer? "Stirring up more shit," he said, answering his own question.

Gene is not "down on" all black leaders or strategies for racial change. He likes Martin Luther King, although he is not too familiar with the man's philosophy. He knows King is nonviolent. But nonviolence itself does not appeal to Gene; that would be too hypocritical. What he likes best is that King's approach does not involve him. As he put it, "King is not trying to be *better* than me."

He has no problem with the idea of black power, either. As he sees it, black power is black people "bringing themselves to a position where if a white man says, 'I'm going to throw you out,' he can't." Gene defines the idea with one word: "equality."

His notion of equality is concrete. "It means that you ain't no different than me; ain't nobody any better than anybody else." But equality does not mean intermarriage.

As far as Gene can tell, as long as the earth rolls around, a majority of white people will be against that. But with regard to other things in life, like having opportunities, equality means things will be "even." And black power is the means for achieving it."

Black power is also an attitude toward white people. Gene thinks the black man is "registering his independence; his indignation with his treatment." And where there is a possibility of achieving this objective, "black power is that group movement." Black power is "the banding together" of black people. And Gene respects that.

Alex detected a problem with this formulation. "Do you realize black power originated from Stokely Carmichael?" he pointed out. Yes, Gene was aware of that.

"But yet you disagree with Stokely Carmichael and you prefer Martin Luther King over him. How do you explain that?"

"Cause Martin Luther King is not trying to be better than me. And hell, King's really a do-nothing. I mean what did the March on Washington do? Wheee. People took a big walk and wore out their shoes. Maybe if he was making shoes and selling them then he'd be doing something. But he's not doing nothing. What's he done?"

"You ain't gonna put me in the bag of having to defend King, man. But what you say raises a problem. I'm talking about what they can do for black people and you're talking in terms of how they relate to you. Now you believe that Martin Luther King isn't doing anything for black people?"

"Right."

"You believe black power *is* doing something for black people?"

"Right."

"But you disagree with Stokely?"

"Right. Look, what I'm saying is that as relates to what either of those two people are doing for black people I feel

Stokely is doing more for them by virtue of the fact that he is doing *something*. Even if it's nothing but just stirring up shit — and he's sure doing that! But King? What's King doing? If Stokely's doing anything he's doing more than King."

"I don't understand, man. If you think King ain't doing nothing why do you disagree with Stokely?"

"Because he's trying to be better than me and he's trying to be better than everybody else."

"Why do you say that?"

"I don't really know any specific instances. I just get the feeling from reading about Stokely Carmichael that he wants to be the best of everything, of *everybody*. And everybody includes me. I don't like nobody to think he's better than me. Like big Dave down at the hall; he thinks he's better than everybody, man. As far as he's concerned, his shit don't stink. Big Dave ain't no better than me either."

"I'm having trouble pinning you down, Gene. I'm trying to get at this discrepancy because first you say you believe that he's doing something for black people but then you say what he's doing for black people ain't half as important as what he's saying in terms of being better."

"He's not doing anything constructive that I know about."

"But yet you think that's better than King."

"Yeah. What's King doing for black people? He's doing nothing. At least Stokely's stirring them up; they're getting mad."

"But yet you prefer King over Stokely!"

"Yes."

"So what you're saying is that the most important thing isn't that he's doing something for black people. The most important thing is how he relates to other people — specifically *you*. And you're saying that how he relates to you is more important than what he is doing for black people."

"To me it is, yes."

"Why is that more important than what he's doing for black people? Why should you give a damn *how* Stokely relates to you? Why would you give a damn about how he helps black people? Why would you even concern yourself with Stokely Carmichael and his superiority over everybody? Why, man?"

"Look, man, what Martin Luther King is doing cannot possibly ever come back on me. You see. Because he's not doing nothing. He's leading a march down the street. Well walk down the goddamn street. I don't give a fat rat's ass. But what Stokely Carmichael is doing is better for the black people because he's stirring them up. He gives them energy and ambition to do something. You see? And if I was a black man I would *have* to relate to Stokely Carmichael because he's stirring things up; he's getting me going see? And he's getting all my brothers going. See? He's making things roll. But as he relates to *me,* and *I* am white you know, the way I see what Stokely Carmichael does is stir up a lot of shit that could break out into something that might *involve* me."

"Involve you how?"

"A riot. I'm driving down the street in Oakland and somebody throws a rock through my window. Oh I'd be mad. Ohhh, I'd be mad! Understand? See, I get pretty hot. But I don't mess with nobody else and I don't expect them to mess with me. You see? What Stokely Carmichael does is likely to involve me in something I dislike; something I would definitely not agree with; something I would not want to be a part of. Now that's as opposed to what Martin Luther King does. I don't see any way in the world he can wrap me up in what he's doing. In other words Martin Luther King is not likely to do anything that would involve me in a riot, a fight, burn my house down, or anything like that. Does that make it clear?"

"Yeah. I guess so."

"I hate to make it hard for you man," Gene sighed, "but it ain't easy. I mean it just ain't easy."

For the most part Gene's feelings about racial controversies are ambivalent; his clear-cut attitudes toward King and Carmichael, black power and separatism are exceptions to the rule. When Gene hears people talking about "integration," for example, he thinks of schools. And he has a rather self-serving notion of what that means. It means that kids go to the school "closest" to their homes. If the school system in his town were not integrated, that would mean black kids in his town were being bused to Oakland and white kids living in Oakland were being bused to his all-white town. Gene would be a "mad son of a bitch" if his son had to go to school across town; "someone would pay for it."

Nevertheless, Gene's feelings about the matter are tangled up by conflicting emotions. He feels his kids are "disadvantaged" because they have few opportunities to associate with black children. If they went to integrated schools they would gain "understanding"; something he never had until the Marines. Yet he is not sure he would be willing to have his children bused in order to attend integrated schools. He might be willing if some "purpose was achieved"; if the kids got something out of it. But why pay to send them miles to school and then not get something out of it? He cannot see what is being achieved by busing programs that currently exist. Politicians may get black votes; but he wonders what the children get. He saw an idea on television that he liked. Some black students from a San Francisco high school went down to an all-white school on the peninsula and they all spent the day getting to know each other. Gene thinks "that's great." He would have "given anything" for something like that when he was their age. But busing for its own sake? He "can't go for that."

Integration means schools to Gene; it definitely does

not mean interracial marriage. In his estimation, interracial marriage is not a very significant strategy for helping blacks. The way he sees it, if colored people are ever going to have the opportunities other people have — "if my opportunities are yours and if my son's opportunities are your son's," he explained to Alex — "then it's got to be in the schools." As far as Gene can tell, mixed marriage is quite a rare thing. "Nothing that small could ever be as important as something as big as integration in the schools."

Gene has other reservations about interracial marriages. He thinks white people are very sensitive about it. White men feel "impugned" when a white woman goes to bed with a black man. From what he can tell, instead of getting mad at the Negro they get mad at the white girl for even being around a black man.

Gene finds it difficult to talk about the topic; Alex had to push him to be specific. Gene has a daughter of his own and Alex asked what his feelings would be if she were to marry a black man. Gene sighed and then thought about the question. He did not think it would bother him one bit if it happened in the future, some other day and age. He "wouldn't like it to happen right now" and he has one main reason for that feeling. He would worry about her children. From what he gathers, white people "would put them kids down." He is especially concerned about the treatment they might receive at the hands of other kids. He knows kids can be rough on each other and when a couple of them gang up on another, that one has it bad. If his daughter were married to a black man and they had children, other kids' parents would "talk about it." The kids would overhear it and it could only be a "disaster" for his potential grandchildren. He does not want his grandchildren exposed to that.

But what if the children were raised in the black community, Alex wanted to know. That way they might have a place; they might not be ostracized. Gene's voice grew small. "If they had a place that would be great." In his estimation "kids are fabulous, they got to have everything"; kids are "all we got, there ain't nothing else. Once you're gone, that's all you got left." He would be for whatever is "best for kids."

But Gene was not really happy with that formulation. He does not think it is feasible for kids to spend their whole lives "hiding from everything else in the world"; spending their lives in some ghetto so "nobody'll talk about them." What if they just stayed in the ghetto, Alex asked? Gene was not too sure about that either. He wanted to know if the kids could come out one black and one white. "I don't know how they come out," he laughed nervously. "It varies," said Alex. But if one were colored and one white and they brought friends over to the house there would still be problems, Gene insisted. What if they both had dark complexions, Alex countered. That was fine with Gene; those two kids would have a place, a community of their own.

He was not convinced that was possible, however. He could not get a handle on the "full story." "I don't know Negro people," he said, running out of patience, "I don't know how they feel." He was not sure the kids would be accepted in the black community, or even if there was a black community. But he does know how white people feel, and that sooner or later the kids would have to come in contact with them. That would be "disastrous." When Gene thinks about all the possibilities he goes in a circle and ends up where he began. Interracial marriages are possible in the future where they could be a "perfectly normal, natural thing." But not now. The kids would "suffer."

Riots are something else Gene goes round and round about. He has strong feelings about the issues they raise;

but nothing as simple as whether he is for or against them. He is not sure that taking things, breaking windows and stealing furniture, is necessary. But he also wonders if there is any other way for people living in riot areas to get "that stuff." He does not know; he has never seen places like Watts or Chicago. So riots might be "all right." He is still troubled by the issue because he knows "it ain't right to steal." He is caught between conflicting senses of morality. Should he evaluate riots by the biblical notion of thou shalt not steal, or by his own standards of fairness? Gene wonders whether the people who own stores in the ghetto have been giving black people a "screwing"; "14 percent every week or something like that." If that is true, the guy is "supposed to get robbed." The way Gene sees it, "he's supposed to be a loser 'cause he's been putting it on people." But he is not really sure which picture is the correct one.

He is convinced about one thing, however. He does not "go for throwing rocks at firemen." "That's crazy"; "it's wrong as two left feet." As Gene sees it, "that cat's in there risking *his* ass to put out *your* fire" and hitting him in the head with a rock is "stupid." What good does it do to shoot him, Gene wonders. "The poor son of a bitch is just doing his job." As far as Gene can tell, all firemen do is put out fires. Shooting at them, throwing rocks, "that ain't right."

Shooting at cops, on the other hand, might be justified in Gene's estimation. He can imagine a situation where a cop gets a couple colored guys "up against the wall" and starts hitting them with his stick. "That cop's *supposed* to be shot," as far as Gene is concerned. He believes black claims about police brutality — "there can't be all that much smoke without some fire" — but he does not accept *all* the talk about police brutality. His younger brother is a policeman in a South Bay town and sometimes Gene can see things from the policeman's angle. He thinks cops are sometimes brutal because they see so much and have to put up with "bull shit" from everybody. As far as Gene can tell, an honest cop's job is "just like riding down a sewer in a glass-bottom boat"; they see all the "worst" society has to offer. He thinks this probably helps make them brutal, but is not really sure it is the only reason. Some of the cops he knows around town are "more interested in being all-powerful unto themselves, like a god, than they are in doing a job."

Their job, as far as he is concerned, is to "protect the property and the lives of those persons who pay taxes in their jurisdiction." Whether Gene consciously meant to exclude people who do not pay taxes is uncertain, but he clearly feels that police should use any means necessary to protect at least the people who do. If somebody beats up on his kid, cops are supposed to "get that stopped," no matter how.

As Gene sees it, the cop's job is "to maintain law and order." And by that Gene does not mean "to keep blacks in their place." He is talking about something that is both more general and more personal than that. Why should certain demonstrations be stopped and not others, he asked. Should they be stopped because they offend the mayor or the police? No. If people are holding a demonstration in a park where no one is being bothered, "well let that one go." "That ain't got nothing to do with law and order." But if people demonstrate in front of the tunnel connecting the East Bay with Walnut Creek, and people cannot get to work, "*that* demonstration got to come to a stop." In Gene's mind, law and order is violated when "something causes trouble for most people." And then the cop's job is to stop it.

Gene feels rather "selfish" on the topic; "if something gets in *my* way," he said, then it is against law and order. When a teenager abandoned his "junk car" across the street from Gene's house, it was offensive — not only to the neighborhood, but to Gene personally. People see the car in front of his house and "relate a bunch of junk" to him. Gene is bothered by that because he has $20,000 invested in the house and does not want people to associate his investment with "junk." Maintaining law and order in this instance means that the police have "got to get that car removed" because it offends Gene and he is a taxpayer.

Gene has not figured out what to make of the Black Panthers; he has not sorted out a stance toward them with which he is comfortable. Compared to his feelings about Martin Luther King, he "totally disagrees" with them. He thinks "they're like the cops; they would rather be god than do a job." He also gets the impression that "they want to be these all-powerful beings." And Gene "just doesn't dig all-powerful beings; that's all there is to it."

But that is not really all there is to it. Gene "kind of goes along with" the Panthers' idea of arming the black community to protect itself. He thinks black people need "to do something" to help themselves. He agreed most with "the original intent" of the idea; it was right for them to "give a guy a twelve-gauge shotgun and teach him how to use it." That way if some "son of a bitch" came in his front door, the guy "knows just what to do"; he could "take care of business." But Gene is strongly opposed to using firearms for any other purpose. "You don't need to go around stirring up shit with a shotgun," in his estimation. People should not take shotguns to demonstrations "like them dudes that went up there to the legislature in Sacramento." Gene thinks that was a "*big* mistake."

Firearms are a big part of his life. He has over forty rifles, pistols, and shotguns in his bedroom. He has had them since he was a kid; they are part of his hobby. He makes his own guns and loads his own ammunition; he "really digs the sport." When Panthers walked into the State Assembly packing shotguns, "putting on a big show," they "messed things up" for Gene. The legislators passed a law saying it was illegal to carry guns "just on account of them dudes that went up there making like gang busters."

Epilogue

Were Gene to be interviewed in a survey, he would probably be found ranking high on somebody's prejudice or authoritarianism scale. He certainly has his prejudices; his daughter marrying a black man is one. He also displays streaks of authoritarianism: shit disturbers in his estimation should be shot. We *expect* people like Gene to be prejudiced and/or authoritarian. That is what working-class life in America does to people.

If that was all we said about Gene, what a distorted, oversimplified, caricatured picture of him it would be!

Concepts such as prejudice or authoritarianism fail either to shed very much light on people like Gene Danich, or to describe them accurately. Gene departs from the authoritarian—prejudiced personality prototype in critical ways. He has the ability to criticise his father, for one. While Gene has no hostility toward his father, he is able to say, in terms of an ideal, that he is more of a man than his father. Gene has some anxiety about putting down his father; he stammered and paused a good deal throughout this part of the discussion, but he would not idealize him. Authoritarian people are ostensibly incapable of doing this. They are supposedly unable to be objective or critical of their parents, whom they need to idealize.

Gene's thoughts about black people are also not categorical — another supposed trait of prejudiced—authoritarian thinking. Gene makes distinctions among black people. He is favorably disposed toward blacks who espouse ideas he finds to his liking and adamantly opposes people he feels threatened by. He has no objections to certain black people living next door to him: "people who don't throw their garbage outside." And he would not live in a neighborhood with people who did. Gene does not perceive black people as an undifferentiated mass. He does not generalize about them in the categorical terms we would expect of a prejudiced person.

Rigid thinking may be a defining characteristic of prejudice. It hardly characterizes Gene Danich's thinking, however. If anything, Gene is remarkably open and flexible about some very controversial and emotional subjects. He favors law and order but he feels that policemen who brutalize black people "deserve to be shot at." He is ambivalent about riots. In his estimation people should not steal but there are mitigating circumstances. Businessmen who exploit black people "should" be robbed. His mind is not made up about the Black Panthers arming themselves. He can see a need for black people to know how to protect themselves from abuses of authority. Nevertheless, Panther demonstrations did result in legislation that restricted his use of firearms. We could say many things about Gene's thoughts regarding black people, but one of them would not be that they are rigid.

To talk about Gene Danich in terms of prejudice or authoritarianism would not only be inaccurate — it would also miss, if not obscure, what is essential about him. It would not capture the essence of the dynamic and complicated way in which he relates to the issues posed by black people.

Gene is quite aware of racial inequality in American life. He sees that blacks have a "rougher" time than whites. The jobs they hold are not as good as the ones white people have. They have less money than whites. He does not minimize these facts. Nevertheless, the situation is understandable to Gene; he can explain it. He thinks that the educational opportunities open to black people are "insufficient." He also feels that many whites are "down on" black people; they are prejudiced. In his estimation, these factors explain the situation of black people, and he is opposed to this state of affairs; he does not think it is right that black people should be treated in this fashion. Gene has a very strong commitment to what he considers fair play.

The most compelling feature of his thinking is his intense sense of self-interest. Above all else he is concerned about how issues affect him personally. It is through this lens that he filters all questions. Thus he is able to make the remarkable admission that if he were black he would be a Stokely Carmichael supporter because Carmichael is doing something for black people. He is white, however, and opposes the man because his actions might come back on Gene. The feelings Gene holds toward blacks are thus not dictated by prejudice or authoritarianism. Instead they follow from his evaluation of how his interests are affected. And because Gene recognizes inequality as blocked access, rather than as a form of privilege, he is open to some policies that will change the situation of black people. However, he is only open to policies that do not alter institutions from which he receives benefits: He favors integrated schools as long as busing is not involved; black people should be armed as long as firearms legislation is not increased.

Gene's openness to black power strategies is understandable in this context. As he chooses to understand the strategy, it is a very nonmilitant, nonviolent one. He sees it as equality, as solidarity. It is almost a legalistic, gradual approach to change. Gene can favor such a strategy because it barely affects him. Why he interprets it this way, how he has come to this understanding, is frankly puzzling.

Gene's posture toward black people is somewhat unique among our respondents. Most people develop ways of minimizing racism when they explain the situation of blacks. In this way they put distance between themselves and the problems involved. They get themselves off the hook. But Gene confronts the issues head on. Where there is a conflict between his interests and those of black people, he explicitly opts for his own. He makes no pretense about it and does not "pretty up" his formulations with fancy disclaimers. The uniqueness of Gene's "strategy" for defending his privileges is its simplicity and straightforwardness. He will resist anything that undercuts his self-interest.

This may explain his hostilily toward Malcolm X and Stokely Carmichael — but not its intensity. Gene is bothered by their cockiness and what he thinks is their pretension to be all-powerful gods. They behave as if they want to be "better" than he is. The special threat is not because they are blacks who are cocky and arrogant; whites who are arrogant and bossy also bother him. On the other hand, Gene is not at all hostile toward Martin Luther King who he feels is not trying to be better than he. None of this answers the question of why he likes King. Is it because King is not arrogant, or is it because his actions do not affect Gene?

Perhaps Gene's intense feelings about Carmichael are related to his deep desire to remain uninvolved in matters that evoke his violent propensities. After all, many of the key events or turning points in his life have been associated with physical confrontations. At age ten or eleven he defied his father and hit some neighborhood toughs over the head with a board. At sixteen or seventeen he punched a high school teacher and consequently received no diploma. His first personal contact with blacks was a fist in the mouth at age eighteen when he was in the Marines. That resulted in his becoming "prejudiced." A fight with another worker at the farm machinery company made it necessary for him to look for a new job. The job turned out to be the best one he has ever had. Maybe the reason Gene feels so strongly about Carmichael is that he fears the consequences of his involvement in the issues raised. He knows he is prone to violent encounters. He may be trying to conquer this tendency. As he remarked with some relief about longshore work, "you can't fight on the docks."

Gene reflects some of the characteristics sociologists find among working-class men. He is physically expressive; has a sense of fair play; strives for control over his work and dignity in his life; and has a feeling of camaraderie toward his fellow workers. He is an outdoorsman. But there is another side to Gene. A side that is not always associated with working-class life but which may be becoming more and more characteristic of young American workers. It perhaps helps explain Gene's concern about people like Carmichael. Gene may be a member of the working class, but he has a very bourgeois orientation toward life. He is far more concerned about property, property rights, and individual freedom than he is about collective rights or social justice. In this sense he is his father's son. Like his father, he is an intense individualist. Carmichael's appeal to black people as a collectivity is undoubtedly threatening.

Gene's fears are probably attributable, in part, to the process of embourgeoisement that segments of the American working class are experiencing. He earns a comfortable living. He will own his own house in only seven years. He drives a new car. His children go to a good school and have an opportunity to do better than he did if they wish. He has a stake in the process that makes all this possible, and Carmichael is challenging it. Perhaps it is fear of this challenge that Gene expresses when he says, "Carmichael wants to be better than me."

Gene's feelings about racial matters, like so many other issues in his life, mostly boil down to how they affect him personally. In areas where implications for his self-interest are unclear, his feelings are characteristically ambivalent.

When an issue appears to involve him, however, Gene's feelings are predictable: He wants to maximize his self-interests as he sees them. If there is a "logic" or "consistency" to Gene Danich's way of handling the world, this is it.

A study of this type cannot assess the extent to which Gene Danich is representative of young American workers. Indeed, that is not its purpose. Nevertheless, Gene's experiences, feelings, and formulations seem quite typical of many workingmen in his generation. Gene is neither authoritarian nor prejudiced. That is too simple. He is terribly ambivalent and confused. He is constantly beset by competing values, loyalties, goals, and realities. He is confronted daily by a world he does not always understand, one which often offends him, but over which he wants to exert a certain degree of control. He knows from experience that social resources are not infinite, that people are competing for them, and that he wants his fair share. His sense of fair play prevents him from relegating black people to perpetual inferiority, yet he is aware that their gain could be his loss. He has worked hard to get where he is and has suffered in the process; he has a great deal invested in what he believes to be America. The contradictions in his life and feelings put him in a difficult position. The only reasonable articulation he can live with is one that combines equality or fair play with his self-interests. It may not be consistent, or even logically possible. But it is honest. It is not the conjured creation of an authoritarian—prejudiced personality.

4 "The trouble is all this suspicion between us." Darlene Kurier

Prologue

If someone had told Hardy Frye in 1960 that he would be working on a Ph.D. in sociology eight years later, he would have looked at them in disbelief and said, "Sure man; and I suppose my father will also become a rich white man." In his mind one was probably as likely as the other. He was living in Compton at the time, driving a truck for the U.S. Postal Service, and felt he was doing quite well for a black man who had been raised by a working-class family in Tuskegee, Alabama. His father had worked as a security guard for the then-segregated Veterans Administration hospital in town. Most of his brothers and sisters were not as well off as he. With the exception of one brother, a high school teacher, they were all doing semi-skilled work or pursuing military careers. Frye figured he was doing all right. He was steadily employed and making pretty good money.

He certainly did not look forward to driving trucks the rest of his life, and he was bitter about the racial discrimination he encountered in Los Angeles. He was also attending a school for chefs; and although he graduated third in his class, a white Hungarian refugee at the bottom of the group landed a job that was denied to Frye. Nevertheless, he figured that was life for a black man living in a white world, and working for the post office was not such a bad deal.

The civil rights movement changed all that. When the Student Nonviolent Co-ordinating Committee (SNCC) began voter registration projects in the South, he was excited by the idea. He knew the South; he had lived there most of his life. He wanted to be a part of a movement to change it. And so he went to work for SNCC in 1964. For two years he was one of the group's most effective organizers in Mississippi.

During his stint there, he met a number of white volunteers from the North who were impressed by his mental as well as organizational capabilities. One was a professor at Sacramento State College in California. He encouraged Frye to attend college if he decided to leave the South.

I met Hardy in 1966. He had taken the professor's advice and was a student at Sacramento State College. He also continued to do organizing for SNCC in Sacramento, which is how I met him. We worked together on a SNCC newspaper (*The Movement*) published in San Francisco. Frye and I rapidly became close companions; we were intimate friends as well as political comrades, I, like many others, was extremely impressed by him. I thought he was a natural sociologist and encouraged him to go to graduate school.

Two years later Hardy was admitted to graduate school at the University of California at Berkeley. At the time I was research coordinator for the project on which this study is based. Most of our interviews were to be conducted with black people and I thought Frye could help. I had observed him organizing and was impressed with his ability to break down barriers between people and get to the heart of issues with them. He liked to talk with people and was good at it. No matter what the situation, Hardy could provoke an exciting, often controversial, conversation. He had also developed excellent and extensive contacts with black people in the Sacramento area through his organizing activities. I thought he would be able to arrange interviews with people who are normally inaccessible to sociological researchers. My hunch proved correct and Frye conducted numerous interviews with black people.

He also had contacts with whites he met while organizing poor people in Sacramento. When he asked me if he should interview them, I agreed. My apprehensions about black people interviewing whites were minimized by Alex's success. I also thought that people who shared experiences with Hardy probably respected him. His color would make no difference to people who knew him.

The interview with Mrs. Darlene Kurier indicates I was right. Mrs. Kurier worked in a Head Start program as an assistant and became acquainted with Hardy when he was organizing welfare mothers. They had been allies on some issues and opponents on others. She respected him in either capacity. When he began working with us, he told her he was doing research on racism and asked if he could interview her. She agreed and the interview took place one afternoon at her house in a Sacramento suburb.

The interview was not one of Hardy's best. It was one of his first attempts and he was a bit mechanical. He seemed overly concerned about covering all the issues we had discussed in connection with the project. He consequently jumped from topic to topic without going into sufficient depth on some important ones. He was also somewhat nervous in his new role as sociological researcher and sometimes had difficulty getting Mrs. Kurier to understand his questions. Hardy's pronounced southern black accent probably contributed to the confusion as well.

Mrs. Kurier also made the interview difficult to conduct. Sometimes she seemed unable to answer his questions; at other times she seemed unwilling. She had to be pushed in many instances and often disarmed Hardy with insistent claims of ignorance concerning potentially embarrassing issues. She giggled nervously throughout, apparently trying to defuse the situation. Hardy pushed her, often only to end up with an "I really just don't know." The interview frustrated him intensely. When he gave it to me he quipped, "I just don't know about you white folks, Dave. Can't you answer simple questions?"

Because of its problems the interview proved to be an important one. The frustration, indecision, and ignorance contained in it reflect problems that go beyond the interview itself. The problems are representative of how Mrs. Kurier deals and does *not* deal with racial issues in American life. Frye's frustration often caused him to be more direct than he might normally have been. In turn, his directness forced Mrs. Kurier to be more candid than she intended to be. The interview was consequently a very revealing one.

Growing up unaware

What is going on, wondered Mrs. Darlene Kurier when she realized there was a serious civil rights movement happening in her country. Why are people rioting? What is all this talk about black power? The world in which she had grown up was changing and she was having difficulty with the consequences. She was confused, and she was also very fearful.

Mrs. Kurier was not really prepared for the racial showdown that occurred late in the 1960s. From childhood through maturity she had lived in a kind of racial vacuum. Mrs. Kurier is fifty-two years old; she has spent most of those years in relatively small or suburban communities. She was born and raised in Hawthorne, California, a suburb of Los Angeles. That is where she spent her childhood and a good part of her married life as well. Sixteen years ago the Kuriers left Southern California, tired of city life, the traffic, and all that it implied. They moved north to Fresno where they could live in the "country." But Fresno was more of a city than they expected and five years later they moved even further north to the suburb of Sacramento where they currently live.

Mrs. Kurier was not born into a wealthy family; her father was a moderately successful minister. He met her mother in Germany while doing missionary work before World War I. The family lived in a relatively comfortable, although not totally white, neighborhood. There were a few "colored children" in any school she attended, but Mrs. Kurier never associated with them. For one thing there were so few of them; for another — well, she just never did.

When she was about nine years old, however, a little Negro boy tried to associate with her. He was smitten by a minor case of puppy love and sent her little notes. His love offerings not only embarrassed her, they made her furious. Looking back on it now, she is not sure what provoked her wrath. She does not know if it was because he was Negro or just a boy. She recalls being unreceptive to receiving love notes from any little boys at the time; she did not appreciate it one bit. So she was furious when the boy left notes on her desk and she tried to ignore him. Except for this one instance, she never associated with her colored classmates.

"Why not?" Frye wanted to know. Mrs. Kurier did not think she had acted that way "purposely." It was just that there had *always* been "racial discrimination"; it was simply a "fact" of life. "*What* was the fact?" Hardy asked. "The fact that there had been racial discrimination," she replied. And then, chuckling, she added, "There *still is,* you know." Hardy knew. But there was still something he did not understand: How did she *know* that discrimination existed?

"Did someone tell you?" Perhaps, but she really did not remember.

Maybe her parents talked about it in the house, Hardy suggested. No, Mrs. Kurier did not remember any such conversations. They never discussed whether white people were any better than Negroes, or anything like that. In fact, it was a subject that was more or less ignored. Mrs. Kurier could not think of a reason *why* she did not associate with Negroes. Except, of course, because there was discrimination in the school. "Otherwise how would we *feel* there was a difference?" she asked. Hardy laughed, "But that's what I'm asking *you*." Mrs. Kurier struggled with her memory. There must have been some reason for the feelings, she thought out loud. And yet she really could not put her finger on exactly what they were.

The feelings were not peculiar to blacks, she noted, as if that might somehow explain them more adequately. There were also Japanese people in the area where she was raised. They worked on truck farms in surrounding communities and were more numerous than Negroes. She did not associate with them too much either. Hardy was beginning to sound like a broken record. "Why not?" Mrs. Kurier giggled nervously, giving him an answer she thought he wanted to hear. "Because for some stupid reason people seem to think that one group can't mix with the other." Hardy began to bear down on her. "We're coming to a fence here," he said sternly but respectfully. "You say you felt there was discrimination and I ask how did you know this. Then you say it was discrimination. We're going in circles."

Mrs. Kurier could see that. And she was frustrated by it too. She tried to maintain her composure but her voice was rising nonetheless. "I don't remember why!" she exclaimed. "It's just something I guess you grow up with when you're very young. And you don't really realize it. It's there; that's all!" Still, she was convinced that her mother never told her not to mix with certain people. The woman would not have done that because she was foreign born, spoke with an accent, and felt people looked down on her because of it. Hardy persisted: "But you picked it up somehow; how did you know not to associate with blacks or Japanese?" Mrs. Kurier tried another angle. "I guess it just seemed like this was the thing in our culture." But she could not put her finger on why or who or where it came from. She thought maybe it came from people she associated with, the kids she played with. She imagined that was where it came from more than anything else.

Frye was still unsatisfied. "How does it happen?" Mrs. Kurier's patience was being pushed to its limit. "There must be homes other than the one I came from where there *is* a stronger feeling," she said curtly. "I probably picked it up from their children."

Knowing when to leave well enough alone, Hardy suggested they talk about her high school experiences with black people. "Were there any Negroes in high school?" There were a few, she recalled, a very few. She remembers being friendly to them; she was never rude. They were never rude to her, either. But as in elementary school, she never associated with them socially. Frye raised the troubling question he had just dropped. "Why not?" Mrs. Kurier started to say it was because her white friends had insisted on it. But then she corrected herself. No, as a matter of fact one of her good friends had gone with a boy who "appeared" to be colored. He insisted he was not and was so embarrassed by the accusation that he had blood tests taken to see if there was a strain of Negro blood in his family. There was not. The tests "showed" the family was of French ancestry. But most of Mrs. Kurier's friends did not accept the proof. They still could not understand why the girl would go with a boy who looked as though he was Negro.

Frye was confused. "Why couldn't you understand it?"

Mrs. Kurier returned to her earlier explanation. "It goes back to the same thing," she said. "Our society wouldn't accept the intermingling, the amalgamation of races." Hardy still was not satisfied. "Why not?" It just was not the "accepted" thing to do; that's all. "But who said you shouldn't do it?" Hardy said, getting frustrated again. Mrs. Kurier did not know. It was just something people grew up with; she did not know where it started. The only explanation she could come up with was that racial discrimination had always existed.

They were back in the circle they had failed to break before. "You keep coming back to this," Hardy pointed out. "But what I want to find out is how did you *know* racial discrimination existed?" Mrs. Kurier could see the frustrating bind they were in. "That's what I'm saying," she laughed. "I don't *know*." She did not feel she could go far enough into her background to really explain where it started. As far as she could tell, it was due to the "makeup of our society." It was something that was accepted because it was "the way of society."

Actually Mrs. Kurier grew up mostly unaware of blacks and the issues they posed for white people in America. The questions Frye was raising were not issues for her during adolescence. She never really thought too much about black people until much later in her life when she was married and living in Bremerton, Washington, during World War II. Until that time there were so few blacks in her life that they hardly left an imprint on her consciousness. Her first "real" contact with blacks came during the war when she worked in the personnel office of a Navy shipyard. She did not work with blacks, but she traveled on buses with them to and from the shipyard. It was a new experience for Mrs. Kurier. She found the blacks very "overbearing"; they were "pushy." People would start to board the bus and the blacks would push them out of the way.

Just prior to this experience, Mrs. Kurier had become

"aware of the great injustice done to colored people all through the years." How she became aware is not clear because Hardy did not ask her. But because of this awareness she could understand why colored people were acting in this manner. Most of them came from the South, she explained. Being in the North was a new experience for them; they were living in an area where they had some rights; there was no segregation. And because they suddenly had freedom, it went to their heads. That is why they were so pushy and overbearing on the buses. But it was not their fault, she quickly pointed out. It happened because they lacked social graces which until then only white people had the advantage of learning.

Mrs. Kurier "understood" this, but many of her white coworkers did not. These people felt the coloreds were pushing them around, trying to take over. A lot of them thought the colored people were trying to be better than they were. That was hard to take. It made them furious.

While Mrs. Kurier understood the reasons why Negroes acted this way, she still felt "pushed around." She would be standing in line waiting to board the bus and a group of colored people would shove her out of the way without recognizing that she had been waiting for her turn to get on. No one likes to be pushed around, she laughed. Colored people do not like to be pushed around by whites, she pointed out; and they have certainly been pushed around all these years. So naturally, she concluded, whites feel angry when they are shoved by blacks. Her personal anger, however, was directed toward the act of pushing, not the color of the person doing it. If a white person had pushed her she would have been equally mad. But many of the whites she had worked with had felt the color of the pusher was all important.

"Why?" asked Hardy. Mrs. Kurier thought it stemmed from prejudice that people had lived with all their lives.

The idea that white people are a superior race was pretty much accepted by all when she was younger. Mrs. Kurier had to admit that even she was affected by it. She supposed that every white person felt that way during her youth. It was an "accepted" fact; people did not start questioning it until they got older. She realizes now that it is a false idea. But when she was young the idea was "there"; it had been "created" by society.

Perhaps that is why she never associated with black children in school, she thought. She did not think it was a conscious decision, however; children do not really make those kinds of decisions for themselves. But once she was older and began to make decisions for herself, once she understood the nature of prejudice, she never acted on the belief that whites were a superior race. She has never refused to join a group simply because black people belong to it. She associates with blacks now.

In fact, she is still friendly with her high school friend who went with the boy everyone thought was colored. They are married now. Mrs. Kurier is polite to him; she even visits with them. They come up to Sacramento and stay with the Kuriers on occasion. She no longer feels that his color is something that should separate people. And when the Kuriers were building a house in Southern California, they hired a colored draftsman to draw up the plans. Mrs. Kurier even asked him to come in the house. His visit seemed perfectly all right to her despite the fact that many white people would not ask a colored person into their house. As far as Mrs. Kurier was concerned, if he could do the work there was no reason why she should not invite him in.

Her attitudes sometimes cause problems with her husband. They have differences on the subject of black people. She thinks his attitude is a very narrow one and they argue about it. He contends that colored people are given too much leeway these days, and if things continue to move in the same direction, white people will have to step aside for the coloreds. He is just prejudiced, she concludes; these are ideas he was born into.

But she gets awfully mad at him about it. She feels that a person should be judged by himself; by his own education and what that person is himself. People's color should be irrelevant. She thinks it is unfortunate that all white people do not agree with her. Many of them insist on judging people by their color. She thinks that is wrong; it is an attitude that must be changed.

Personally, Mrs. Kurier would accept an educated colored person in her all-white neighborhood — if that person had an education equal to hers and lived in the same manner she did. She especially admires people who have at least one college degree and possibly more, but she would be friendly with anyone who had her interests and could talk intelligently about them, even if they did not have a college education. But she would not want a neighbor who did not share any of her interests and was not very intelligent. The issue, as far as she is concerned, is an individual one. It is not a matter of race. People should be judged by their personal merits, in her estimation.

Coming to grips with the 1960s

Mrs. Kurier's thinking had undergone some pretty important changes between her youth and the late 1960s. But when the civil rights movement exploded on the American scene, she was confused. Just as she was coming to evaluate black people as individuals, they demanded to be treated as a group. When she came to recognize that black people needed equal opportunities, they were demanding political power. As she began to locate the causes of discrimination in individual prejudice, black people were referring to the entire society as racist. By the time she recognized that blacks needed help, they rejected it. The period during the civil rights movement troubled Mrs. Kurier. It complicated and contradicted the position on black people she had been working out for almost thirty years.

Mrs. Kurier found urban rioting particularly difficult to deal with. In her estimation, the riots were a "pretty sad" situation; they were "terrible." She was equally upset by the mayor of Chicago's response to them. She thought it was terrible for a person in his position to say that all rioters should be shot. But what bothered her most about the riots was that the colored people were hurting themselves.

America is finally ending racial discrimination, she thinks. "We are working to give the colored people in the South the vote now. We are trying to give them more advantages and an equal education." Mrs. Kurier feels strongly that the government is trying to do something about racial inequality. The problem, as she views it, is that Negroes are getting too impatient. That is what causes riots. And riots disturb her because she feels if they keep up, America will become a police state. "What good would come from that?" she asked.

"The labor movement was violent in its early organizing stages," Hardy pointed out, "and look where they are now." Mrs. Kurier thought labor violence took on different proportions. She agreed there had been riots. She also knew that police and even the National Guard had been called in, but she still felt the labor violence had been on a much smaller scale. "Now you have whole cities being burned," she said. And she feared that if the National Guard had to be called out every time that happened, it would make America into a police state.

"But many black people feel it's already a police state," Hardy replied. Mrs. Kurier had to disagree. "Not to the extent that Germany was under Hitler," she argued. "We don't have a fascist government." Hardy concurred, but he still wanted to pursue the violence issue. "What about the argument that America has a tradition of violence? Look at the treatment of Indians and black people. Maybe violence is the only thing this country understands." Mrs. Kurier sighed deeply. She did not agree with that formulation either. As far as she could tell, America had made real strides through means other than violence. "Violence has been used in the past," she concluded, "but it isn't really part of the American tradition."

Mrs. Kurier does not deny that the police are sometimes brutal. But she feels that police brutality stems more from "our society's prejudice that has been with us for so many years" than any tradition of violence. She feels that the primary function of the police is supposed to be upholding law and order, protecting people. Nevertheless, she realizes that when police departments are predominantly white they think their role is to protect whites from the black community. "It shouldn't be that way, though," she added.

Black radicals do not make Mrs. Kurier much happier than do prejudiced white policemen. Stokely Carmichael is "too militant" for her; she was a great admirer of Martin Luther King. Carmichael is in too much of a hurry. Of course she can understand *why* Negroes are in a hurry to improve their way of life, and does not "blame" them for this. She can really understand why they riot and why "all of this is going on." It is just that she does not think it's a "good thing." And as far as she is concerned, "Carmichael is too anxious to overthrow all the bounds." Change has got to come an awful lot slower than that, Mrs. Kurier feels.

While her feelings about Carmichael are clear, her sentiments concerning black power are not. She is not really sure that she knows just what it is. When she hears the "term" black power she thinks it has a "wrong connotation." It automatically builds up resistance among Caucasians because they think it means blacks want power over whites. But Mrs. Kurier is not sure that is what blacks mean by it. She tentatively thinks that it means bringing blacks into their own. "Is this right?" she asked Hardy.

"Well that's what I *thought* it meant," he laughed. "But evidently most whites took it differently. How did you feel when you first heard the phrase?" She felt the way most whites did. It sounded to her as if black power meant blacks would have power over whites. And she did not feel blacks should have that power, any more than whites should have power over blacks. But of course, she added parenthetically, "the power has always been on the white side, hasn't it."

Mrs. Kurier is also ambivalent about busing children in order to integrate schools. And like most topics, she talked about it in terms of white people other than herself. She supposes that some families would resent it, while others would feel it was the only way to achieve equality. How would she personally feel about having black kids bused into her neighborhood? If this is the only way Negroes can get an adequate and equal education, she replied, then it should be done. On the other hand, if they can get the same education, have the same quality teachers and the "same everything else" where they live, why bother? Thinking out loud, she began to answer the question she had posed. But then the schools that colored children attended would be predominantly Negro, and that would keep "voluntary segregation," wouldn't it? So maybe busing is all right, she concluded.

When the busing issue was first raised in the news media, she felt it was not the right solution to the problem. She did not think it was good to have children bused so far from their homes. She questioned the purpose it would serve, thinking colored kids had the same advantages in their schools as whites did in theirs. But she is not sure about that now. She thinks that in a way busing is perhaps breaking down some of the segregation that exists in America. So Mrs. Kurier is beginning to think that maybe it is a good thing.

Interracial marriage is another issue that gives Mrs. Kurier pause. She is not of one mind on the subject. Eventually, she thinks, it will be an accepted practice in America. She doubts, however, that it will be broadly accepted. Nevertheless, people will go along with it. The situation of Japanese war brides is an example. When servicemen first came home with them there were strong feelings against the couples. That changed over time, and now they are accepted. But regardless of how other people feel, Mrs. Kurier would not personally discriminate against any person. If she had a friend who came home with a Japanese bride, Mrs. Kurier would "accept" her. "What if he came home with a Negro bride?" Hardy asked. Mrs. Kurier thinks she would accept that woman, too. "What if your daughter came home with a Negro husband?" She would also accept him.

"Perhaps it would be a shock," she added quickly. She would be concerned about what friends and relatives would say and feel about it. They would ask, "Why has she done this?" They would wonder a great deal. She recalls that people made many disparaging comments when Dean Rusk's daughter married a Negro. They asked how the child could possibly do that to her father. In spite of this, Mrs. Kurier feels that people should be judged on their own merits. The question should be how do they fit into a society or cultural environment, not what is their color. "If we ever get to a place where the races are on an equal basis," she pointed out, "then why should it make such a difference?"

Hardy asked her how she thought black people felt

about intermarriage. "Perhaps they don't want it either," she replied. Her daughter's boyfriend had recently returned from Vietnam and told her that in the service, Negroes discriminate against whites. "They will have nothing to do with the white fellows," he told her; "they stick strictly to themselves." Whenever there is racial trouble over there, "the Negroes band together and protect their own interests." The white guys do not act that way, however. Segregation in Vietnam must be caused by Negroes, she feels. So maybe the American situation exists because of both groups.

Frye wanted to return to the topic of intermarriage. "How do you think a black mother would feel if her daughter were to marry a white guy?" Mrs. Kurier thought the woman would probably feel that she did not want it. It would cause too much of a hardship on her and the daughter. The woman might feel that the situation would bring her daughter nothing but heartache; the girl would be "segregated against," she would not be accepted into the white society. "So perhaps she might feel as strongly against it as the white mother," Mrs. Kurier concluded. But she does not really know; she is not sure.

The issue troubles her. It is complex. "Colored people are suspicious of white people," she noted. They have good reasons to be. They never really let white people know exactly how they feel. Mrs. Kurier does not think that is wrong; it is merely a fact. "They are even suspicious of the white people who are trying to help them," she pointed out. "They wonder about white people's motives." So she guesses that colored people are not much happier about intermarriage than whites. And she wonders how things will ever work out with all the suspicion that exists between the races. Things were so simple as she saw them in the past. They are so much more complex and complicated now.

Education is the solution

"I guess everybody is going to have to change their attitudes," said Mrs. Kurier with a great deal of conviction. The issues are complicated. The civil rights movement has muddied the water for a lot of people. But this is the only way out of the impasse, as far as she can tell. The only problem is that it cannot be done overnight. It will be a long, slow process and it will have to start with education. Colored people will have to be educated up to the same level as whites. They will have to be given the same advantages as white people. In Mrs. Kurier's estimation, "the solution has to come through education."

"Yes, Negroes are the ones who have to be educated," she continued. They are the ones who have not had the advantages in the past. That is why Head Start programs are necessary, and that is why most of the Head Start students are Negro. She realizes, of course, that some of the students are white, but they are poor whites, people who also lack advantages. In this respect they are the same as Negroes.

The crux of the matter for Mrs. Kurier is education. If Negroes become educated they will be accepted by white people. They need the same advantages as whites. And when they have had a chance, the problem will be on its way to being solved. "But you see," she said, "education really takes a generation, doesn't it? It starts with the baby and continues until the time when the baby reaches adulthood. But it just can't come overnight." People who are rioting and causing trouble do not have the background or the proper education to see that this long-term process of education is working out.

Mrs. Kurier thinks the process will take almost a generation. She also knows that people are not going to wait that long. "The Negro is impatient." And she added firmly, "I don't blame him!" She began to chuckle at the observation, which contradicted her prognosis. "Really," she said as if to underscore the irony, "I mean I can understand and I can see why we are having riots." She can understand it and she is afraid they will continue. "All this hate has been bottled up for so long. Now that people are beginning to get a few advantages and the road turns a little upward, they're impatient to have more."

She wanted to use an analogy to make her point, but feared it would insult Hardy. "I hope you'll excuse me for using it," she said.

"Go ahead," Hardy insisted.

"I'm sorry to use it, but . . ."

"Go ahead."

"It's just sort of an example."

"Look, I can take it."

"You take a dog that has been penned up, tied and chained all his life," she bagan, "and then you turn him loose." The dog would have had no training. People could not take it into the house and expect it to act like one that had been housebroken. The dog would want to run loose and explore, for this was its first experience with freedom. Mrs. Kurier felt the analogy applied to the colored . . . the Negro. It was not until ten or fifteen years ago that they really started to get freedom. Voting restrictions in the South were not lifted until 1960. Negroes are experiencing something new, she explained, and they are impatient.

"Many blacks don't want the kind of freedom whites offer them," Hardy suggested. "Some people are saying 'we want to be separate from whites because they will never accept us as equals.'" Mrs. Kurier sighed. She guesses that is something America is going to have to face in the next five to fifteen years. She feels Negroes have a right to think this way; after all, "white people have done *this* to them." She maintains nonetheless that eventually "we'll have to become one society where we *all* accept one another." Mrs. Kurier does not think America should have separation between the races. If people are going to live harmoniously together, they are going to have to be together, they are going to have to learn to live together.

"But what about the whites who move out of neighborhoods when blacks move in?" Frye asked. "Should they be allowed to move out?" Mrs. Kurier had to think about that question for a moment. "Well," she began, "a person has his own rights. This is what our country is based on. Freedom is dear to us all." She paused again. "Yes," she decided, "people should be able to move out if they want." But she refused to concede that this contradicted her opposition to separation by blacks. "I just feel that eventually this will not be," she said before Hardy had a chance to point up the discrepancy. "There *will* come a time when we'll all accept each other."

Frye was getting exasperated. "Through what method?" he asked in a wry tone of voice. "Through education and advantages so that everybody will have an equal opportunity," she said as if it were the first time the thought had dawned on her. And the solution also applied to the high unemployment rate among colored people, she continued. The reason they do not have jobs is because they lack an education. But she could also see the employer's point of view. "You can't blame the manufacturer for not wanting to hire them," she said sternly, "because they haven't had the training or the learning yet." As far as she can tell, the problem will persist until coloreds are brought up to the equal of the white labor force. "We just *have* to do something to solve this problem!" she said excitedly.

Frye thought educating whites might be a good beginning. "Yes," she agreed. "Whites have to be educated, too. They have to be educated to accept the fact that we have got to eliminate discrimination."

"But there's all this suspicion between the races."

Mrs. Kurier realizes that educating whites in this day and age is going to be difficult. "Whites have always had the upper hand," she noted, "and many of them are suspicious of blacks now because they're afraid that maybe the blacks are going to get the upper hand!" The thought amused her and she laughed, saying, "perhaps they might reverse the conditions." Her voice became more somber. She thought fear was a serious force to be reckoned with in the white community. It was a particular problem among working-class whites because they are not intellectuals. As she sees it, white intellectuals are accepting colored people more than the nonintellectuals. It all goes back to the secret behind the problem: education. Whites who have not been educated are not as tolerant of Negroes as those who have been. "You mix with both types, Hardy. Don't you find this to be so?" Hardy laughed. He would have to raise questions about that formula. "Didn't whites in California vote three to one in favor of Proposition 14, the proposition that repealed the open housing ordinance?" he asked.

Mrs. Kurier realizes this was true. But it concerned property rights. People felt they had the right to decide what should be done with their property. Personally, she feels an open housing ordinance is necessary if there are to be any real strides toward equality. It is another step in that direction. But she can understand why people voted against open housing. It has to do with money. "An awful lot of people are fearful that if one Negro family moves into their neighborhood this will bring others. And then their property value starts dropping." Mrs. Kurier knows of instances in which this has happened. She has friends in Southern California who used to live in strictly all-white neighborhoods. Colored people started moving in gradually and pretty soon the area became almost totally colored.

When some of her friends decided to sell their houses they had to settle for prices they felt were far below the values of their homes.

"Why didn't they just stay?" Hardy asked, making the alternative sound so simple. Mrs. Kurier's friends felt the neighborhood was being taken over by the colored people, that's why. She thinks this is the way most white people feel; they are afraid colored people will get the upper hand. Negroes will move in and take over. There will be so many of them that the majority will be colored instead of white. And because they are white, they feel they should be the majority.

Mrs. Kurier shares some of these concerns herself. The thing that worries her is that if whites became the minority — "well, you know," she said laughingly, "the fact is that majority rules." She giggled uncomfortably at the implications of the hypothetical situation. "If you have a predominantly Negro society, then *they're* gonna make the rules and they are gonna say what can be done and what can't." She switched the frame of reference back to her friends. Perhaps they are afraid that maybe the Negro will want to get even for what has happened in the past. Mrs. Kurier thinks there are good reasons for believing this. "Look what happens when you have a large grouping of Negro people and only a few whites. There've been cases where they've *beaten* up the white people." She thinks this is why whites fear Negro people.

Working-class whites, in her estimation, have other fears as well. They are afraid that work will be given to colored people instead of whites. Then it will be the whites who are discriminated against; the tables will be reversed. Maybe this is why they keep Negroes out of their unions, she suggested. But she thinks there is more to it than that. Somehow or other they feel they are better than the colored fellow. "They think they should have the choice of everything. But don't ask me why, please!"

Mrs. Kurier's friends are not the only people who fear black majorities. She does, too. The mere fact of Negro membership in an organization would not persuade Mrs. Kurier to avoid it. She would belong to a group that had colored people in it. But she would not join a group that was predominantly Negro. Her reasoning is simple: "Because then I would be the minority!" If black people want to join groups that are predominantly white, that is fine with Mrs. Kurier. They should be allowed to. She belongs to groups like this. But she would not do the opposite. She is prevented by fear. "I feel they don't trust us; they wouldn't trust *me*."

Mrs. Kurier is inhibited from joining a predominantly black organization for yet another reason. "I wonder if they would accept me. I'm afraid that they might not." If she were positive that they would, she might feel free to do it. "The trouble is," she said in a tone of voice verging on defeat, "there is all this suspicion between both of us. There are the suspicions that colored people have of whites and the ones whites have of coloreds." But she would not allow her optimism to dissipate completely. Momentarily perking up, she said, "I think eventually these suspicions will disappear. When we've had time to amalgamate I guess."

Her concern about black neighbors is related to these fears. Returning to the topic, she said, "I wouldn't have any objections to living in a black neighborhood if I felt that I was completely accepted." But what bothers her is all the suspicion between the races. She does not feel she would be accepted. And to complicate matters, she does not know what form acceptance would take if it were expressed by blacks. She is aware, however, that some whites have been accepted. She knows there are whites who are sympathetic to the colored movement. They have been accepted. Perhaps they have lost their fears and inhibitions, she guesses. Mrs. Kurier paused for a couple moments. She shook her head. "I only know what I feel. And I feel that there is so much *anger* in the Negro people toward the white people. I mean . . . it's as though in our whole country we're walking on a powder keg right now!" And then she laughed nervously, as if frightened by the realization she had just verbalized.

The fears expressed by Mrs. Kurier intrigued Frye. They were emotions he struggled with daily as a black man but he could not understand them coming from a white person. He wanted to tell her this but felt it was inappropriate in his role as interviewer. So he did the next best thing. "Let me ask you a hypothetical question." he said. "Suppose you walked into a courtroom and everyone in it was black: the judge, the bailiff, the clerk, everybody. How would you feel?"

Mrs. Kurier laughed. "I guess I'd just pray and hope the saints would be with me because I would feel the deck was stacked against me!"

"In other words, if you were black, you'd be prayin' all the time!"

"Yeah," she laughed. "Yeah!"

"Okay then!" Hardy said in an amused tone of voice. The point had been made.

Epilogue

Darlene Kurier totally frustrated Hardy Frye. Each time he thought he had her thinking pinned down, she wiggled out and said something else that complicated or confused an earlier formulation. She contradicted herself throughout the interview. Frye found it particularly difficult to

cope with the two faces Mrs. Kurier presented. At times
she seemed blind and bigoted, other times she appeared
well-meaning and flexible. Which was the "real" Mrs. Kurier, he wondered.

People like Mrs. Kurier *are* frustrating. They do not present themselves in neat packages tied together with a consistent bow that nicely pulls together all of their thinking
on a subject. But what makes Mrs. Kurier frustrating is also
what makes her interesting. The question she poses is:
How do people handle the various, and often contradictory, aspects of their racial thinking? The ways in which
she manages these inconsistencies represent her approach
to the contradictions set in motion by the black presence.

It is easy to point out the apparent contradictions in
Mrs. Kurier's thinking. The interview was filled with them.

She thinks America is moving toward racial equality but
that Americans are walking on a racial powder keg.

She is opposed to separatism for blacks but she is not
opposed to whites moving out of integrated neighborhoods.

She is opposed to racial discrimination but she supports
property rights that effectively maintain it.

She "understands" militancy but she thinks it is "self-
defeating."

She recognizes that black people need jobs but feels employers are justified in not hiring them.

She "understands" riots but thinks they are "sad."

She wants to relate to people as individuals but fears
blacks.

She sees America essentially as an egalitarian society
but recognizes that most Americans are prejudiced.

If we assume that Mrs. Kurier is sincere, and there is no

reason to believe otherwise, then two things become apparent. One: None of the issues are logically contradictory. One can consistently subscribe to both sides of these issues. For example, America can be both egalitarian and contain prejudiced people. Or, logically speaking, one can favor both property rights and human rights. Two: The "contradictions" do not represent misperceptions or distortions in her thinking. They are contradictions that can be located outside her head and inside American society. For example, black people *do* need jobs but, given the universalistic standards that business people are legally obligated to live by, they *are* justified in not hiring black people. The "contradictions" in Mrs. Kurier's thinking reflect conflicts of interest and ideals in the society itself. They do not represent mental or psychological problems on her part.

But to establish that the contradictions in Mrs. Kurier's thinking are neither imagined nor problems of logic does not mean she is consistent. In terms of how she presents herself she is not. I have only staked a claim on the sociological dimension of the problem. Thus the question of how she handles these contradictions is still an open one.

Reconciling contradictions: black people need to be educated

America is basically a healthy society as far as Mrs. Kurier is concerned. The government is working to eliminate racial inequality; voting restrictions on blacks have been lifted. The society is moving in the right direction. Mrs. Kurier believes this very strongly. It is an article of faith for her. As she puts it, "there *will* come a time when we'll all accept each other." She feels no compulsion to argue or demonstrate the point. It will occur sometime, that's all.

Mrs. Kurier is not, however, unaware of racial problems in America. Her faith does not reduce her to blindness. She recognizes problems: There are discrepancies between what America professes to be and the situation in which black people find themselves. The factors she recognizes as defining features of these problems are instrumental in her ability to reconcile the contradictory aspects of her thinking. In her estimation, America's racial problems are attributable to the following things. (1) Black people lack the advantages white people have. (2) Black people lack social graces. (3) Black people are too impatient; they are in a hurry and some of them want to overthrow all bounds. As a result, black people sometimes hurt themselves. (4) White and black people are afraid of each other. (5) White and black people are suspicious of one another. (6) White people have prejudiced ideas toward blacks and think one group cannot mix with another. Whites believe they are better than blacks. (7) The idea of racial discrimination has always existed; it is an accepted fact, a part of society.

In Mrs. Kurier's thinking the issues that account for America's racial troubles share one of the following two characteristics: either they exist in people's minds (are problems only on the level of ideas), or they refer to the *dis*advantages of blacks rather than the *ad*vantages of whites. Problems with these characteristics can, of course, be solved without structurally altering the society. Changing white people's thinking and correcting black people's disadvantages can happen by tinkering with individuals rather than societies. And this is exactly what is suggested by the solution Mrs. Kurier advances for the elimination of racial problems.

Educating black people is the solution, in her estimation. Over time education will change white attitudes toward blacks and give them the same advantages as whites. Nothing else needs to happen, as she sees it. The solution she suggests, then, solves the problems that she feels cause America's racial troubles. But it does much more than that.

(1) The solution validates her faith in the basic goodness of American society. It gives her reason to believe that there will be a time when racial harmony will exist. Thus her faith is not misplaced or utopian.

(2) The solution places the responsibility for change on black people rather than whites. The changes whites must experience are indirect. Whites will change their thinking when blacks are better educated.

(3) The entire social apparatus that is related to racial issues is untouched by the solution. Since racial advantage or privilege is not the issue, elimination of it is not part of the solution.

(4) The solution resolves most of the apparent contradictions in her thinking about racial issues. She can, and does, explain seemingly inconsistent sentiments and formulations by saying that they will be worked out over time when blacks are as well educated as whites. Thus what would otherwise be contradictory statements become consistent, given her overall "logic."

Copping a plea: "I just don't know."

Mrs. Kurier cannot resolve all her inconsistencies with appeals to the educational process. Her childhood experiences with people of color testify to that. And when this happens, she usually cops a plea of ignorance. Perhaps if she appears ignorant or unaware of the sources of her behavior, then she is not responsible for them. This was clearly how she handled questions pertaining to her early childhood. She persistently claimed ignorance regarding how she knew not to associate with black children.

Certainly a case can be made that a fifty-two-year-old person might legitimately forget the details of her past. But Mrs. Kurier should probably not be given the benefit of that doubt. She seems to selectively forget certain parts of her life while actively remembering other details. She does not remember how she knew about discrimination, but she can vividly recall the details concerning a boy in high school who everyone thought was black. Mrs. Kurier seems to "know" what she wants to and claims ignorance about issues she finds unsettling. Her knowledge is thus conditional upon the response she anticipates it will provoke in the person with whom she is communicating. This is another important way in which Mrs. Kurier reconciles inconsistencies in her thinking.

The way in which she implicitly defines prejudice is also related to her plea of ignorance about certain matters. She assumes that prejudice is conscious and purposive. She went to great lengths to explain that she was always friendly, not rude, to the black children with whom she did not associate in school. Racial discrimination was something she grew up with, she repeatedly pointed out, but it was not something she was aware of at the time. She was not conscious of the reasons for her actions. Her refusal to interact with blacks was not based on anything about which she was aware. It was part of the culture. She never "thought about" blacks until her World War II experience, and then she tried not to act in a prejudiced manner because she understood why they were pushy.

The implication seems to be that if you are unaware of why you act in a certain way and do not harbor any malicious motives, then you are not "prejudiced." Since she was "unaware" until adulthood, she apparently wants to be absolved of any racial liabilities incurred during childhood. Mrs. Kurier did not say what church she attends, but this may well be a racial twist on the theory of original sin.

This position can be extended to matters beyond childhood. If people move from an integrated neighborhood because they fear property values are threatened, and if they are ignorant of the racial consequences of that action, then according to Mrs. Kurier's conception they are not prejudiced. And if white workers discriminate because of ignorance they are similarly off the hook. The neat thing about this formulation is that it fits nicely with what Mrs. Kurier considers to be the solution. Ignorance can be eliminated through education. Perhaps Mrs. Kurier has read Myrdal. She has certainly figured out a solution to the vicious circle contained in the American dilemma.

The reality of fear

Ignorance and education may resolve contradictions, but they do not settle fears — and the fears Mrs. Kurier expresses are real ones. They are not conjured excuses to rationalize a dislike of black people. Like the inconsistencies that mark her thinking, her fears have their roots in the fluidity of American racial organization. She knows white people have traditionally held the upper hand over blacks. She also knows the situation is untenable or is at least changing considerably. But she does not know what will be changed, how it will occur, or what will be its consequences. Despite her well-meaning intentions, she does not want to give up the rewards of majority status. She realistically, in my estimation, assesses the consequences of change as meaning the rules of the game will be changed. She fears that in that process blacks may want to "get even."

Mrs. Kurier also expresses a very reasonable emotion: She wants to be accepted. She fears rejection. A good deal of her indecisiveness can be attributed to this fear. She is ambivalent about intermarriage because she worries that the arrangement will not be accepted by either race. She hesitates to live in an integrated neighborhood because she is afraid she will be rejected by blacks. In short, Mrs. Kurier's thinking is in large part influenced by her fears.

In fact, while the major characteristic of her thinking is

an appeal to education, the overriding quality of her character seems to be fear. She has faith in America, to be sure. She feels that ultimately blacks can be educated, which would eliminate most of America's racial troubles. Until that time, however, she lives in real fear: fear of rejection, fear that the rules will be changed, and fear of black retribution.

Her fears are revealing. They reflect an incipient awareness of the privileges she has enjoyed as part of her racial status. To date, whites have been able to define what is acceptable, dictate the rules of the game, and contain black resentment. Whether all this will in fact be changed is not at issue. But on one level or another, Mrs. Kurier is aware that if black demands for equality are implemented, then white power and privilege will be curtailed. This is ultimately what she is afraid of. And her fear is realistic. In this respect, all her talk about educating blacks may be more a plea than a solution.

5 "If I could do it, why can't they do it?" Dick Wilson

Prologue

I met Dick Wilson in a business administration class at the University of San Francisco. It was summer session and Dick was taking graduate classes in the evening to advance himself on the job. I had published an article the previous spring in which I strongly criticized a government-funded job training program. Dick's professor was impressed by it and asked me to speak to his class about job opportunities for minority people.

Normally I would not agree to speak at a business administration class. I do not think of businessmen as open people. They certainly are not my "kind" of people. Their button-down demeanor clashes with my bearded, semi-long-haired appearance. I do not even own a tie. I am not very sympathetic to their interests or concerns, and do not see myself as a sociological missionary. I doubt that much can be accomplished by a meeting of this sort. But I wanted to interview businessmen for this study and figured I might meet some willing people at the class. So I agreed to address them and decided my remarks should be low key and as nonantagonistic as possible; I did not want to eliminate interview possibilities.

When I arrived at the class I realized it would not be so easy to maintain a nonantagonistic posture. The professor had also invited a successful black entrepreneur; a man who had made it from rags to riches. He was supposed to rebut me. I could not help but be tickled by the absurd irony of the encounter: a white sociologist arguing why job opportunities for minority people were severely restricted; a black man arguing why they were not. It was a difficult position to be in. If we took off the gloves and really engaged each other it might be good theater, but it certainly would not change anyone's mind and I probably would not get interviews. I wondered if this was the way young black men felt in earlier periods of American history when they were paid to fight in front of drunken southern businessmen. Nevertheless I enjoy a good debate; I am not "liberal" or paternalistic enough to avoid an argument with someone simply because he is black. Interviews or not, I knew I would not agree with the man on basic issues.

So we "got it on."

Before class ended I announced that I was working on a sociological study concerned with white people's attitudes toward blacks and that I would like to interview anyone who was willing. I did not expect to be taken up on the offer. Who would want to be interviewed by someone with a position as "outrageous" as mine? I had made it quite clear that I thought the business community was instrumental in keeping minorities out of meaningful jobs. I was quite surprised, then, when a number of men came up and volunteered — some of them challenging me — to be interviewed.

Dick Wilson was one of these people. He left me his business card and said to call him about a mutually agreeable time and place. One evening a couple of weeks later I went to his house to interview him. He lives in the hills overlooking Oakland, in a rather expensive house that struck me as being modestly furnished. He had worked hard that day and seemed a little tired. Nevertheless, he was friendly and looked forward to the interview. There were some things he wanted to get off his chest, he smiled. We sat in his living room; his wife periodically gave us some snacks. It was a relaxed atmosphere.

I felt confident about the interview. The normal apprehensions associated with any interview were under control. I had had interviews with others from the class, and they had gone well. The men had disagreed with my presentation but were more than willing to be open and candid about their feelings. They seemed to welcome the interview experience. They liked the chance to talk about racial issues that troubled them. Dick was no exception.

Interviewing him was relatively easy. When I posed an issue he took off with it. I rarely had to push or probe him, but when I did, he did not seem personally threatened. It was more like a conversation between two adults getting to know each other than an interview. I felt comfortable and he appeared to feel the same way. He listened carefully to my questions and thought about his answers before he spoke. He struck me as a rather intense person: someone who felt very strongly about issues. At times his voice would rise when he became emotionally involved in what he was saying. He spoke with conviction. The presence of a stranger in his living room apparently had very little effect on his candor.

We never became really friendly. I did not presume to laugh at humorous incidents in his life. He was older than me and perhaps our age difference was inhibiting. He seemed to relate more on a professional level than a personal one. He asked about my feelings "as a sociologist" concerning certain issues. Obviously I felt differently about things than he did. Nonetheless I liked him.

I found Wilson a compelling person, someone I respect-

ed. He was self-made, proud, and articulate. Perhaps I
identified with him. I come from a working-class family
myself; neither of my parents have a high school education. I was in graduate school working on a Ph.D. and often wondered how that happened. Here was a man who
had also moved from one class position to another. He intrigued me and we spoke for better than two hours.

I learned a lot listening to Dick. He challenged some of
my notions about middle-class businessmen. They still
were not my kind of people, but they were no longer a
unified mass either. Furthermore, they were not any more
close-minded than anyone else. They were troubled by
some of the same issues I was and their solutions were as
tentative as mine. They were not all born with silver
spoons in their mouths, but neither had they cornered the
market on enlightened liberalism.

Making it the hard way

Richard Wilson knows what it is to be poor; as a youth he
was "down there" himself. His family survived the 1930s
depression because the government helped them; they
were "poor white trash" on welfare. But Dick decided to
"get out" of poverty. In his estimation he is "not anything
special." Perhaps he was lucky in some respects, but he
thinks the main reason he got out was because he decided
to do it. Dick did it and he is no longer poor; he is now
assistant to the district manager of a major food-processing
company located in the Bay Area.

Dick is not very sympathetic to poor people — regardless of their color. Richard Wilson made it the hard way.
"If I could," he reasons, "why can't they?"

Dick was born in the early 1930s, a depression baby.
And like so many other people in that period his folks
were poor. When his dad could find a job he worked as a

laborer to support Dick, his mother, and a younger brother. Dick had little opportunity to know his father very well because his parents got divorced when he was seven or eight. Child-support laws were not enforced very strictly in those days, so the burden of family maintenance fell mainly on his mother's shoulders. She did whatever work she could find to support the struggling family.

Every two or three years, life was complicated by a black family moving onto their block. The Wilson's lived in Richmond, Virginia, and at that time its neighborhoods were not integrated. The Wilsons would have to move. But they never wandered very far and always lived in poor neighborhoods. In fact, they lived in the "poor white trash" section of Richmond called Oregon Hill.

Dick knew Oregon Hill was the poor white part of town; people told him that all the time. When by chance he happened to stray from the neighborhood, something about himself always gave away his origins. "You sound like you come from Oregon Hill," someone would usually point out derisively. When Dick would confirm the observation, somebody else would quite likely insist, "Why don't you go back."

Dick resented life on the Hill. He felt like a marked man. Most young men started wearing long trousers in their young teens. Not Dick. His clothes were provided by welfare agencies and the only pants they had were knickers extending to his knees. Since all the other kids wore long trousers, Dick's knickers identified him as someone on "relief." Not until he was fifteen did he own his first pair of long trousers.

Just going down to the local store to buy groceries for his mother identified Dick as someone different from other people. Most people paid for groceries with money; the Wilsons bought food with stamps. The stigma associated with walking up to the cash register and handing the cashier a book of tickets "embarrassed the hell" out of Dick. He would do anything in the world to get out of going to the store for his mother.

Living on Oregon Hill meant trying to live with very little money, and Dick dramatically learned what his family's financial position was at a young age. To this day he cannot forget the time he lost a dollar. At the time he did not know what a dollar represented; he was only seven or eight. The Wilsons had an ice box and Dick's mother (having no small change) gave him one dollar with which to purchase a block of ice from the neighborhood ice house. It was a hot summer day and the firemen had opened up fire hydrants so that kids could cool off and play in the water. Dick stopped to watch the kids playing, but he did not join them because he had to go to the ice house. When he finally arrived at his destination he discovered he had somehow lost his money. The discovery did not mean too much to him; the value of a dollar was unknown. He simply returned home and informed his mother that he had lost it. But he was shaken when she began to sob uncontrollably. One dollar bought a lot of things in those days and that was the last cent she had to her name. He had lost all of their food money for the rest of the week. Dick learned an important and bitter clue about his family's financial condition that day.

There were other clues as well. Dick noticed quite early in life that his mother walked to work every day. Carfare was only seven cents but his mother felt the money would be better spent on food than on a ride for herself. Whenever the family used public transportation they rode on streetcars rather than buses. The buses ran much smoother and had upholstered seats, but they also cost eight cents a ride. The trolley car was a penny cheaper and Dick's mother literally could not justify spending the extra penny to ride a bus. That is how poor Dick's family was.

Living on Oregon Hill ultimately meant that the Wilsons were poor white trash. Looking back on this period Dick thinks his situation was quite similar to being black: The only difference was that there was no skin color to identify him. Yet Dick assured me that white trash could be readily identified. Except for the clothing, which obviously gave them away, Dick was unable to specify just how "other people could tell"; yet he was always aware that "people knew." At the time he knew little about black people and he never compared his situation to theirs. He knew only that being poor white trash meant being poor and having to move many times. It also meant having a horrible feeling of embarrassment about being on welfare. While many people were on welfare during the depression, it was obvious that not everyone was. The Wilsons were conspicuous and Dick was embarrassed.

There was only one group in Richmond that was worse off than white trash: "These people were niggers." Dick remembers the pecking order vividly. At the bottom were the "niggers." One step above them were white trash. And one step above white trash was "the whole rest of the world." To Dick being poor white trash meant being one step from the bottom.

"Niggers" did not figure very prominently in Dick's life at the time. There was absolutely no communication between the races, so he never had to relate to them. Dick had never seen a Negro woman wearing a new dress until he was ten or eleven years old. He did notice it, and then he wondered "where in the world did she get a new dress?" He never questioned whether she was entitled to it, he just could not figure out how she had collected enough money to buy it. Throughout his life he had only seen black people clothed in rags. Exceptions to this simple rule caused wonder and amazement.

Dick had no strong feelings one way or the other about

black people when he was living on Oregon Hill. There was no social relationship between the races. Black people were just "them." They were "kind of a formless mass" over "there." Whites only related to them as garbagemen who came into the neighborhood once a week.

Getting off Oregon Hill

As far back as Dick can remember, he wanted out of Oregon Hill and all that it represented in the worst way. One day stands out in particular. He was only ten years old but he can recall details as obscure as the angle of the sun on that day. He remembers looking around the neighborhood and making a decision. He was going to get out of that place somehow. He was not going to be trapped in it for the rest of his life. Dick is not sure what particularly prompted the decision but he vividly recalls making it. From that time on Dick was determined to leave Oregon Hill and cease being poor white trash.

Deciding to get off the Hill was one thing; doing it was quite another. Going to school seemed ill-suited as preparation for the task. Dick could not see the relationship between studying books and making money. As a result he dropped out of school at age 15. He thought that perhaps if he worked in a factory he could develop the means to escape. But by the time he was sixteen he realized that industrial work was not leading anywhere.

The Marine Corps seemed to be a natural escape: Joining up would get him out of Oregon Hill and he could see the world as well. For six and a half years Dick was a Marine. For five of those years he did see the world; he was stationed overseas. The only frustrating aspect of his tour of duty was the Korean War, which extended his enlistment by six months.

While the Marine experience changed many things about

Dick's life, one aspect of it remained unchanged: his contact with black people. In that respect Dick had not moved very far from Oregon Hill. The Marines were strictly segregated most of the time Dick was with them, and until he and a couple of his friends got into a scrap with some black Marines, he did not know blacks could be in the corps.

One of Dick's friends picked a fight with some black Marines and was subsequently stabbed. Later that week, the white Marines went to an ammunition depot to try and identify the assailant. There Dick saw an entire detachment of black Marines: two or three hundred of them. Dick had never seeen so many black people in one place.

When Dick's enlistment period was up he left the Marines. It had been a good experience; he had seen the world and even received a high school diploma through GED. Although the Marines helped get him off Oregon Hill, he had no desire to make a career out of the military.

Dick was no longer poor white trash, but he was also a long way from where he wanted to be. He figured the only way he could put enough distance between himself and his childhood circumstances was to get a college education. So he took college entrance exams and on the basis of his high scores was allowed to enter the University of Richmond on probationary status. Dick went to school during the day and to support himself worked a full-time job in the afternoon and evening.

Four years later Dick received a degree in business administration. His first job took him to Cincinnati, Ohio, working for a large soap manufacturer as a job study engineer — in common terms, an industrial engineer. The company had a policy of rotating management people through various positions and during the five years he worked for them he held different jobs. At one time he was chief of standards; during other periods he was production supervisor.

Dick began to see black people in a different light while working for the soap manufacturer. Until that time blacks continued to be "them"; they remained a formless mass. But while Dick was employed by the manufacturer, they hired the first black person to work on their production line. Before that no blacks had worked for the organization in any capacity.

Dick Wilson had never had a working relationship with black people until the company's minimal integration. He had never before communicated with black people person-to-person, although he was in his late twenties.

Dick's initial enthusiasm at being a member of management decreased during his five years with the company. It is a highly structured organization and, their policy of job rotation notwithstanding, Dick felt as though they were confining him to a box. He felt that the company had boxes into which they fit people and the box in which someone found himself pretty much defined the small area in which that person could operate. Dick had been confined for sixteen years in a box called Oregon Hill. He was not about to exchange one box for another.

Jobs at the company were strictly defined; in fact everything was written down in a book. As far as Dick could tell, "they've got manuals 'til hell won't have it." No matter what the question was, a person could find the answer to it in one of the manuals. That is, if he could figure out which one to use. The company was inflexible. Everything was spelled out in a manual of manufacturing standards and formulas and his job was to make sure things went according to the book. There was no room for uniqueness or deviation. There was even a correct way for someone to have a new idea. The person had to fill out an "EO," an "experimental order," and obtain the appropriate signatures. Dick found the company very frustrating to work for.

The company's organizational rigidity was exceeded

only by its paternalism. The company was not simply a business organization; it was a social organization as well. Employees were expected to relate to the company in much the same way as they might to a large extended family. Once a year, for example, in the summer, the company would take over an amusement park and hold a big celebration called "Dividend Day." Employees were personally handed checks for dividends earned on company stock. The celebration was fine with Dick, but the requirement that all members of management be there, dressed in white shirts, ties, and suit coats, violated his sense of himself as an adult individual.

Dick began to realize that the company was not only dominating his work-day life, but his social life as well. All his friends worked for the company; whenever he went out, he did so with company people. He knew no one outside the small circle within which he worked. The company liked things that way; and many of Dick's colleagues found it a very comfortable little world. But for Dick it was too confining and he refused to adapt to it. The soap manufacturer was a good first job, and Dick enjoyed certain aspects of it. He had learned a lot about management, but it was time to make a change.

Finding rewarding work

Dick wanted a job that would allow him to use his unique abilities, whatever they might be. He looked for a job in which he would be free, within broad limits, to pursue the things for which he had particular talents and skills, things in which he had an interest. He wanted out of a job that built a box around him and closed him off to personal and occupational development. Dick discussed these concerns with potential employers during his job search. The people for whom he currently works had a job that met his needs, and seven years ago Dick moved to the Bay Area to be with them.

Dick is assistant to the district manager for Northern California. As with many positions entitled "assistant to so-and-so," his responsibilities are nebulous. Dick finds the looseness of his job attractive; it allows him to work at his own pace and in his own way. His work activities depend mainly on what his boss will let him do and his particular skills and interests. Dick is basically interested in working on the production end of food processing, but a significant proportion of his time is taken up with the economic aspects of the business.

Food processing is a highly seasonal business. Most of the canning takes place during a four-month period. Dick especially enjoys working during this period because production time puts him in the plants. He finds working in the plants most challenging because one of the big problems in canneries is what he calls "people problems." He has to show people what to do; there are labor difficulties to iron out; he has to mediate between levels of management.

During the past seven years Dick's feelings about black people have solidified considerably. He no longer sees them as the formless mass he once did. This is to be expected; he comes into daily contact with them since a large percentage of cannery workers are black. In this respect, things have changed a great deal since Dick lived on Oregon Hill, or even since he worked for the soap manufacturer. Nevertheless, Dick does not feel that there has been a "hundred-and-eighty-degree turn" in his thinking. He still thinks of people in group terms. He no longer cares about what group they belong to; but he thinks of Italians, or Jews, or blacks in "somewhat ethnic terms." At the same time, he sees them as individuals. Dick now sees black people on two levels. There are individuals with whom he has dialogues; and there is a mass. Dick admits that maybe the mass of black people are a "little more formless" than any other ethnic group as far as he is concerned, but he cannot really say for sure.

Most of the blacks Dick recognizes as individuals are people with whom he works. He knows they are individuals because he has had conversations with them and as a result he sees their distinctiveness. The individuality of black people is also evidenced through the particular jobs they hold in the plant, and Dick recognizes them in different roles. When he walks through the plant and sees black seamer operators, he recognizes them as individual seamer operators, not just as black people. Dick sees many "individual blacks" in the canneries.

Off the job, Dick mostly sees a mass of black people. The mass is not formless, however; he now sees differences among blacks. He takes pride in the fact that he divides the mass — evaluates it — according to color-blind criteria. A black family lives in the second house from the corner on Dick's block. They are pretty much invisible as far as Dick is concerned; he hardly ever sees them and he knows next to nothing about them. They leave for work quite early in the morning and return home late at night. The people across the street think the black family works in a factory because they leave so early in the morning. Dick does not know for sure; hell, he doesn't even know how many people there are in the family.

There is another black family in the neighborhood that lives down the hill from Dick. He does not know their name and has never spoken to them. He knows they have at least one son who is about fourteen years old, because the young man visits the daughters of his next-door neighbor. Dick has never met the youngster's father; in fact, he has never seen the man. "It's just like they didn't live here," Dick told me. He certainly did not arrange it that way, but he did not consider it unusual either, at least not in California. As far as Dick can tell, in California people live right next door and never speak to each other. The only people on the block he speaks to live across the street. Dick has never been inside their house and they have never been inside his. Most of the people in Dick's neighborhood are indifferent to each other, regardless of race.

I asked Dick if he had known black people lived in the neighborhood when he bought the house. He had. He discusseed the fact with his wife and they decided they did not particularly care one way or the other. The houses owned by the black families are worth about $48,000. As far as Dick is concerned, if the man can afford a $48,000 house, "he's my kind of person."

The black people in Dick's neighborhood are mostly invisible to him, but when he does see them he evaluates their visibility in color-less terms. For example, the evening I interviewed him, a little before my arrival, some neighborhood boys, including a black youngster, were fooling around in front of his house. They were throwing rocks at an old dog who lives across the street. The dog is a neighborhood institution and all of the kids play with him. Dick objected to the youngsters throwing rocks at the old creature. "Stop it!" he yelled as he poked his head out of the window. "The dog doesn't have any teeth and he's not a threat to anybody. Put the rocks down!" The kids looked defiantly at Dick, but they stopped harrassing the dog. Dick mentioned the incident to make a point. "I'll bet you from the expression on that black kid's face, and his whole attitude when I told them to put those rocks down, that he thinks I was yelling at him because his skin is black," he said to me. I would not take the bet. But Dick insisted that was not the reason he yelled at the youngsters. "The fact is," he said, "if *any* kids came up here and acted like hoodlums like those kids acted, I would do the same thing."

*"I can relate to people whose backgrounds are
similar to mine."*

Dick's opinions about people are not based on the color of
their skin; he is more interested in what they have done
with their lives. His "kind of person" is somebody who
starts out poor and can afford a $48,000 house; someone
who "makes it on their own." Dick is most impressed by
men who have accomplished something in life. Not that
he evaluates people simply by how much money they
make: Money is just a common denominator; it is objective — something that can be measured. It is conceivable to
Dick that his kind of person might not have a lot of money.
Wealth is not the issue; the question for him is can the person make it — however that person defines success — "on
their own."

Dick knows of people like that, and some are black. In
his estimation, the black man who addressed the business
administration class with me is a good example of one such
person. Dick does not think of him as a black man, but
rather as someone he can "relate" to. Dick feels that in a
broad sense their experiences have been similar. The black
man got where he is because "he went out and dug for it."
He worked for what he has and Dick thinks "he deserves
every bit of it." The man's skin color is immaterial. Dick
can "relate" to a person like that; color is not a "problem"
for him.

People who have not made it are not Dick's kind of
people. What Dick finds distasteful is their poor showing,
not their skin color. When Dick thinks about society's failures he does not consider their race. He does not distinguish between "poor Negroes and any other people in this
sense." The point for him is that there are some people he
would like to associate with and others he would not. Dick
resists using stereotypes and he dislikes putting labels or

handles on people. Nevertheless, he thinks the words "trashy," "hoodlums," "shiftless," and "lacking ambition" are appropriate descriptions for the people he wishes to avoid.

The color of these people is irrelevant to Dick. He wants to avoid contact with all the people who fall into these categories. Dick lived among such people when he was on Oregon Hill and he would never live there again; he would not want his family exposed to that. The issue is not color, as Dick sees it; his objection to living on Oregon Hill "proves" that, since the Hill is all white. The point is that it is a *poor* neighborhood.

As far as Dick can tell, the majority of blacks are like the people on Oregon Hill, who he thinks are "bums." They are not people with whom he wants his family to associate. But Dick has to admit, "in all fairness," that many of these black people "have been denied the opportunity to do the things which would permit them to rise above their current circumstances." He thinks that is "wrong." Dick is "all for" equal opportunity. He favors it because there is "no such thing as equality." He feels that people are not born equal; they are born with different economic, physiological, and mental capabilities. Because people are not the same, they are not equal to each other. Nevertheless, Dick believes that "everybody should have an equal opportunity to make the most of whatever unique talents he has as an individual."

Dick realizes that many blacks, and whites like the ones on Oregon Hill, have not had equal opportunities in society. But he thinks their number is exaggerated. Most of them remain poor, as far as Dick can tell, "because they lack the ambition or determination to get out of their situation." Dick is not rigid about the subject. He admits that his opinion may be "unfair." But this is offset by the examples of people who have been able to get off the Oregon

Hills and out of the West Oaklands of America. He considers himself one of these people, and he knows of many more. "So what's the difference between the guys who make it and the ones who don't?" he asked. The only conclusion he feels comfortable with is — "ambition."

"Blacks need pride in themselves and genuine
jobs — not the indiscriminate use of ideological
phrases like black power."

Dick is extremely unsympathetic to militant proposals for change in the black community. He does not think they come to grips with people's motivations, which he sees as the heart of the problem. When people talk about black power, he thinks of the Black Panthers and the Stokely Carmichaels. His feelings on the subject are straightforward: "It just burns me up." As we began to talk about black power Dick's tone of voice became impassioned; he spoke rapidly and with a great deal of emotion. Black power to him means "the indiscriminate use of ideological words, phrases, and terminology." Black power is not about helping the black community, he argued; it is a "grandstanding play." He was particularly bothered by the way black power advocates speak about police brutality. Nothing makes him angrier, he said with conviction, than to hear someone yell "police brutality" when they get their head knocked with a police club. As Dick sees it, the newsreels and newspapers always show the police officer hitting somebody. But they never show the officer getting hit by rocks and bottles. This kind of grandstanding really "burns up" Dick. Just talking about the subject with me made him noticeably angry. He knew where I stood and I got the feeling he was speaking to me as one of "those people."

I asked Dick why this angered him. The slogans, words, and actions of black power advocates, he shot back, are not consistent with what they claim are the abuses. As far as he can tell, demonstrators provoke and trigger off the police. Then they turn around and say "look how you abuse us." They do that all the time, he proclaimed, not just with the police. "Look how they handle demonstrations," he announced loudly. "You have to have a permit to parade, right? Fine. But not these people." From what Dick can tell, black power demonstrators turn up their noses at such regulations. They say, "We're not gonna get a permit to parade, and we're gonna parade anyhow." "That's not fair!" Dick said, standing up as if to make his point more forcefully. "If I want to parade, I'm going to go down and get a permit for it." But not these demonstrators. They say, "We're not going to obey the law, we are going to disobey it. We're going to parade or demonstrate or what-have-you regardless of whether we've got a permit." "That's wrong," he concluded, sitting down again. "If people are going to violate the law, they can't complain when they are punished for it."

Before I had a chance to ask another question, Dick spoke again. He wanted to point out that he was not opposed to demonstrations and parades. People have every right to do that, he said. However, he also wanted to point out that they have an "obligation to follow whatever restrictions have been imposed on their right to do this for the greater good of the rest of society." It would be absolutely wrong to deny people the right to demonstrate, he thinks. But he also feels that when this right is exercised, people "don't have the right to trample on other people's rights in the process." People's rights, in his estimation, imply an obligation. "If you have the right to petition, you have an obligation to the rest of society to do it in a manner which does not disrupt their lives."

I thought Dick was raising the issue of law and order and I began to ask him about that. But before I completed the question he interrupted me. "Let me give you one more point about why this black power talk infuriates me," he said. He related an incident to me in which seven black men who work in one of his warehouses took two days off, without authorization or notification, to participate in "Free Huey" demonstrations in Oakland. Their absence annoyed the hell out of him. He expects workers, regardless of their color, to be on the job because the company has a task to perform and "we can't perform it without them being there." These blacks had an obligation to the company to be at work, in his estimation. Their absence prevented the company from meeting shipping orders for two days.

Dick was not only annoyed by the situation, he was frustrated by it as well. He could not discipline the seven black workers the way he might others. "Can you imagine what would happen?" he asked me. If he brought in the seven men and said, "You guys were down at the Huey Newton trial, weren't you?", they might say, "Yeah." But what could he do then? He did not want a big scene on his hands. If the men said, "No we weren't," he still had no real comeback. To say, "I don't believe you," would give them cause to respond, "You're calling me a liar because I'm black."

Dick feels the men were using their skin color to "rationalize irresponsible actions." He points out that he is not talking about all black people. But he feels very strongly that "some of these people better thank God that their skin is black. Because if it weren't, they would have to face up to the fact that their failures are due to themselves as individuals and *not* because their skin is black." Black power rhetoric gives these people something to "fall back on," in Dick's estimation; they do not have to face the reality of their personal failure.

Dick sees the Huey Newton demonstrations as another

kind of irresponsibility. The slogan "Free Huey Now" in-furiates him. "Huey doesn't have any more business being freed than any other guy that shoots a police officer," Dick said intensely. I pointed out that the demonstrators are only yelling "free Huey"; they were not doing any-thing that would free him. But Dick was unimpressed. "Look at the threats they're making," he said, "Free Huey now or else!" He realized the "or else" was ambiguous. "Or else what?" he asked. But he did not find the ambigui-ty very settling. "They've been very careful not to spell that out," he noted, "and that's irresponsible as hell."

"Change has to occur within the law — and people have to be motivated to do that."

Dick realizes there are no simple solutions to racial prob-lems. He has none to suggest. Nevertheless, he feels that black power rhetoric is leading to a situation where people want things but refuse to consider the relationship be-tween ends and means. People who yell black power only see the ends; they "don't care how they get them, they just want them now." Until people consider what they want and think about how to achieve the objective, Dick thinks "they're not anywhere." There has to be a connec-tion between an end and how it is achieved as far as he is concerned; people cannot continue to say, "I want it now, give it to me."

When the connection between ends and means breaks down, the result is riots. People who riot "go out and get the ends — the television sets and radios, the dinette sets and the clothes." They never consider the means for ac-complishing these ends within a lawful society. That is what the riots are all about to Dick: the decline of a "law-ful society," the breakdown of law and order.

This bothers Dick because he was raised to respect the

law. He was taught as a child, and even as an adult, to say "yes sir!" when addressed by a policeman. "Obviously people don't do that now," he said sullenly. He lamented that the police are called "pigs" today; he attributed this to the events leading up to the Black Panthers.

"Where do you stop," Dick asked me, "when an individual reaches a point where he feels that he can violate what he considers unjust laws?" As he sees it, the problem started in Montgomery, Alabama, when Martin Luther King organized a bus boycott. Laws were violated at that time and people went out and "deliberately got themselves arrested." Those demonstrations were pretty quiet, he admits; "they didn't disrupt things too much." "But then look where it's progressed to," he continued. Now people are rioting all over the country; Watts and Detroit are the two biggest examples. "Once you have rationalized to yourself that it's all right to break what you define as unjust laws," he concluded, "then there's no stopping them."

I pointed out that some southern laws maintained segregation. Was it wrong to violate unconstitutional laws? If they were not violated how could they be ruled unconstitutional? Dick had to qualify his earlier statement. He would be "sympathetic" to their violation, but it was still wrong. He could "understand" why laws had to be broken; but he would not "condone" it.

I was persistent. But how could change occur within the law when the law supports segregation, I asked? Dick said that he had no really good answer. Then he suggested that the Constitution provides for change under law. The Supreme Court school desegregation ruling in 1954 was a good example of that. "This was all done within the law," he pointed out. Some schools are still not desegregated, he volunteered; some people continue to defy the ruling. But "ultimately they'll have to come around," he said.

Dick anticipated my reaction to the validity of this example. "You're going to ask me where would black people be now had they not broken the law in the first place, aren't you? You'll probably want to know would people really be concerned as they profess to be now had blacks not broken the law?" I nodded. "I would have to say, no, they wouldn't be," Dick said in a tired tone of voice. He was finding political solutions difficult to come by. "These questions are just not easy to answer," he sighed.

Dick is more sure of himself when he thinks about solutions that involve motivation and work. He thinks it is most important to get jobs for poor people. By that he means "genuine" jobs, not make-work activities. He emphasizes genuine work because he feels that, "a job is something that gives a man status and dignity." In Dick's estimation, it is a bad thing to tell a man he is totally unemployable. In effect, that says he is "worthless," "nothing." Dick thinks giving people jobs is a "reasonable approach" to the problem.

In this respect he finds himself in agreement with Lyndon Johnson. Although not an LBJ fan by a long stretch, Dick agrees with him on a crucial point. Johnson addressed the business community and told them that unless business gave poor people jobs, the government would have to. Johnson did not want to do that, but felt it would be necessary if large corporations refused to assume the responsibility. Dick agrees with LBJ that giving every one of these people a job in government would be the worst possible thing that could happen. Dick thinks they already have a job in government: "It's called welfare." Johnson's proposal would be no better. What is needed, Dick thinks, is something "real." "How can a man have any pride in himself if he knows that he's just being given something to keep him quiet or keep him from burning something or from looting something or tearing something down?" Dick asked. "He can't."

The problem is twofold in Dick's mind: It calls for short-range and long-range solutions. In his estimation the issue is "no different from any other problem in business." The first thing that has to be determined is "what is the problem"; the second question is "how does society keep it from happening again." In the short range, Dick thinks businessmen have "got to face up to the problem" that many black people lack the kinds of skills business normally looks for. The appropriate response to that realization in Dick's mind is, "all right, they don't."

The second question — which leads to the problem of "what are we going to do about it?" — is more difficult to deal with. But it is the crucial issue. He thinks society cannot afford to leave people sitting at home all day. He is convinced that idleness is the very thing that breeds the problems facing America. The nine or ten hours a day when people would normally be working allows them to "sit there and think and feel sorry for themselves." The next thing that occurs in his scenario is that people get bored. And to relieve their boredom and monotony they go out and create a little excitement: "riots usually." Dick thinks these people have got to be "organized in the sense that they have to meet time schedules and show up to work." They have to learn the meaning of time on the job: "When they go on a break, they go for ten minutes. When they go to lunch, they come back in thirty minutes." In short, poor people need to assume responsibilities and obligations "just like the rest of the people in the whole world."

In Dick's estimation people need to be motivated before that will happen. But the question, as far as he can tell, is: "How do you motivate somebody that has nothing to lose?" His answer: "You can't." When people have no pride, no dignity, no status, they "really have nothing to lose." And as he sees it, if people have nothing to lose they are willing to do virtually anything. Dick thinks people must have something to lose, something of value to themselves, and a job is a very important thing of value that they should have. He feels the second thing people should have is a home. "Not very many people burn down their own home," he reasoned.

Long-range solutions to the problem are needed, in Dick's estimation. Black people are not going to get out of the ghetto in one generation; too many of them need homes for that to happen. There are twenty million black people in the United States and as he figures it there are not twenty million houses in the entire country that could "possibly be built in any reasonable location in any reasonable period of time." He therefore feels that blacks will probably live in ghettos for several generations. This being the situation, he thinks society has to provide "a means for these people to be as comfortable as possible within this environment." One way that might happen, he suggests, is to help people acquire the property on which they live. That way they can "take some pride in it, fix it up."

Doing things "*for*" people is no solution in Dick Wilson's way of thinking. He recently read about some people in New York City who went into the slums with buckets of paint to clean up buildings for ghetto residents. "That doesn't mean a damn thing to poor people," Dick exploded; "it's something that somebody came down and did for them." The only people who got anything out of it, he feels, were the people who did it.

As he sees it, people only have an interest in things they earn themselves. He offered a parable to make his point. If somebody had a brother who was worth a million dollars and every Christmas the brother gave him a brand new Ford, it would not be enough. The person would say, "That cheap son of a bitch; why didn't he give me a Cadillac!" When people are given something, they always want more.

Dick feels that somehow a relationship has to be established between means and ends, between the work people do and the money they receive. When that happens, "people will take care of what they have."

Dick realizes that black people presently lack the wherewithal to achieve this. "Where would they get the down payment for a house?" he asked. Dick believes some provision has to be made for blacks to acquire houses with low down payments or no down payments. There are all kinds of programs like that for other people, he points out. The GI Bill is a good example. Dick once bought a house himself under that bill without putting down a nickel. He thinks a "GI Bill for the ghetto" would be a good idea. That way blacks could own the homes in which they live and develop some pride.

Tax policies also need revision, as far as Dick can tell. Policies that encourage people to let property run down need to be changed. As things stand, the more dilapidated a piece of property is, the less taxes people have to pay on it. Policies like that cannot help black people develop pride in their homes, "and that's wrong."

Dick understands that the solutions he envisions are long-range ones. They cannot be accomplished overnight. In the meantime, however, he will not countenance rioting. Moreover, he feels public officials should not vacillate on this point. "When people break the law, destroy property, infringe on the rights of others," Dick proclaimed, "they should expect to receive the full penalty of the law." If city officials hesitate to execute the law swiftly and completely, it only makes matters worse. Riots have become fun and games, in his estimation; people like to "get their picture on television." Dick thinks people know what the law is. They also need to know that when they break it they are going to be penalized. He doesn't agree with everything San Francisco's Mayor Alioto says, by a long shot; but Alioto is a forceful man and he has said in no uncertain terms: "Thou shalt not riot or else!" Dick feels that is the way matters have to be handled in the short run. The other alternative is to "hope" there will not be riots.

And that is no alternative for Richard Wilson.

Epilogue

America has been good to Dick Wilson. It has delivered on the dream that a poor boy with motivation can, through hard work, achieve anything he sets out to do. As far as he is concerned, people in America are pretty much free to live up to their potential. Dick is not unaware of inequality, however; he realizes there are people not fulfilling their abilities. While he knows that everyone is not as successful as he, Dick does not consider himself an exception to a more general rule of inequality. He does not think these people "prove" that inequality is built into the fabric of American society. They do not show that the American Dream is untrue. The problem in his estimation is that these people have not *tried* to be successful. He "explains" inequality, then, in personal rather than structural terms. In his mind unsuccessful Americans lack determination and motivation.

Dick does not respect these people. He does not want to associate with them; they are not his "kind" of people. His kind are like himself: They are people who have done something with their lives. Dick insists that skin color is irrelevant in his evaluation of people. Instead, he is interested in how people use their capabilities. If someone has not made something of his life, he is a "bum." The fact that many black people fall into this category is irrelevant. It is not their blackness that leads to this designation, it is their lack of motivation. He respects black people who are like himself. Blacks who can afford to live on his block are his kind of people.

Dick Wilson is relatively uncomplicated. A self-made man, he has rapidly moved from poverty to semiaffluence. He has done so, moreover, in the face of some pretty serious obstacles. Dick has made it. And he has done so on his own.

Dick sees the world in rather simple terms. He divides it into two camps; those who have "made it" and those who have not. His standards are "universalistic"; they apply to people regardless of "ascribed" traits such as skin color. In his estimation race has very little to do with a person's lot in life; motivation is far more instrumental. Dick considers his own experience a case in point. If he could succeed, anyone can.

As an individual, Dick Wilson is obviously unusual. Few people move so rapidly and effortlessly through the American class structure today. His position on racial inequality is not so unusual. In fact it is a very common formulation of the problem. Why Dick Wilson should pose the issue in this manner is obvious. His stance directly reflects his own experience. Why the position he articulates should be so widely held — even by people with less dramatic mobility patterns — is another, more important question.

Dick's position expresses a classic American strategy for maintaining privilege. The notion that if-I-can-make-it-anyone-can "resolves" the contradiction that racial inequality poses to American ideology, without denying that it exists and without having to alter society. It is a "perfect," almost foolproof formulation.

(1) The formulation puts distance between the speaker and the problem. Racial inequality stems from black people themselves rather than from a system of racial stratifi-

cation. More specifically, the problem exists because blacks are not motivated. The white person subscribing to this position can thus hold to the belief that white people are irrelevant to the question of racial stratification.

(2) The formulation blames the victim for his or her own victimization. It argues that black people are responsible for their second-class status.

(3) The formulation ignores or discounts social structural arrangements that may be relevant to racial stratification. Because society's victims are responsible for their situation, the social order is left entirely out of the picture. This is a crucial component of the position expressed by Dick Wilson. Discounting structural elements allows him to ignore the possibility that he may be unwittingly involved in the racial ordering of society, that his achievements may be the result of black people's lack of achievement. So it is that Dick expresses almost no understanding of privileges that might accrue to him because he is white.

(4) The formulation insures the status quo. It is a self-serving interpretation of inequality. Dick recognizes that black people have different opportunities than white people, but he recognizes only *individual* inequality. The implication of this position is that black individuals must change, rather than the society. This of course insures that the structure that facilitated Dick's success will be unchanged, and in the process Dick's racial interests or privileges will not be challenged.

(5) The formulation is self-enhancing. Dick obviously feels good about himself. And he should; his feats are no minor achievement. His explanation of racial inequality contributes to his good feelings, and because he sees the problem as a personal one, his own individual situation is enhanced. In his estimation there are no structural limitations on mobility, only personal ones. He has competed with people under equal conditions and has outdistanced

them. Thus he feels that his character, and nothing else, accounts for his success. His achievements are then taken to be an indication of his outstanding personal qualities.

(6) The formulation is seemingly nonracist. The basis upon which people are evaluated ostensibly has nothing to do with their race. The criteria for respecting someone are "objective." When Dick assesses worthiness, he wants to know what people have done with their lives, not what color their skin is. Thus when Dick says the majority of blacks are bums, he cannot be accused of racism, for his observation is based on nonracial criteria. Black people who live up to his notions of worthiness are his kind of people.

(7) The formulation fits in very nicely with American ideology concerning the relationship between equal opportunity, hard work, and social mobility. The position suggests that America is true to its egalitarian ideals. It assumes that structural inequality is not an important force in American life. People possessing the Protestant work ethic are rewarded handsomely for their efforts. Because inequality is the result of personal inadequacies, the situation of black people in no way contradicts these ideals.

(8) The formulation rests on a very Protestant notion of work. In Dick's view, work confers dignity on people; idleness leads them astray. People need to do something; they need to feel they are pulling their own load.

(9) The formulation is also consistent with and reflects a kind of Social Darwinian, laissez-faire ideology to which many Americans of Dick's class position subscribe. It holds true to the ideal that the essential responsibility for a person's station in life lies *within* the individual. In this view, people are captains of their own ships, masters of their own fate. Society facilitates the process, it does not inhibit it. Black people have no one to blame but themselves for their poor showing in life.

Dick's feelings about what should be done to eliminate racial inequality are strongly tied into these assumptions. In his estimation blacks need economic motivation, not ideological exhortation. He realizes the difficulties involved in motivating people who have nothing to lose, who have no stake in the system. He therefore thinks it is essential that they have genuine jobs in which they can take pride, and homes in which they can invest themselves.

When he talks about solutions, Dick speaks not just as a self-made man, but as a businessman as well. The problem as he formulates it is no different than any other problem facing an executive: What are its parameters; what are the feasible alternatives? There are no problems that cannot be solved, given this pragmatic business orientation. And like a true businessman he poses the issues in terms of obligations as well as rights, means as well as ends, and the proper relationship between both. In his estimation people not only have rights, they also have obligations to the larger society, and ends cannot justify means in this relationship. When they do, the very fabric of a lawful society is threatened.

Thus radical solutions to the problem outrage Dick on two levels. One: The problem does not measure up to the solution. The situation does not call for them; people can succeed in the present situation if they try. Two: They constitute poor business practices. Group solutions like black power will only succeed in rewarding incompetence. When the relationship between ends and means is violated, people are not motivated to work within existing rules. Unless people are properly motivated they will neither fulfill their obligations to the organization for which they work, nor to the society in which they live.

6 "Convincing people that this is a racist country is like selling soap – if agitators say it enough times people will believe it." John Harper

Prologue

How were we going to get interviews with "respectables": community leaders and prominent businessmen? I became increasingly concerned with this question as the research project moved into high gear. Most of our interviews had been conducted with young people, so-called hippies, and working-class people; we had also spoken with a smattering of businessmen, but none who could be considered prominent or public people. We were short on "responsible," "upstanding" American citizens.

Matters were complicated by the composition of our staff: Politically it leaned considerably leftward and by respectable standards we were a scruffy-looking lot. This included the principal investigator, an associate professor of sociology at the University of California, a semi-long-haired person who sported a full beard. I thought we lived up to respectable people's stereotypes – or nightmares – of typical sociological researchers, and suspected that our chances of getting interviews with the local prominenti were quite low. Even if we were able to interview them, the exchanges would be guarded, the discussions less than candid.

For a while I toyed with the idea of someone cutting his hair or shaving his beard, but that seemed like too much to ask. I was unwilling to make that sacrifice and it hardly seemed fair to ask it of someone else. Besides which, I reasoned, the transformation would be transparent; the lack of authenticity would be obvious to both participants and the interview would suffer accordingly. But the fact remained, my reasoning notwithstanding, that we needed these interviews. I was nearly at the point of changing my outward appearance when someone told me about a "straight looking" graduate student in the sociology department who needed a research assistantship.

In comparison with the other members of our research team, Ed Price was unique. Superficially the differences were striking: Ed is soft spoken, shy, short haired and traditionally dressed. Unlike the others, he had recently completed his doctoral examinations. Ed is also from Texas and speaks with the traces of a southern accent. The differences ran deeper than that, however. Compared to other people on the staff, Ed's ideas about politics and sociology were conservative; he was planning a dissertation on right-wingers. Despite our differences, we shared common needs. He wanted to interview conservative people; we wanted interviews with people often found among their ranks. He was interested in some of the questions we were posing and we were interested in some of his.

Ed conducted a good many interviews for the project. Serving as our "straight man," he mainly interviewed fraternity men, businessmen, and communtiy leaders. He also spoke with some workers and a number of avowed right-wingers. Ed located respondents by attending meetings of Kiwanis and Rotary clubs, unions, and hanging out in right-wing bookstores. He told people he wanted to interview them about their feelings toward controversial issues of the day. Ed had relatively few problems getting "takers." Either people were thrown off guard by his appearance or the local respectables were more willing to cooperate with researchers than we had anticipated. Most of his interviews were obtained through contacts he made at these meetings.

Ed met John Harper at an East Bay Rotary Club meeting. A loquacious man, Harper was excited by the prospect of speaking with a university researcher. He suggested that Ed arrange a time for himself and two friends to exchange their ideas on tape. Harper impressed Ed during the group discussion. He was talkative, opinionated, articulate, and had a vivid memory for details. "Would you be interested in doing a more personal interview?" Ed asked when the discussion ended. That suited Harper just fine. A couple of days later, in the late afternoon, Ed met him at his city hall office in an East Bay town. Because the time was late and Harper worked long hours, Ed expected the interview to be relatively brief. But once Ed turned on the tape recorder Harper's penchant for talking took over and the interview lasted over two hours.

Ed provided an interested ear and Harper provided the rest. Ed pointed him in the study's general interest area and Harper verbally meandered until Ed stopped him. He spoke for almost an hour about his life history alone. Every so often Ed would intrude, bringing Harper back to an issue and pointing him off in another direction. The interview lasted until Harper was talked out.

If I had done the interview I would have pushed Harper more on details and tried to focus on some inconsistencies. Ed let him off the hook too easily on a number of points. But I also doubt that I could have listened as patiently as Ed did. Which may be why I never interviewed people like John Harper.

Having to work for what you get: a
three-generation California tradition

John Harper works between 10 and 15 hours a day. He is the assistant finance director for a medium-sized East Bay city. He handles all the city's money, makes all the investments, and supervises all the collections. Harper holds the job for one reason — he enjoys it. He likes being involved in these activities; the job captures his interests. If he did not enjoy the work, he would not do it. Harper no longer has to do work he dislikes because he has been financially independent since his early thirties.

Actually John Harper was born financially independent; his grandfather left the family quite a bit of money. It was of no particular help to John, however, for no one in the family ever touched it. The Harper family is composed of rugged individualists with a tradition of working for what they get. Each generation has had to work, and work hard, all their lives. That is the way John was brought up, and that is what he believes in.

John Harper is a proud, third-generation Californian. His grandfather left Luxembourg in 1846 and moved to California, settling near the small town of Mariposa, south and east of the city now known as Fremont. Fremont did not exist as a city in those days. In fact, John's grandfather bought his land from John Fremont, the American Army officer who was instrumental in colonizing California, for which assignment he was rewarded a handsome land grant. Harper's grandfather started out as a teamster, the land being used to support animals he maintained for the business. He worked hard and was successful, and soon he was in the stagecoach business conveying passengers and hauling freight into the Yosemite Valley. He also ran the stage line out of Madera. In 1908 the railroad forced Harper out of the stagecoach trade but not out of business. The old man was too crafty for that to happen. He began hauling baggage to and from the railroad stations. Later on, when the automobile was introduced, he became involved in selling and renting cars as well as horse-drawn rigs. Harper's grandfather worked until he died. It was a period during which, for white people, money was there to be made if a person was willing to work hard. The first Harpers in America were willing; and they were rewarded for their efforts. Harper's grandfather died a wealthy man.

John Harper may have been born with a silver spoon in his mouth, but he was not allowed to use it. Like the Harpers who preceded him he earned any money he had. As a young man growing up during the depression, he delivered all three of the newspapers published in Oakland: one in the morning, one in the afternoon, and one in the evening. By the time he went to high school he was accustomed to working hard. When the city of Berkeley opened an aquatic park near the Bay, he worked there picking up trash and hoeing weeds. He made "four bits an hour," which was good pay at the time.

There was never any question as to whether John would go to college. The issue was *which* college. Although John's father was a Stanford man, he never resented John's decision to attend the University of California. Originally John intended to become a doctor, but the idea of studying for twelve years dissuaded him and after one year he switched from premed into engineering. College life was not a time for frivolity with John Harper. He went at it in a characteristic hard-working Harper fashion. When World War II began John wanted to do his share. In the evenings he worked for Pan-American Airways in the engineering department. Each semester he took twenty-two units of classes including Naval ROTC. In order to complete college as quickly as possible he attended summer sessions. John crammed four years of work into two and when his class officially graduated he was not present to receive his diploma. He had already been in the Navy two years.

When Harper left the Navy in 1946, the requirements for a practicing engineer had been changed: His bachelor's degree no longer automatically admitted him into the profession. He needed a professional engineer's license, which required a certain amount of work experience and a state-administered examination. Because Harper had no experience he was unable to take the exam. Even if he had had the experience, Harper felt he probably would have flunked the exam because he had not studied the subject in many years. So he did the next best thing. He went into business for himself as an industrial consultant.

He started out working primarily with sawmills. The postwar period was a good time to be in that business. Lumber was a money-making proposition. It was also an industry that had experienced very little technological change. Mills needed to change if they were to keep up with the demand for lumber, but few of them could afford the staff to do this. Harper studied the problem carefully. He figured out certain innovations, suggested new machinery, and managed to increase production in numerous mills. He also shared their profits.

It was a relatively lucrative business until 1949. That year there was a lumber strike in California. There was no inventory in the yards, and Oregon lumber completely took over the California market. Large-scale technological change was also taking place that year, for lumber conglomerates from the East had moved into the vacuum and had begun to buy many of the small California lumber mills. The situation turned out well for John Harper. He moved into the industrial appraisal business — appraising the mills he had formerly advised.

Harper's industrial appraising operation grew. The organization soon included seven engineers in addition to himself. The company was transformed into an appraisal organization that widened its horizons to involve other kinds of properties and industries beside lumber. They did total appraising. They considered the machinery, equipment, buildings, and land of a particular business. For some industries they did market evaluations, for others they considered potential future locations. They relocated certain industries and advised labor relations with others. The job required twenty-hour days seven days a week and eleven months of traveling each year. It also brought in a good deal of money.

Working hard was nothing new to John Harper. He had been doing it all his life. But the twenty-hour days seven days a week caught up with him and he got a little tired by 1955. Running a business was becoming too much of a chore. He was spending most of his time locating work for other people. To complicate matters, the men who worked for him would eventually decide to go into business for themselves. They soon became his competition. When a Southern California–based appraisal company offered to buy him out, John Harper was interested. They proposed that he stay with the company for a period as general manager and he agreed. After two and a half years they agreed on a lump-sum price for the original business and a percentage of the renewal business. Harper has had no financial headaches since that time; his income is handsome.

John Harper decided he would go home and sit on the front porch awhile, and he did.

For about two weeks.

Then one day the local newspapers carried an announcement that said an East Bay city was looking for a tax assessor. The idea of doing something he was interested in attracted him. Besides which, he had not really kicked the work habit. He had too much invested in the hectic life. It had taken him a long time to find a spouse who was willing to put up with that sort of life and he had not married until he was forty. He had found someone willing to share his busy world, a woman with her own interests, and they had built a life around work, not leisure. He also wanted an opportunity to meet people and a chance to perfect his skills. He liked the potential of the assessor job for combining personal desires with community service.

The job proved to be a stepping stone to his current position of assistant finance director. By and large the position has fulfilled Harper's expectations. He considers himself an organizational "joiner" and the city is happy to have an official who belongs to the Kiwanis and Rotary clubs, who sits on the board of directors for a local hospital, and who participates in De Molay and Boy Scout activities. He enjoys being in a position from which he can look at the city's operations as a totality. He has an overview of the entire operation and participates in most of its functions. In his estimation the vantage point of an assistant finance director is broader than that of a police or fire chief. He makes more decisions in a day than the city manager does in a month. All of which makes the job an exciting one.

Of course, certain sides of city administration are not to his liking — they conflict with his aggressive predispositions. There are many demands made on city administrators, but they have relatively little decision-making authority. Most decisions are guided by ordinances that have been passed by the city council, with the consequence that the work left to many administrators is largely public relations.

As assistant director of city finance, Harper is specifically mandated to oversee the operation of divisions within that department. Formally speaking, he is in charge of all activities that pertain to the city's finances. These activities range from collecting parking fines, to assessing people's property, to making municipal purchases, to writing the city's budget. As Harper sees it his real job is to sell service.

The job involves two problems: He has to make the

people receiving the service "believers"; and he has to make the people offering the service "doers." His biggest obstacle is making the people who work for him into doers. In his estimation many of them take the job for what they can get, not what they can do. Some people simply spend eight hours in an office. Harper feels the hiring process contributes to this problem. Because the jobs are civil service, after six months probation a person is virtually guaranteed a lifetime job. As far as John Harper is concerned, many of them look upon it as social security. He feels his hands are tied because, unlike a private employer, he cannot dismiss an employee very easily. It *is* possible. However, there are so many areas for appeal, and so much latitude in the system, that dismissal rarely occurs.

Despite the obstacles, Harper works hard to make his employees understand that their job is to provide a service to the public. He feels that when someone calls the office with a question, that person deserves an answer — a courteous logical one that gives them some kind of satisfaction. If the staff are not adaptable to that procedure, he does not want them around. Harper realizes that not too many places do business that way. Nevertheless, he is happy with the philosophy. He does not have people complaining — writing letters to the city manager and city council saying they have been kicked around — and he thinks that is important.

John Harper sees himself as a very fortunate man. He has a job he enjoys, a wife who understands his hectic life and puts up with it, and all the money he needs regardless of whether he works or not. He is particularly pleased about his current work. It turned out much better than he anticipated, and he thoroughly enjoys all its challenges. Because he has no need for the income and could leave at any time, the only reason he continues to work is because he enjoys it — and because that is the way he was brought up, just to keep working.

"Aside from skin color, there's no difference
between black and white people."

Harper does not understand how people can accuse America of discriminating against black people. The charge is contrary to his experience and he rejects it. In his estimation America is not a racist society because the criteria upon which people are judged recognize only ability, not color. As far as he can tell people with ability are rewarded, and rewarded well. Such people are treated that way because of their abilities and not their race.

He recognizes that there are a lot of racial "feelings" throughout the country. And he agrees that the South certainly made a point of making black people "aware" of their blackness by imposing limits on their activities: Some places were off limits to them; separate facilities were created for them in the areas of housing, transportation, and education. All that he knows. What he does not know for a fact is if these facilities were unequal. Is the education received at black schools less of an education than the one offered at white schools? He is aware of allegations to this effect, but when he thinks of the outstanding graduates that black institutions have produced he does not believe they were slighted. So perhaps black people did have educational opportunites in the South, he concludes.

He is quite sure that educational institutions in California have not discriminated against black people merely because of color. Educational opportunities definitely exist for blacks in his state. The only discrimination that exists applies equally to all people. Everyone, regardless of color, has to pass an entrance exam. Harper thinks the entrance exam, more than anything else, keeps people out of the university. Grade point averages and the passing of required exams may keep some people from graduating. When Harper attended the University of California, a student needed a "B" average to take upper-division courses, and had to pass an exam on American institutions. It is true that there were other factors that kept students out of California colleges. Stanford, for example, accepted only a limited number of people each year. He remembers a time when a student's name had to be placed on a list at birth if he or she wanted to attend Stanford. That was also the case with Mills College. Of course, he notes, enrollment has been expanded since then. While all these factors discriminated against people, Harper argues, it was not discrimination based on color.

That kind of discrimination was not unfair, in John Harper's book. He thinks if a school is going to operate at a certain level of instruction there has to be some way of determining eligibility. No one wants a "dummy" to go to school merely because he is old enough.

If that was the case, Price asked, then how did he feel about university policy that admitted a small proportion of the student body who did not meet the entrance requirements? Harper had to think about that for a moment. He was aware, he said, that universities had always waived certain requirements for some groups. The example of foreign students immediately came to his mind. Some people were admitted because they had high potential, even though they lacked specific credentials. Now universities are admitting mostly black students under these provisions, he mused. Harper questions this new policy; he is not sure of its rationale. He wonders if blacks are admitted because universities think they have the ability to learn and get along — that their only difficulty is in communication and that over the course of instruction this can be overcome. While he hopes this is true, he really suspects there is some other reason.

In his view, the problems black people face stem from their inability to effectively communicate with white society. To Harper, blacks have great potential; they are not less intelligent than white people. However, somewhere along the line, they have failed in America because of their inability to communicate.

The problem exists to a large extent because blacks have a language of their own. In that respect, Harper quickly pointed out, they are no different from certain other ethnic groups such as Italians. Both groups speak in a way and use idioms that outsiders cannot understand. They use words that only have meaning among themselves. This problem, Harper explained, is passed on from generation to generation. He wonders if this is the reason why they have not been able to understand and comprehend all the education that has been given to them. That raises another question for him: If teachers have not been able to communicate to blacks in a language they understand, what is being taught?

Harper toyed with a number of solutions to the problem he posed. None of them were entirely satisfactory to him, however. Perhaps teachers should be hired who speak all the languages and dialects in America. No. That would be very difficult. It would be very costly, too. Maybe the best thing to do is take blacks out of the home when they are young and bring them up in a sterile environment. Mold them just the way you want to mold them. He laughingly concluded that there would not be very many real people if that happened.

Harper has simply never given a lot of thought to the problems black people face and pose. Until his present job, John Harper rarely came into contact with them. Blacks were not an issue for him. In fact, during the first hour of the interview, in which he talked about his experiences leading up to the present, he never mentioned black people once. Now, although he is in daily contact with blacks, he attaches small significance to problems ostensibly associated with race.

John Harper sees everything in personal terms, and personally he has never knowingly discriminated against anyone because of their color. The only association Harper has with black people is at work: Some are employees, but most are people who have to do business with his department. They come in to pay parking fines, tax bills, garbage bills, or the charge for sewer service. Harper is a little defensive. The black militant charge that city government is racist does not ring true for him. People come into his office not because they are black, he feels, but because they have bills to pay. Harper does not see how his association with blacks in that situation can be considered a reflection of discrimination or racism. His office does not select people to come in because of their race or ethnic background, they come because they are citizens. The city does not even know who owns a car when it is ticketed until they look up the license number. So Harper cannot see how his work involves discrimination.

It is true, he candidly volunteered, that by and large people are hostile when they come in. After all, they part with money in his office. They want good justification for the transaction. If his office is nice to them and gives them an explanation they understand, he sees no reason why people cannot get along. He generally sends them away satisfied, and that applies to all the people he deals with at work — black as well as white.

Sure, he admitted, some black people come in distrustful of city government. He cannot deny that, but in most instances he eventually gets along well with them, too. In Harper's estimation, they are no different than white people who have a gripe with the city. He gives them the same logical arguments he gives whites. They understand him. Why shouldn't they? he wonders; most black people are quite intelligent. Some may have been held back, or not had opportunities to advance themselves, and some may have been too timid to take a chance — but other than that, blacks are no different than whites. He does not treat them any differently, not even the black people who initially distrust him.

Harper has no problems with the black people who work in his office. As a matter of fact, he proudly pointed out, of all the minority people who have worked in his office the only person who ever indicated that she "considered" herself a minority was a Chinese woman. "Oh, she felt she was real put upon," he said in a disgusted tone of voice. She thought she was being discriminated against. Harper feels that sometimes it takes a long time to convince people that discrimination is not an issue. He is quite successful at it, though; he gets along very well with the Negro men and women in his office.

In fact, he got one of his Negro employees a better job. The fellow really had talent and in Harper's estimation was wasting his time working for the city. Harper was instrumental in getting the man hired by one of the Bay Area's major banks as an appraiser. It was a difficult task. He had to speak with a lot of banks before he got any results. They would hesitate, asking him if the man was really that good. They said things like, "It's going to be hard for people to accept," which annoyed Harper considerably.

Just recalling the incident brought back the strong emotions he felt at the time. His voice rising with conviction, he told Price how he had responded. He told them:

> I don't believe it! That happens because *you* believe it. But that's a pile of hogwash! The man is capable, he's adaptable, he will do a fine job for you and this is the thing that's going to impress your client. Your client isn't going to look at it the same way you do. You're part of a conservative institution. You're not willing to accept change or even to

recognize it when it exists. You're kind of like os-
triches: You bury your head in the sand. It's only
when you get kicked in the rump that you finally
find out that burying your head in the sand doesn't
help you.

He badgered people that way until the man was hired. To
Harper's knowledge they have been happy with him ever
since. At any rate, he is still working for them and to
Harper's way of thinking that is the important thing.

But issues like that do not arise in Harper's office. The
way work is organized and evaluated does not permit him
an opportunity to discriminate against people. As long as
employees courteously provide taxpayers the service of
answering questions and are able to handle the heavy work
load, they have a job. Harper has had many black people
work for him; he refuses to notice a difference between
people. To his way of thinking, "Other than the fact that
their skin is black, I can't see that they're any different
than anyone else."

The problem is agitators, not inequality

While Harper discounts the impact of racism in America,
he does not take racial turmoil lightly. *His* head is not bur-
ied in the sand. He believes that unrest does not stem from
injustice or inequality — other factors account for it.

People have become impatient. Things move too slowly
for them. They fail to realize that time is the essence of
satisfaction, and in a modern society like the United States
any meaningful change is going to take time. It has to. The
society is an involved one and there are a lot of strings to
be cut. Harper thinks the laws regulating internal revenue
are a good example of the problem. Instead of removing
the bad features of the laws, the government adds to them
with amendments and compounded ordinances; and be-

cause special-interest groups influence the lawmaking process, "the same thing happens with damn near every piece of legislation in America." The problem, as Harper sees it, is that as young people come along they do not understand this.

Harper thinks public schools are culpable. They are much too permissive these days; especially at the lower levels. For instance, when he went to high school no one left the campus during school hours. They were expected to be in class and they were. Now when he drives past his alma mater he wonders "when the hell students go to class; they always seem to be hanging around outside the school." Education was more regimented when he was a student; that no longer appears to be the case. He recalls feeling his first sense of freedom when he started at the university. Classroom attendance was no longer mandatory. As long as students did the work and understood the material they could pass. No one guided students along the way as had been done up to that point. For the first time, students were really on their own.

It seems to Harper that young people are given a lot more latitude in elementary and high schools today. Opportunities for learning have been expanded; he is open to the possibility that perhaps young people are brighter for it. Their all-around education is improved and they are developing interests in many areas. Maybe they are even accomplishing a great deal more because of the new system. However, he also detects a problem with the system. Young people have experienced so much freedom in public schools that when they start college or work these activities seem restrictive. When they come of age and become entangled in the maze of social responsibility, they feel that all of a sudden the brakes have been put on them. They are not expected to adhere to some code of procedure until they are already adults. Since they have never been held responsible, when they disagree with something they think the thing to do is get rid of it. Some of them say things like: "I will obey what I want to, what I agree with. That which I don't agree with has no use for me." In Harper's estimation, then, the schools are partly responsible for the unrest in black communities.

Only part of the problem is thus accounted for; another part of it has to be attributed to agitation. As Harper sees it, "there has been an awful lot of agitation in the black community." It has been at all levels: from the clergy to the militants. There are even some white people, he pointed out derisively, who promote the philosophy that whites ought to cut off their hands because years ago their ancestors were involved in slavery, "or whatever you want to call it." "Maybe I should have my head cut off," Harper exclaimed sarcastically, "because my great, great grandfather at one time or another had indentured servants." His grandfather, Harper notes parenthetically, more than likely *was* one. Harper's grandfather had supported Bismarck's attempt to annex Luxembourg. When the move failed, he had to leave.[1] "So I guess you'd say we're political fugitives," he concluded. In spite of this fact many young people have the attitude that white people like Harper are responsible for the current situation of blacks.

The biggest problem, in Harper's estimation, is activists who constantly remind black people that they are black. Black militants continually say: "You are second class; you're black; you belong over there; you're not part of this society." Harper thinks it is like selling soap: If people hear it long enough they begin to believe it.

The tactic agitates him on a number of levels. He thinks it is divisive: It certainly does not work toward integration. It also arouses mistrust and hostility. What really annoys him most is that the accusations are untrue. There were no

[1] I realize this event occurred some twenty years after the time Harper in another context (p. 171) reports his grandfather came to the United States. Evidently Harper is unaware of this discrepancy.

problems until agitators began to manufacture them. Take
the problem of the "so-called ghetto," he suggested. It is a
misnomer. The word has always applied to the Jewish
quarters in Europe. It was a pretty concrete concept. By
today's definition, however, any place that has old houses
is a ghetto. Harper does not think Negro neighborhoods on
the West Coast can be called "ghettos" — not if someone
has been anywhere else. California has no neighborhoods
that compare with those in New York, Chicago, or cities in
the South. In his estimation ghettos just do not exist in the
West, even though agitators act as if they do and keep saying that to black people. He feels they are just like people
on television trying to sell a product. The item that is
hawked the most is bought the most. After a while people
begin to believe it is the only product and when they go to
the store that is the one they buy. That explains why there
are so many racial problems.

It also explains some of the problems his office faces in
its relations with the black community. Not too long ago
he placed community workers in black neighborhoods to
organize in favor of a parks and recreation bond issue.
Harper felt the black neighborhoods would be the sole
beneficiaries if the measure passed. He had a lot of support
in the community. There was a great deal of positive feeling toward the plan; many community groups endorsed it.
Yet the measure was defeated. It was defeated in large part
because of the "no" votes of the black community. In Harper's estimation the bond issue lost because one man single-
handedly defeated it — a white preacher who agitated a-
gainst it. The preacher played on the community's suspicions by saying the bond measure would steal property
from community residents and they would not receive a
fair price for their land. He campaigned for the view that
all the money should be spent in black neighborhoods.

Harper thinks it is agitation, not racism, that is pushing
people apart. In previous years the area had a nice group of

blacks and the community was a pleasant place in which to
live. People got along together pretty well; they understood each other. Black people always lived in the area,
but there were certainly no problems. He grants that the
proportion of blacks has increased in the last decade, but
maintains there was always a substantial black community
— 25 to 30 percent of the population as far back as the
1930s. The area was home base for Pullman car workers and
many of them resided there. They were people of substantial means. There were never any problems.

"It's not that way any more," Harper said sullenly. "Now
they've chosen sides." He no longer sees people intermingling and it bothers him, because he thinks the area could
have disproven the myth that integrated neighborhoods
mean a reduction in property values. In his judgment when
black people move into white neighborhoods it does not
hurt real estate values. Blacks have not been gouged by
high prices and whites have not lost money by selling.

Sure, Harper admitted, some people want to move at
that time, because they do not like the type of people
coming in — color is not the issue. Besides which, he
pointed out, there is as much trash among whites as there
is in any race. It is the trash that drives people out — black
as well as white — not the color. Harper feels that this,
more than anything else, causes people to move into certain
neighborhoods. How else can it be explained? he asked.
No one has been able to enforce a racial covenant.

Price pointed out that the President's Commission on
Civil Disorders (the Kerner Commission) decided that the
root of the problem was ultimately white racism. He asked
how Harper reacted to that conclusion. "I'm not too sure
that I understand what white racism is," Harper responded
simply. The newspapers talk about it a good deal and he
often wonders what they mean by it. Perhaps it is just a
phrase that is popular these days. But he is not really sure

what it means. He wonders if maybe it refers to people who advocate racial superiority — people who are trying to encourage division among races: "separatism, if that's what you want to call it." Perhaps it refers to a movement that is trying to instill confidence in a group. Harper is not satisfied with either of the definitions. He still does not understand what people mean when they talk about racism.

He does not think the unrest in black communities has much to do with racism, regardless of how it is defined. In Harper's estimation the groups stimulating dissension, activism, and revolt — "or whatever you want to call it" — are doing it merely because they want to. They want to collar and destroy institutions — destroy the progress that has been made up to now. Their actions have also pushed people to recognize that there are all kinds of people and that groups have to get along with each other, but that was not what activists were trying to do. In his view their desire was to upset "our way of life," to disorganize the community.

Racism is not an issue in Harper's mind. Activism is. And the problem is not restricted to the black community. White people are involved as well. Activism knows no color. Its objective is to destroy institutions regardless of the community in which they exist. "Look what Jerry Rubin and his bunch are trying to do to Berkeley," he pointed out. In his judgment the white community has faced these problems since at least the "Savio days" of the Free Speech Movement. As far as Harper can tell, society's problems are not racial, because militants want to change institutions in both communities.

John Harper does not understand why people should want to do that.

He has particular difficulty understanding the purpose behind proposals for Third World colleges and black studies programs. He does not see how a course in Watusi, soul, or black history is going to help anyone. What does it do for people except promote understanding, he wants to know? And if these studies fall under the heading of history, he thinks they should be taught by history departments. There is no need to segregate them or turn them into special courses. The main question he has is: What good are these courses going to do kids in later life? "So fine," he said sarcastically, "I have three units in black studies; I have fifteen in Watusi; and I have six units in soul studies. All my meals have been cooked by an expert in soul foods. But what has it really done for me?" The only thing he can see is that perhaps they can work in a black studies program or join the Peace Corps.

What are they going to do later on in life? He doubts that they will have many alternatives. They will not know math, they will not have an in-depth education. What will they be able to do? Harper does not think black people are doing themselves any favors demanding these programs. In fact, he thinks such programs hurt them.

It is not just the goals that bother him. He also takes issue with their methods of implementation. In his view the goals are an excuse for something else. The only purpose he can see for raising them is that they give people a banner to rally around. "They don't really know where they're going," Harper exclaimed. He likens their actions to youth movements in fascist states. He feels their minds have been captured by strong leaders who they feel can do no wrong. "The leaders won't accomplish anything for any of them individually," Harper said, "but they'll be followed to the death."

Harper feels that things cannot go on like this forever. "Ultimately, somewhere along the line, someone will come along and set them down." In his judgment, people will reach a point where they are a little too offended and they are going to think they have to resist. That will be the point at which mass confrontation will occur, and Harper thinks the consequences will leave the nation pretty well fragmented for a long time afterward.

He does not know at what point people will become sufficiently offended so that they will resist. That is rather hard for him to say right now. No one is trying to push him at the moment. Right now they are pushing on the educational institutions. It might be different if people pushed his city the same way they are pushing for black studies. Were that to happen, he would try to maintain a line of communication to them, and be responsive to their needs. He thinks a city should at least give them the idea that they are getting a part of its resources; they should not feel they are a closed community that is being ignored. When that happens, riots, burning, and looting occur. "But granted you can't give them the whole damn city!"

If that were a demand?

Well, things have not reached that point yet, have they....

Epilogue

It hardly seems plausible that a person living in the United States in the late 1960s could honestly dismiss the impact of racial inequality on the life chances of black people. For someone to say they do not know what racism is seems ludicrous. Yet that is precisely what John Harper says, and I believe he means it.

How can he maintain this view that seems so out of touch with what most people see as reality? Is he blind? Does he systematically distort facts? Are his beliefs a cover-up for deep-seated prejudices?

I think the answer to the last three questions is no. There is nothing pathological or distorted about Harper's views on racial issues.

His biography suggests some obvious explanations for his

viewpoint. Harper hardly had any contact with black people until late in his life. His current association with them is minimal. This accounts to some extent for his ignorance of racial problems. His class background is another factor. Success was his for the asking even though he did have to work for it. Perhaps problems of the ascribed sort are incomprehensible to him. Both these factors contribute to his position.

They hardly, however, make up the whole story — in fact they do not carry much explanatory weight. Harper is, after all, not totally ignorant of racial problems. He is aware of segregation in the South. He has had difficulty finding meaningful work for qualified blacks in his office. If his personal experiences with work accounted for his position on blacks, I think his contention would be that since he has been successful, anyone can be. Much of his history lends itself to such an interpretation. The Harpers were undoubtedly a hard-working lot who successfully faced some pretty tough obstacles. But strangely enough, John Harper never makes this claim. He does not even hint at it. Obviously, then, other factors are operating.

I think Harper's position reflects a curious mixture of certain typically American beliefs concerning how the society operates and how people should relate to one another. One part of the mixture is Harper's expression of upper-middle-class liberalism. He suggests that all people are created equal: The only difference between black and white people is their skin color. Were it not for that difference, people would be the same. The other component of Harper's position is his commitment to universalistic criteria for evaluating people. He feels that in America people are judged by standards that do not recognize color. When these two positions are combined, they add up to the idea that America is essentially a very healthy and just society. To Harper, America *is* the land of freedom, equality, and opportunity. These concepts are not ideals for him, they are the reality. That is why he gets so angry with people who in his judgment are trying to destroy American institutions. He evaluates the situation of blacks *as if* formal rights and legal ideals were *in fact* the norms by which society is governed. In essence, he projects a truly color-blind view of the world.

Of course, this point of view quite often bumps up against an opposite reality. Racial unrest and turmoil are hard to ignore in a period as turbulent as the 1960s. And this state of affairs represents a potential contradiction for Harper, at least on a theoretical level. How can he maintain his color-blind view of the world and his positive evaluation of American society in the face of seemingly contradictory evidence?

The answer is that there is no contradiction for John Harper. The problem, as he sees it, is not racial inequality or racism but rather agitators, impatience, and a failure of communication. Racial unrest reflects *these conditions*, he feels. As far as he is concerned, there would be no racial problems were it not for agitators. The problems that exist independently of activists are mainly breakdowns of communication that can be solved once people begin to speak the same language and use the same concepts. The only major problem he sees in America is permissiveness in the schools, a problem that is related to race only insofar as it contributes to impatience among young black people. While it cannot be proven, Harper's concern about permissiveness may be related more to the challenge it presents for Protestant theology regarding family authority, than to race relations in American society. Be that as it may, for John Harper there is no discrepancy between his color-blind view of the world and racial unrest. As long as he subscribes to a theory of agitators, the apparent contradiction is reconciled.

Attributing racial problems to agitators and communication blockages fulfills other functions as well. (1) Harper's logic allows him to recognize the existence of racial issues without calling into question his beliefs about racial justice in American society. In his view, racial issues are manufactured by militants and not generated by social inequality. This leaves intact his belief that America is a universalistic society.

(2) He can deny that blacks suffer from racial discrimination without appearing as a "racist" or reactionary. In his judgment, the problems blacks face stem from insufficient communication, not racial restrictions. Thus Harper can maintain a liberal posture of wanting to help and get along with blacks while at the same time denying that their problems have any structural basis in American society. In this respect, his "liberalism" is somewhat unique. Traditionally liberals recognize the need for social reform.

(3) Harper's insistence that agitators come in all colors also contributes to a seemingly liberal stance. He can claim that his hostility toward agitators has no racial motivation. He is annoyed with *agitators,* not just black ones.

(4) Because the only legitimate racial problems he sees are communicative ones, there is no need for him to entertain social reform as an issue. Successful communication can be accomplished without having to alter society in any meaningful way.

(5) Since communication failures originate on the black side of the color line, it is blacks rather than whites who need to change. Thus Harper can argue that black people, not whites are responsible for the racial situation.

(6) When he is forced to recognize racial troubles in America, Harper can minimize them. In his estimation, they stem from impatient, disgruntled individuals well versed in the techniques of hard sell rather than any basic characteristics of American society.

(7) There is a personal as well as a political payoff in Harper's stance. Invoking the spectre of agitators and communication failure permits him to feel that he is in no way implicated in the racial ordering of American society. In fact he is hostile to the suggestion that white people are somehow responsible for the racial situation. The privileges from which he has so obviously benefited never enter into his thinking. That is the way it should be: As long as the issue is agitators, privilege need not be considered. Nor does he have to take into account institutions that facilitate privilege.

At first blush it seems strange to find a person of John Harper's class background subscribing to an agitator theory of racial turmoil. We expect to find this belief expressed by lower-class or working-class people. That has been the conclusion of many sociological studies concerning authoritarianism. Everyday observation appears to confirm the finding. It always seems to be the red-neck or blue-collar ethnic who is looking for the "red under the bed" or the "commie" behind the civil rights leader. Sometimes it is a bitter and beleaguered FBI director. And yet in the case of John Harper we have a western blue blood subscribing to a sophisticated version of the same scenario.

This is not really so strange. As long as racial divisions in America provide white people with privileges, they will be defended. As long as it is illegitimate to defend racial privilege with crass references to biological factors, people will invoke more acceptable rationales. The rationales will vary, but particular rationales are not the exclusive property of one class or another. They are part of American culture and therefore accessible to anyone. In John Harper's case, the agitator explanation fits most comfortably into his world view, his biography, and current circumstances. If it did not, he would articulate another explanation.

7 "There wouldn't be any problems if people's heads were in the right place." Roberta

Prologue

Finding "hip" young residents of San Francisco's Haight-Ashbury district, who are willing to speak with sociologists, is not an easy task. The community is quite suspicious of and hostile toward university-based social scientists. In the eyes of these young people, sociologists are not only members of the "straight" community – they are "spies" for it as well.

Lincoln Bergman, who conducted a series of interviews in the Haight, was able to partially break through this barrier. He was able to do this through the good offices of his sister and brother, who lived in the community. All three were raised in the district; Lincoln's brother and sister still lived there. Lincoln has a number of qualities that evoke confidence in him. He is a quiet, thoughtful person and a good listener. He is someone who apparently evokes the confidence of the people he interviews.

Lincoln had other qualities as well. He was raised in San Francisco and was quite familiar with the city – its politics, diversity, and temperament. He had been a civil rights activist in San Francisco during the early 1960s and had a feeling for the difficulties hip young people were experiencing in the closing moments of the decade. But Lincoln did not participate in the various struggles that gripped the Haight. He was now a graduate student in the school of journalism at the University of California at Berkeley, across the Bay. Lincoln's ability to get interviews seemed to be enhanced by this geographic separation from the community. He was not identified with one or another faction in the Haight; people apparently felt they could speak openly to him.

Lincoln spent a lot of time in the community. He "hung around" various communes, went to numerous community meetings, and talked to a lot of people. He made no secret of his intentions. When appropriate, he told people why he was there: He was working for some sociologists who wanted to know how white people felt about racial issues.

All in all Lincoln interviewed fifteen persons living in Haight-Ashbury. The quality of his interviews is difficult to assess. This stems in part from the frustrating way in which America's counterculture participants choose to express themselves. They speak in a manner that can only be described as studied inarticulateness. Words like "trip," "far-out," "scene," "too much" are mainstays of their vocabulary, and concrete referents for such abstractions are difficult to pin down. While in most instances the interviewees actively resisted Lincoln's attempts at clarification, Lincoln himself contributed to the uneven quality of many interviews. He is not a social scientist and often felt ill at ease probing about in the unexplored regions of people's minds. As a result he sometimes did not push people beyond clichés. He was also overly conscious about his interviews being comparable with each other. He seemed to equate comparability with a uniform wording of questions and he tended to formulate his questions rigidly in accordance with this principle, regardless of the person with whom he was speaking or the context of the interview. Thus many of his interviews have a wooden quality.

The interview upon which the following portrait is based was one of Lincoln's best. He seemed to hit it off well with Roberta. She responded to his questions in a thoughtful manner, gracefully transcending the rigidity of his questioning. She took his questions seriously, answering them in depth without being pushed. The interview took place in her apartment a couple of weeks after the two had been introduced by Lincoln's sister. Roberta did not know Lincoln very well at the time. She had seen him around but had never spoken with him very much.

Perhaps this is why the interview worked — she was telling him about herself and that was something he knew little about, yet wanted to. The interview succeeded for yet another reason: Roberta is relatively articulate. To be sure, she has affected the style of hip stuttering that characterizes her comrades; nevertheless, she can be lucid and concrete when she wants to. For some reason she often chose to be so while talking with Lincoln.

*"I want to devote my whole life to like
spiritual things."*

No one in Roberta's family was surprised when they found out she was living in San Francisco. Most of her young life had been devoted to seeking "some kind of harmony" with herself and other people. She had done a lot of traveling, lived in a lot of different places, and experimented with different ways of "doing" her life. So in 1966, when many young people migrated to San Francisco's Haight-Ashbury district, Roberta's family expected her to be among them. Like most Americans, they considered her a "hippie."

The road Roberta followed to San Francisco began in a small Louisiana town across the lake from New Orleans where she was born twenty-one years ago. It was a typically southern town: rural and lazy; dominated by one-family rule. Most people earned their living off the land as farmers and sharecroppers. Roberta's parents were exceptions. Her father owned the local feed store; her mother was a socialite. They were "old timers" in town. To Roberta's way of thinking, most of the townspeople were "ignorant." The basis of their ignorance was not stupidity; they knew the land and "could feel things through growing crops." They were ignorant because they had never been outside the town; "they were people who just stayed there all their lives."

The local social scene was "nowhere" for Roberta. "It was sickening." Her social life revolved mainly around church functions and country clubs. By the time she reached high school, churchgoing had become a bone of contention between Roberta and her parents. They insisted that she attend the local Presbyterian services weekly and when she refused she was punished by being confined to the house.

Local race relations conformed to the southern norms that prevailed in the 1950s: The town was segregated. Whites were paternalistic toward blacks and on the surface, at any rate, blacks accepted the arrangement. Accordingly, Roberta did not come into contact with black people very often. Blacks had their section of town and whites had theirs. Blacks went to their school and whites went to theirs. The only blacks Roberta knew were people who worked for her parents. Her father had an amicable, albeit paternalistic, relationship with the black men he employed. He always seemed to be helping them out when they scraped up against the local law enforcement officials. One young black man seemed to end up in jail every Saturday night and "Daddy would always bail him out."

But the black lady who cleaned their house made the biggest impression on Roberta. In fact, "she was one of the few people in town I could identify with at all." Roberta felt "at home" with the lady; it was a comfortable relationship. She did not have to constantly explain herself or account for her various activities as she did with her parents. She could joke with the black woman, who was always ready to laugh. The woman liked Roberta, her sister, and two younger brothers. Roberta felt she enjoyed watching them grow and Roberta got pleasure out of giving her clothes she had outgrown. When Roberta left Louisiana and then returned for occasional visits, she always looked up the lady — much to her mother's amazement and displeasure. They would share cake and coffee and talk about Roberta's latest venture. "Mother couldn't understand it; she thought it was terrible." But as far as Roberta was concerned, the lady's house was the only place that felt like "home" in small-town Louisiana.

The town was a peaceful one, racially speaking. When the United States Supreme Court announced in 1954 that public schools would be desegregated, "people talked an awful lot about the decision." But black people did not indicate to whites that they were especially interested in drastically changing things. They were conciliatory toward whites, their feelings evidently tempered by the paternalism that had characterized race relations in the past. Roberta was impressed by their "peacefulness," their gratefulness to whites who had helped them, and their indifference to edicts emanating from Washington, D.C. She thought it was "really nice that they wanted to be peaceful." "But, you know," she added, "they didn't really owe everything to us. They were just groovy people."

Roberta had outgrown small-town Louisiana by the time she graduated from high school. While she could not "put her finger on why," she was beginning to feel that she was different from the other folks in town. She was appalled at the thought of living out her life in rural America; there had to be more to life than that. She felt at odds with herself, and that was an uncomfortable feeling. There was no one in town to whom she could turn, no one with whom she could communicate except possibly herself and she had just about exhausted that alternative. No matter how she figured it, Roberta's hometown simply did not add up to be enough . She wanted more. Although she was not sure how much was enough, or even what enough would look or feel like, she knew there had to be other ways of "doing life." She decided that when fall came she would begin looking for them. Even if she never found them, she promised herself, she would still keep on trying to find out more and more about herself and the world. She would continue until she reached "some kind of harmony with myself and others." At that time Roberta did not realize that her search would be a life-long project and that it would take her to San Francisco. She only knew one thing: "I couldn't wait to get out."

When Roberta enrolled at Louisiana State University that fall, a whole new world began to open for her. It did not happen all at once, however. At first glance LSU was just a larger version of the small town from which she had just escaped. People were mainly interested in petty sorts of things: fraternities and sororities; clothes and cars; football games. Roberta gravitated toward people who were "looked down upon" by others at the school. They were "like hippie people" even though they were not called hippies at that time. "They were just free people": people who said, dressed, and lived as their spirits dictated. Unlike folks at home, they were people who thought and had feelings that they expressed. They lived in accordance with their beliefs, unconcerned about what others thought or said of them. Roberta was fascinated; she wanted to be like them. They were "into art, into music"; doing things that made her "feel," made her "grow" — "into real things, not any phony society-type things."

Roberta began to feel that some of the ideas she had brought from home were better left there. She had been taught that she was "above" black people because she was white; "better" than they were because her family had money. At Louisiana State, her friends were "into brotherhood and love — integration." Some of them were even organizing marches in Bogalusa in support of black groups like the Deacons for Justice who were protecting black people from local whites. One of Roberta's newly found friends headed up the marches and he gave parties to which black people would come. People got to know one another at these parties and felt "free" around each other. Roberta had a feeling of excitement, "like at last it's going to happen. We're going to always be comfortable together; be equal to one another." She thought it was a "beautiful thing," and along with everyone else she was very excited.

Black people began to take on a new meaning for Roberta. They were no longer in the background of her life as they had been back home, where they were used and abused like props in a stage play that are rarely directly involved in the drama. She saw them with different eyes and black people took on a special kind of significance for her. They are the personification of "feeling," "freedom," "soul," "togetherness," "expressiveness" — all admirable qualities in her estimation: qualities very few white people express, yet which she hopes to be able to. Roberta is fascinated by black people: "They're really far-out." Black music, the blues in particular, is one thing Roberta finds intriguing. "They have such a nice way of expressing their feelings — they just say it and feel it." The music gives her a certain kind of feeling that she enjoys. She thinks maybe it is the music in black people's lives that helps them survive adversity. She also likes what happens when blacks get together, the way they talk, laugh, and dance. "They just be-bop around having a good time." It is not very often that white people act like that, she thinks, and those who do are either rare people or "stoned."

There are a lot of ways in which white people are less free to express themselves, she concludes. White language — the "King's English" — obscures things, hides people's real feelings, especially in comparison to the vivid terms in which blacks speak. She rarely sees white people show true feelings toward each other the way blacks do. Blacks seem to be less "hung-up" about sexual matters than whites. Fatherless families and families fathered by different men do not stigmatize black children as they do whites. Black people are "basically freer among each other" than whites, she concludes, and she "dug that."

Blacks also have "soul," a quality she has difficulty defining but nevertheless feels is "something real." It is not a physical object, something one can touch or feel. It is more spiritual — "above all that." She sees it as a kind of bond that "would tie them together." Soul is not the exclusive property of blacks, however. Some white people have it too, although not too many of them. Perhaps some of her friends do, but even they do not show it too often. White people just do not like to "open up in that kind of way." They would get embarrassed.

Roberta is not completely of one mind about blacks, however. In some respects she is ambivalent. Certain feelings contradict others. Blacks are too concerned with what she calls "earthly material things" for her liking. While it is true that she appreciates "earthy" things and so do they, blacks put more emphasis on such things than she does. She wants people to be "more into mind trips and looking above all that."

All in all, however, Roberta is quite impressed with

black people. Their approach to life is certainly different than that of most white people she knows. It is an alternative to the small-town life of her childhood that she found so unfulfilling. She wants to be like blacks in some important ways. Roberta wants to be freer, more expressive, she wants to feel things and have her mind experience various facets of life.

Although Roberta wants to live life in some of the ways blacks do, she has never wanted to *be* black. Her experiences have not altered this feeling. There were, to be sure, moments when it might have been nice; they were fleeting moments, however, and never lasted very long. They were times when a lot of blacks got together and seemed to be enjoying soul music and dancing. It was at such times that she felt she could "really dig to be a part of that." Nonetheless, she thinks of herself as a white person, even though she prefers not to think much about it. Being white is not anything she is particularly proud of or ashamed of. It does not have that much meaning to her. Nevertheless, she has to admit that being a white person in America has made a difference in her life. She knows that if she had been born black she would have had more to overcome. Yet she even wonders about that. A person's social class is also pretty important, she feels, and that might be just as hard to overcome as being black. She does not like getting "hung-up with those kinds of things." She prefers to judge people by what is "inside of them," by what they "express." It makes more sense to think of herself as "one more soul who's got to make his way. Just like anybody else."

Roberta dropped out of Louisiana State after about one year. It was becoming too familiar. She thought that perhaps the freedom and feeling she experienced there could best be expressed through art, and the following fall she enrolled in another college specifically to study that subject. But after about six months she "started to leave." She was getting "fed up with the whole college thing." She needed to "experience more and more" and to "grow" in yet different ways. Roberta wanted a new adventure and to meet new people.

First she went East, up to Baltimore, but "didn't dig it." Then she moved back down South; this time to the mountains of North Carolina, where she lived for a while at a lodge. She washed dishes and worked in the kitchen and around the yard. People had large families, lived in log cabins, swung on trees, and played with snakes. It was a good life, everyone had a great time; the folks were simple types, "beautiful people." Roberta was "bored as hell." The time had come for her to move to San Francisco to be with people like herself who were seeking what she sought, living life as she thought it should be lived.

The last two years had been important ones in Roberta's life. She was beginning to see the world through lenses she had been grinding since high school. She had a rather distinctive, if not coherent and final, perspective concerning how she wanted to relate to the world when she reached the city. "Earthly material" things were of little concern to her. She wanted to be "above all that," free to pursue and "feel" matters on a more "spiritual" level. She wanted the world to be "real" and "loving," a place where people could "live together and do their own thing" and be judged by "what they express" rather than the color of their skin. She saw things in color-blind although not color-less terms. She also sought "earthiness" — for people who could be true to themselves and their feelings and, above all, express them openly. She wanted to "grow," to "love," to expand her powers of thought. Life should be a "mind trip" that included lots of feeling, freedom, brotherhood and love, expressiveness and soul. Foremost, she wanted to relate to the world in a *spiritual* fashion.

*"Spades want to see you defend yourself a lot of
times. Like that's their trip."*

It was not easy to live this way in San Francisco. Numerous worldly details insistently interrupted Roberta's spiritual "trips." First there was the matter of supporting herself. Jobs were scarce and the ones she could get were a "drag." She alternated between being on welfare and working in head shops. The police were also a problem. They would, with infuriating regularity, "sweep" the streets for runaways and young people under eighteen. Roberta feared that she would be picked up because she looked so young. Finding housing that she could afford also proved difficult. Also, it hurt her to see the "love scene" commit suicide with speed and heroin-filled syringes. But ironically enough, black people proved to be the greatest obstacle to Roberta's vision of the good life. In the South, black people had turned her on to herself and to feelings that she was previously denied; but in San Francisco young "spades" made that impossible.

Before young white people began to move into the Haight-Ashbury district in the summer of 1966 the neighborhood had a large black population. When Roberta arrived, there were still many black people on the block and many of the younger blacks were curious about Roberta and her six roommates. They wondered what the "hippies" were all about. Roberta and her friends felt this was positive and asked the blacks over to their house. They thought they would "turn them on to some new ideas; help them to grow a little." The idea was to let the blacks know that "everybody is brothers"; people should be "together" and hippies "didn't want any prejudice." Hopefully the blacks would get turned on to things like "sharing with your brother." For a while the young blacks were friendly and when they came around they would bring gifts. It was apparent to the black youths that the hippies were poorly clothed and so when they came over they would bring hand-me-down garments.

This cultural exchange program did not last very long. Inexplicably, the young blacks were soon stealing from Roberta and her friends, taking things when no one was looking. When no one was home they broke into the house and stole things. They also picked fights. One young man, whom Roberta saw as "a big pile of muscles walking around," wanted only to fight. There was no way to get "through his head." Roberta felt they were all "a blank wall you couldn't get through" and she was disappointed that they did not really want to learn. She decided they were "typical juvenile delinquents — ignorant"; it seemed to be the "basic scene with spades anywhere from sixteen to twenty-one years old."

Roberta might have avoided that conclusion had she only been hassled by the blacks on her block, but the problem extended beyond that to the entire Haight Street "scene." Each time she went down there, over and over again she had similar experiences. "If I had dope, the spades wanted to rip me off for it." Sometimes they wanted to rape her and brandished knives to convince her they were serious. She had the feeling they were always trying to see what they could get from her.

Roberta found it difficult to maintain her color-blind approach to the world. She liked to take long walks in the evening and preferred to walk in a white neighborhood rather than a black one, "cause you're not getting hassled as much." Although she tried not to, she began to fear black people for the first time in her life. She was afraid to walk alone in black neighborhoods at night because "there were too many people out there just waiting and watching; waiting to grab you." Each time she passed a group of black men standing on a corner one of them would call out to her: "Hey baby, come over here. I want to talk to you." That scared her. She ignored them, pretending not to hear. She would walk faster, thinking, "Those ignorant fuckers." Sometimes she ran, frightened of their "trip" and her response to it. Roberta built up defenses and that annoyed her.

Although the young blacks have annoyed, scared, and disappointed her, and in some instances even made her wonder if it was possible to disregard color completely, Roberta cannot generate much hostility toward black people as a group. She still thinks they are pretty "groovy," "far-out" people — perhaps more so from a distance than close up. Their music and dancing continue to turn her on. She continues "to dig their expressiveness"; though she wishes some of them would "express" a little less hostility toward her.

Without quite realizing it, Roberta is also dividing black people into two groups. There are the "groovy blacks," most of whom she has known in the South, and to some extent in the North although only abstractly. And there are "uptight spades," the young people, mostly men, with whom she comes into daily contact in San Francisco. When she thinks about black people in general terms, she usually pictures the "groovy" ones. Unfortunately, in the city she has to deal more concretely with "uptight spades" every day. But she refuses to "get too down on them because they couldn't help it if they were ignorant."

Nevertheless, living in San Francisco is not as spiritual as Roberta wants it to be. The city is not a very loving place, and people are hardly free to do their own thing. She finds it difficult, though not impossible, to "grow" and be "for real." It is considerably easier being "above" earthly material issues or questions of race when she is high on pot. She finds it impossible to avoid a world that insistently comes into conflict with her views about how it ought to be. Although this kind of world makes it difficult for Roberta to remain true to the way she wants to see it and live it, she has never given up trying.

"Like it's a drag to have as your whole trip trying
to get your race equal to another."

Roberta is not the only person in the Haight having difficulty reconciling what ought to be with what is. Many of her friends are reconsidering what their attitude toward the world should be. Some of them argue that the "love trip" is impossible; the neighborhood blacks see to that. Others question spirituality as a life force; Martin Luther King was assassinated and the civil rights movement defeated. Change is not going to come through mind trips alone; ghetto rebellions and demands for black power are evidence of that. Some people think racism can be ended only by rearranging economic structures; others feel it is the blacks who are racists. Maybe brotherhood is impossible; perhaps racism is part of the natural order of things. A few friends take these problems to be evidence that their ideals are untenable, hopelessly contradicted by the world that surrounds them. Roberta rejects that. She feels no such contradiction exists. The problems that rage around her are real, to be sure. They can neither be denied nor avoided. People have to cope with these problems, but they do not refute her ideas about the world. She interprets things differently.

Sure, "spades hassled hippies," she conceded. But that does not mean it *has* to be that way. It happens because they are not very intelligent. They are not "stupid," however, she quickly pointed out. It is just that they are "really hung up"on the whole Fillmore scene, which is not a very intelligent scene. They have a "whole brawn idea" toward everything; you know, "like muscles, material things, earthy things." Even so, she insisted, the way they act is understandable. They act the way they have to act because "it's like from their whole environment." She thinks she can see how that "would lead to exactly what they're doing." Not that they all act like that; there are lots of exceptions. "Like there are individuals in every kind of race and that makes up for everything."

Roberta cannot deny that hippies are getting "uptight" about being hassled. That is a natural fact and she includes herself as one such person. Maybe she is even "prejudiced about certain things." As far as she is concerned, the only people who are not prejudiced are people who have not been "hassled by spades." If they had been, they would definitely feel otherwise. She insisted that these feelings do not really mean she is prejudiced. It is simply a matter of "more or less finding out what's better for you." Everyone needs to protect themselves, she argued; to put up some kind of defense. "But that's not prejudice. It's just natural instinct."

Ghetto rebellions sort of "blew" Roberta's mind; she thought black people were really "more together" than that. She does not see any reason to call rebellions "political" or "protests." The people involved were just "burning houses, shooting people, and looting places." They were "into it because they like to feel better than white people." She has spoken with some young blacks who were involved, and all they talked about was the things they stole — the new clothes they got. "They weren't in it for any other reason," she concluded. "They dug the money. Like that's what they were in it for."

She does not think much can be done about the riots, but she worries that if the blacks are allowed to continue on that "trip" they will just "tear up everything, the whole city and they'd kill a lot of people." Although she does not like cops, she feels someone had to "fight against the spades, to protect just the general public, I guess." The alternative, as far as she can see it, would probably "just be a terrible murder scene." She is disturbed by her own thoughts about the matter; she feels it is too bad "you couldn't talk to them about it." She is nevertheless convinced that some of them just "insist upon having riots."

She does not think that these thoughts necessarily contradict her view of the world. Riots were not caused by earthly material forces like racism; the majority of blacks were not involved in the riots, which did nothing for black people as a race. Rather, riots were caused by some "intelligent spades" who could control the mass of "not-so-intelligent spades." The less intelligent spades would then go on the intelligent spades' "trip," thinking that what they were doing was helping their race. But it was not. It was just "each one for himself"; they were not in it for their race. If they were, Roberta thinks she could understand why a lot of people rioted. Since it was an "individual trip," however, she can only understand the intelligent spades; the "leaders like people from SNCC who organized them." Roberta feels that as long as there are leaders like that who rule, "they'll always have their own mass of people to join." She thinks it is unfortunate that some leaders are "into that whole trip" and that "it's their whole life." Nevertheless, she is convinced that is not the trip of all blacks, "just some leaders."

Roberta is not very impressed by talk about black power and demonstrations. She thinks it was "bound to happen"; "everything had been leading up to it." She cannot get too concerned about it, however; it was just there, that's all. As far as she is concerned, it is "a drag to have as your whole trip trying to get your race equal to another." But she can still "see why that might be where some spades are at." Hippies went throu·h a similar stage. For a long time they "put the general society down" because they felt inferior — she had felt inferior for quite a while. She would walk down the street and sometimes a "straight person" would look at her funny, make a comment, and it would "upset" her. She got "over that," however; "like that's not real at all." After a while, she got so that she could "dig where their heads are at and I can dig where mine's at." It does not matter anymore. She just wants to "live" and to get along with people. If they think they are better than she is, she will just ignore them and "be above all that." Perhaps blacks will eventually reach that point, she thinks. However, if they do not, it will not be because it is an unreachable point. It will be because they are not "intelligent" enough.

Roberta is not at all convinced that these events and experiences refute her ideas about the world. Instead she sees them as exceptions; they are examples of fear and ignorance, uptightness and manipulation, a lack of intelligence. They show, to be sure, that many people are not where she is "at." However, they do not show that she is at the wrong *place*.

To some extent, however, her two-year stay in San Francisco has taken its toll on Roberta's thinking. She is no longer the optimistic teenager at LSU who went to parties with black people and thought, "At last it's going to happen: We're going to always be comfortable together." She is more cynical. The integration issue has "lost its touch." Now she wants to know, "Why do you have to be for it or against it? Why don't you just live together and do your thing and stop fighting?" She no longer knows if it is going to happen; she wonders if it is not "like expecting all the wars in the world to quit forever." She entertains the possibility that perhaps things go through cycles and that the situation will have to "get worse before it gets better." She does not particularly like that thought; but then neither does she know "enough people around that you can like."

Even so, Roberta finds it difficult to be too pessimistic. Despite the two years of hassles and disappointment, she still pretty much hangs on to the ideas that brought her to San Francisco in the first place. She still wants to devote her life to "spiritual things," to "see many people do that," and "bring as many people together as possible." One thing she has learned is that "in order to bring people together you have to be together yourself," and she wants to get herself "straight." She does not take her cynicism too seriously, and when Lincoln asked her how she wanted herself described to the world she said:

> Tell them I just want to see peace with everybody —
> which is an outrageous thing to even hope for
> 'cause it'll never happen on this earth. But tell
> them she wants to see as much done towards that
> as can be done; enough people turned onto the
> idea of it that want to work towards it. Black peo-
> ple, white people, you know, everybody. Every-
> body. I'm just so sick of all these petty little
> hassles; you know, like "I got mine, you get
> yours.

Epilogue

One has to give Roberta credit for consistency. She refuses to significantly modify her idealistic vision of life even though she has suffered experiences that contradict it. It is not easy to maintain a spiritual, optimistic view of the world these days; but somehow Roberta manages it. To admit that these ideals are hopelessly contradicted by her worldly experiences would have serious consequences for Roberta. It could mean that the kind of life her parents are living, along with the millions of other people who are weighted down by worldly material considerations, is the only available life-style. As far as Roberta is concerned, that would be disastrous. Perhaps this is why she clings to her ideals so tenaciously. Along with countless other generational cohorts, Roberta wants no part of the boring, humdrum existence she feels characterizes middle-class, affluent America. She is engaged in forging a new world out of the old. She insists upon creating and living by new values, developing unique institutions, living in ways she thinks have never been tried before. Roberta can settle for nothing less. If she could, she might as well return to Louisiana.

Not surprisingly, black people figure rather prominently in Roberta's world view. She is both fascinated and frustrated by them. They represent an alternative life style and a mystery. Roberta's feelings about black people are strongly influenced by her larger world view. She explains the racial situation in the same way that she explains anything that contradicts her ideas about what ought to be: People's heads are not in the correct place.

The criteria against which Roberta evaluates events in the world are quite individualistic and voluntaristic: You can do anything if you set your mind to it. In her view, people act in accordance with their heads or their hearts rather than sociological or economic conditions. The word racism is not even a part of her vocabulary. Even though she was raised in the deep South, she expresses very little understanding of its racial order. She seems only barely aware of segregation. Her assessment of the northern racial situation does not go much further. As she sees it blacks are poor because they are "ignorant." But Roberta does not hold this against them; "they can't help it," she explained. The problem, in her estimation, is that blacks are "hung-up" on "earthly things"; they are "into a brawn scene."

According to Roberta's formulation, there would be no racial problems if people's heads were in the "right" place.

Activities aimed at changing social conditions have almost no meaning for her. She sees politics as a "drag"; something that is not "real." Strategies like black power are simply a stage through which black people must pass; eventually they will get "over it" and be "above all that," as she is. She sees no reason why people have to be "for or against" issues like integration. She feels that people should simply "live together" and "do their own thing." In short, race relations are a "head trip" and she is not a part of them.

Certain aspects of race relations, however, strain the viability of her formulation. She finds it difficult to do her thing, to remain neutral and above racial issues, in the face of ghetto rebellions and black animosity toward people like herself. Thus, she avoids walking in black neighborhoods and was taken aback by the riots, which "blew" her mind. Yet even these realities do not really shake Roberta's insistent claim that the world is governed by ideas rather than structural forces. The blacks who hassle her are "uptight" people; ghetto rebels are "unintelligent spades" motivated by a desire for material possessions and manipulated by the more intelligent elements in the community. She sees no relationship between ghetto conditions and rebellions.

Ghetto rebellions tax Roberta's world view to its limit, and, at least in one respect, threaten it. People can do their thing up to a point and one of these points is rioting. Then the police have to step in and "protect the general public." When the actions of black people touch Roberta directly, she is forced in some instances to seriously modify her spiritual perspective, and in others to abandon it altogether.

Ironically enough, when one strips the euphemisms from Roberta's explanation of racial issues, she sounds remarkably like people of her parents' generation and class background. In such people's view, racial problems are not endemic to American society; they are individual problems of ideology. Black people are not denied access to the resources that are America because of any structural constraints, but rather because they are not properly motivated. There are racial problems in America to be sure; but none that cannot be worked out once people — black as well as white — have a correct understanding of the situation and are willing to try and work it out.

Roberta's interpretation of racial issues is self-serving. As long as racial problems exist in people's heads, they are solvable. Moreover, they are solvable without alterations in American society. Whatever changes are necessary must take place in people's heads. Her perspective is also a rather arrogant one: Everyone except Roberta must change.

Her focus on "head trips," almost to the total exclusion of structural forces, serves another function. Racial issues are articulated in a manner that totally ignores or disregards Roberta's involvement with them. She expresses no awareness of the ways she is implicated in the racial ordering of American society. Were she to formulate the problem in more structural terms, she would have to come to grips with her own involvement; she would have to deal with issues like privilege. As she chooses to interpret the racial situation, however, privilege is not even an issue and she need not be involved in racial matters unless she chooses to be. The fact that she can go to college or not if she wishes, wander around the country trying to find herself, and live in and out of poverty, does not even give her pause.

There is no way of knowing whether Roberta's ignorance of structural forces is a conscious avoidance of them. Indeed, it makes no difference. The fact is, she does not take them into account. By formulating the problem in this way, Roberta puts distance between herself and the racial ordering of American society. She does not have to change in order for equality to take place. Other people have to, and most often those others are black. Society does not have to change; people do. Institutional priorities need not be rearranged; they are not an issue. Thus Roberta can have her cake and eat it as well. Racism, as she understands it, can be eliminated; in the meantime she gives up nothing. In this way Roberta's interpretation of racial issues constitutes an ideological strategy that justifies her privileged position in American society.

Roberta's articulation of racial issues not only justifies her privileged position — it reflects it as well. She can have negative feelings toward material, earthly objects and the people who pursue them, because they have lost their meaning for her. She can organize her world around spiritual forces like love because she has never wanted in material terms. She can say she is above racial issues because she has never had to deal with them. She can transcend earthly considerations because she can afford to.

Roberta can transcend many things in life. One thing she cannot transcend, however, is her class position. In this respect, it is not at all ironic that her ideas should echo the thoughts of the very people she and her comrades see themselves as so different from — their middle-class parents.

8 Toward a sociology of white racism

Introduction: the contradiction

"The American society is faced not just with the necessity of actualizing those Negro aspirations to which it is officially committed," writes Earl Raab, "but of substantially reconciling the contrary and frustrated aspirations of the white community" (1962: 16). White Americans confront quite a problem when they try to reconcile their aspirations with the ones held by black Americans. In crucial respects there is a conflict of interest involved; gains for black people can mean losses for whites. Somehow white Americans must simultaneously attend to black demands and avoid the institutional reorganization that might cause them to lose ground. The problem is not easily solved.

To complicate matters considerably, white people have relatively few publicly acceptable ways to defend their interests. Defenses that vulgarly refer to biological differences are currently unacceptable in public arenas. Arguments that explain the situation in terms of racial subordination, on the other hand, are also unacceptable to many white Americans. Reasoning of this sort implies that blacks are not responsible for racial subordination; it directly

216

implicates white people in the system of racial injustice. Most people are unwilling to accept this harsh judgment of themselves.

This, then, is the contradiction confronting white Americans. The racial advantages they have traditionally enjoyed are threatened and they have few acceptable or legitimate options for defending them. What are people in this situation to do; how are they to respond? The people in this study reflect five different ways in which white Americans come to grips with the contradiction. They justify Gus Tyler's claim that:

> To ask people to be fearless when they have every reason to be afraid is to ask normal folk to act abnormally. They couldn't do it even if they wanted to. They will seek safety — no matter what political ribbon is wrapped around the prized package of survival. Castigating these people as stupid (some are) or racist (others are) does not solve the problem. They will in the end simply conclude that the lofty lecturer who thus looks down on them is himself either stupid or racist, or both [Quoted in Lipset and Raab, 1970: 512].

The ways these people cope with racial issues also suggests that William Ryan was correct when he observed that: "In order to persuade a good and moral man to *do* evil it is not necessary first to persuade him to *become* evil. It is only necessary to teach him that he is doing good. No one . . . thinks of himself as a son of a bitch" (1971: 19).

How, then, do white Americans deal with the racial situation — the troubles and aspirations of black people — without putting themselves at a disadvantage *and* thinking of themselves as sons of bitches? That is the issue facing all the people in this study.

Getting off the hook

Stated simply, the answer is that they resolve the contradiction by minimizing racism. They neutralize it. The
specific ways in which people defuse racial issues are numerous. Dick Wilson blames the victim for his or her own
victimization: Racial inequality exists because black people
lack motivation. Darlene Kurier and Roberta attribute the
problem to ignorance: If black people weren't "into a
brawn scene" (Roberta), if they had more education
(Darlene), there would be no racial problems. Gene Danich
formulates the issue in personal terms: He is in favor of
anything that does not affect him personally. Dick Wilson
and John Harper affirm the viability of America: Dick feels
that if he could be successful anyone can; John insists that
decisions in America are based on qualifications, not skin
color. Both Dick and John appeal to American ideals:
America proclaims that all people are equal and there is no
reason to believe otherwise. Roberta denies the injuries of
racism: Blacks are groovy and soulful; they have more fun
than whites. Harper denies responsibility for racial injustice:
Agitators cause racial problems; white America does not.

Reduced to the basics, each formulation removes the
speaker from complicity in the system of racial organization.
Each of these people is, as Ryan describes it, ". . . most
crucially, rejecting the possibility of blaming, not the
victims, but themselves. They are all unconsciously passing
judgments on themselves and bringing in a unanimous ver-
dict of Not Guilty" (1971: 28). The functions served by
these expressions, however, extend considerably beyond
self-exoneration: They legitimate America as well. None of
them questions the basis of a racial hierarchy; its continuation is taken for granted. The privileges each of these people
have, because they are white, are consequently maintained.

If the people in this study are any indication, white

Americans use many variations and combinations of the above themes to resolve the contradiction that black subordination presents for them. Taken together, organized into a relatively consistent theme, the expressions add up to a formulation that rationalizes, and thereby defends, an individual's racial situation. In this study I have presented five formulations that I think are fairly typical of the ways that white Americans do this. Each position represents a relatively successful accommodation to the problem of how to cope with the existence of racial inequality without thinking of oneself as a "son of a bitch." Each formulation manages nicely to navigate the difficult waters between biological defenses of interests and those explanations of the situation that imply either self-blame or social change that might result in a loss of privilege. Each position is formulated in very acceptable, almost liberal, American terms. With some minor exceptions, there is not a prejudiced-sounding formulation among them.

At first glance there appear to be an amazing number of "integrationists" or "liberals" in the sample. No one insists that blacks be doomed to a subordinate position. No one opposes black demands for racial reasons. In varying degrees they are all open to changing the situation facing black people. Everyone would like to see a world in which skin color makes no difference. On the surface, at any rate, this seems strange. Only a few short years earlier, a civil rights movement based on similar color-blind principles was vigorously opposed by people who quite frequently looked very much like these. Nevertheless, there is little doubt that most of the people we spoke to, regardless of their class position, felt the ultimate solution to racial inequality was some sort of color-blind world in which all people are treated equally.

The finding is intriguing. It runs counter to many studies of racial attitudes that conclude that "liberalism" or "openness" is mainly found among young people and the middle class. Yet we find it among all groups. Could it be that the sample is unique? In part. But that does not explain the sentiments. Could it be the people lied to us about what they really felt? That is doubtful.

The "intrigue" diminishes when the *solutions* these people found acceptable are subjected to closer scrutiny. The following were acceptable solutions to the problems faced by black people: change has to occur within the law; blacks have to conform to and/or be integrated into white society; blacks have to be educated and/or given equal job opportunities and/or become motivated; people have to become color-blind and/or whites have to cease being prejudiced. There is a common thrust to each of these solutions: None of them involves a basic change in the life-style of white people. Were any of them to be implemented, the racial status quo would prevail.

This is seen clearly in those solutions that suggest that change must occur through law or blacks must conform to white society. Legal solutions are obviously prescribed by the "rules of the game." When one accepts these rules, the "game" itself is not challenged. The suggestion that blacks be given equal opportunity at work and education has similar consequences. As long as the focus is on equal access rather than equal results, little has to be changed. The actual position of whites within these institutions is unaffected. R. H. Tawney makes the point nicely. He refers to equal-opportunity measures as "the impertinent courtesy of an invitation offered to unwelcome guests, in the certainty that circumstances will prevent them from accepting it." Even those solutions that suggest that prejudice be eliminated, blacks motivated, integration promoted, and distinctions based on color denied, leave the situation of white people essentially untouched. They speak exclusively to the attitudinal dimension of inequality. None of them call for a redistribution of power, wealth, or prestige.

The proposals most whites suggest for dealing with racial inequality are not, in any basic sense, "solutions" for black people. About the only thing they "solve" is the contradiction that racial inequality represents for white people and American ideology. That, they do well. The solutions allow white people to recognize the need for change without having that change affect them in important ways. They can have their cake and eat it too. They need not be reactionaries and they need not give up anything.

In addition, the solutions these people entertain allow them to be conscious of inequality and injustice without condemning themselves, to recognize a societal problem without implicating the society, and to defend their interests without referring to genes or race. This is possible because they recognize racial inequality either abstractly or as blocked access; they explain it in terms of the problems of its victims; and they "solve" the problem with solutions that do not affect white people. This allows them to put distance between themselves and the problem, explain the situation without implicating themselves, justify their position in nonracist or unprejudiced terms, and avoid the imperative for social change. In short, they get off the hook and defend their racial privilege as well.

This raises a critical question. These are not "prejudiced" people. The distinctive feature of their racial sentiments is neither hostility toward nor faulty generalizations about racial groups. As far as I can tell, their attitudes are not characteristically based on prejudgment or misjudgment. They do not categorically or systematically misinterpret facts. Nevertheless, they do not want social change that will significantly alter their relationship to the racial ordering of American society. If they are neither prejudiced nor amenable to change, what is the problem?

In part, the answer is that racism extends considerably beyond prejudiced beliefs. The essential feature of racism is not hostility or misperception, but rather the defense of a system from which advantage is derived on the basis of race. The manner in which the defense is articulated — either with hostility or subtlety — is not nearly as important as the fact that it insures the continuation of a privileged relationship. Thus it is necessary to broaden the definition of racism beyond prejudice to include sentiments that in their consequence, if not their intent, support the racial status quo.

Legitimacy of grievance and receptivity to change: some differences

Extending the definition of racism is useful. However, it does not explain why the people in this study recognize certain problems and are unaware of others; why they support some demands and reject others; or why they are amenable to only certain proposals. More importantly, it does not explain the differences that exist *between* these people in terms of their understanding of the issues involved and their openness to changes in the racial order — the conditions under which they would be receptive to new arrangements.

The differences are important ones. For example: Gene Danich and Darlene Kurier recognize that some black grievances are legitimate and the problem is "real." Gene feels that, relative to whites, blacks lack good jobs and money. Mrs. Kurier says "power has always been on the white side." Both of these people register genuine concern that something tangible happen: Blacks should be given more educational or occupational opportunities. Dick Wilson also recognizes the discrepant ways in which blacks and whites have been treated. While he admits that blacks "have been denied opportunities," he is less sympathetic than Danich or Kurier: The majority of blacks are "bums." John Harper and Roberta, at the other extreme, are barely conscious of the problems that blacks experience. The only problem Roberta can see is that blacks are "ignorant," "hung-up," on a "brawn scene." Harper says he does not understand what people mean when they refer to "white racism."

There are other differences as well. Neither Gene Danich nor Darlene Kurier rejects the concept of black power out of hand. In fact, Gene is receptive to the idea; it speaks to the need to achieve equality. Mrs. Kurier is more ambivalent. If it means bringing blacks into their own she has no objection; if it means power over whites she is opposed to it. Neither Gene nor Darlene is opposed on principle to school busing, although both of them would prefer that integration be achieved by other means. In the event that no other way was possible and if something positive came of busing, both would reluctantly go along with the strategy. When it comes to individuals, black militants like Stokely Carmichael are personally offensive to Danich and Kurier; but both recognize that he serves a legitimate function for the black community. Mrs. Kurier says she "understands why he is in such a hurry." Gene admits that were he black, he would probably be a Carmichael follower. While neither Danich nor Kurier feel comfortable about social change that affects them directly, both feel that something must be done to change the lives of black people. Gene favors the impossible: anything from riots to better jobs, just as long as it does not touch him. Darlene is more traditional: Her solution is education.

Unlike Gene Danich and Darlene Kurier, Dick Wilson is hostile to the idea of black power. As far as he is concerned it is a "grandstanding play," of no use to the black community. It rationalizes irresponsible behavior and covers up incompetence. The idea burns him up. Dick is equally unsympathetic to black militants: They serve no legitimate purpose. They also burn him up. However, like Gene and Darlene, Dick would like to see things get better in the black community. While the solution he suggests does not directly involve him, it is a sincere one and would alter the situation of blacks. He proposes a "GI Bill for the ghetto."

Like Dick Wilson, John Harper and Roberta have little use for such notions as black power. In fact Harper never even refers to it explicitly. Since he does not know what white racism is, he obviously does not think much about black power. Roberta is not much interested or impressed with the idea either. She considers it a "drag . . . trying to get your race equal." Both Roberta and Harper discount militant black leaders; nothing they do seems justified. For Roberta, militants are "intelligent spades" on an "individual trip" for personal aggrandizement. To Harper, they are agitators; their aim is not to end injustice, but to destroy "our way of life." Roberta and John Harper express the least concern for what happens to blacks in the future. Unlike the other three, neither of them seems very open to serious proposals for concretely changing the situation. As far as Roberta is concerned, blacks should not get too upset about what others think of them; they should be above all that. Harper does not give the idea much thought. He is concerned with agitators, not inequality.

Ranking these five people on some sort of prejudice "scale" would not be a very fruitful undertaking. The scale would be unable to distinguish clearly between them. Yet there are obvious differences between these people.(1) Danich, Kurier, and Wilson are the most aware of the different ways in which blacks and whites are treated in the United States. Roberta and Harper are the least aware.(2) Danich and Kurier are the most receptive to group strategies like black power and the most willing to recognize that militant black leaders raise legitimate issues. Harper, Roberta, and Wilson, on the other hand, do not take kindly to militant strategies and barely tolerate militant leaders.(3) Danich, Kurier, and Wilson feel most strongly that something must be done to change the situation of blacks; all have their own private, concrete solution. Roberta and Harper seem indifferent — if not hostile — to the idea of concrete changes.

The picture is a curious one. In terms of these three dimensions, Danich and Kurier are the most open to changes in the racial order, Harper and Roberta the least receptive, and Wilson fluctuates somewhere in between. That seems strange. We expect people like Gene Danich to be the least agreeable to the idea of change and people like John Harper to be the most approving of it. How might this be explained?

The pulls of race and the pushes of class

Each of these people shares in common the color of their skin. That is why none of them wants changes in the racial order to affect them too directly. Race, however, is only one basis on which Americans either come together or go their separate ways. Americans are also unified and divided on the basis of their class position and their sex. Race pulls the people in this study together; it makes them sound similar. Class experience, however, pushes them apart; it separates people into distinct clusters of sentiment. Thus tension is created between the pull of race and the push of class.

This occurs because certain social possibilities are attainable by virtue of one's race. In the United States, if one is white, essentially nothing is denied on the basis of race. The racial organization of America insures that whites are pushed upward. At the same time, other possibilities are both created and *denied* by a person's class position. Certain groups of white people are pushed upward by the workings of class hierarchy while others are kept down. In some instances the upward push of race and class overlap. This seems to be the case for John Harper and Roberta. More often, however, the upward push of race conflicts with the ceiling imposed by class, producing tension between the two. This is the situation in which Gene Danich and Darlene Kurier find themselves. Dick Wilson lives between both worlds.

The tension between race and class is created "outside" people. It is produced by economic, political, and historic forces. Regardless of where it is created, the tension is *experienced* "inside" people. The dynamic between racial interests and class loyalties gets played out through people's lives.[1] People's willingness to accept changes in the racial order reflects the delicate balance they have worked out between the competing possibilities and restraints imposed on them by two of the three bases of stratification in America. This can be seen when we let Danich and Kurier "stand for" white working-class experience, Harper and Roberta stand for white middle- and upper-class experience, and Wilson stand in between.

Working-class whites like Danich and Kurier are simultaneously privileged and denied.[2] Their whiteness is an advantage relative to blacks; their economic or class situation is disadvantaged relative to wealthier whites. America is organized such that they are pushed up *and* down at the same time. These pushes, moreover, are experienced in contradictory ways. They experience class in individual terms; their situation is interpreted as something peculiar to them. For example, Gene argues that he is a longshoreman by choice. On the other hand, they experience race in group terms. The people below them — blacks — push on and define them as a group. And the people above them —

[1] The resemblance between this formulation and Richard Sennett's notion of the "hidden injury" of class is intentional (Sennett and Cobb, 1972).
[2] My thinking in the next few paragraphs was stimulated when I read Todd Gitlin's paper, "Lower-Class Racism: Its Phenomenology and Transcendence" (1975). It is difficult to say where I leave off and he begins.

middle-class whites and sometimes radicals — define them similarly.

The upward and downward pushes pinch them between simultaneous threats. From above they are squeezed economically. From below they are pushed to make room for more competition over resources already squeezed from above. From both directions they are told they are better off because they are white, but they do not *feel* better off. Surprisingly, then, this is the context that creates the kind of receptivity to change that is represented by Danich and Kurier.

The forces operating on middle- and upper-class whites are quite different. People like Harper and Roberta are disadvantaged only by choice. Unless they decide otherwise, they are advantaged with regard to race and class; they are simultaneously pushed upward. As long as they can maintain sufficient distance from racial and economic problems, they experience their situation in individual terms. They feel they are who they are because of what they have done with their potential; their situation has little to do with birthright. Of course, when they choose to give up economic advantage, as Roberta does, the situation changes. In the Haight-Ashbury, Roberta is treated according to group rather than individual characteristics; to blacks she is a white, female hippie. They treat her as such, regardless of how she feels about it. Thus, despite her class background, to some extent race has been a group experience for Roberta. Unlike Harper, she *feels* the pushes from below.

A different combination of factors affects the ways in which upwardly mobile people like Wilson are willing to rearrange the racial order. Like Danich and Kurier, Wilson has been pinched between the contradictory pushes of race and class. He knows what that feels like. Unlike Danich and Kurier, the pushes from below are no longer felt with the same intensity and Wilson no longer feels the squeezes from above. He is currently elevated by the combined pushes of race and class. If the advantage he presently enjoys is lost, it will be of his own making.[3] Wilson now shares that option with Harper and Roberta.

Personal concerns and the commitment to individualism

The combined and often contradictory ways in which race and class are experienced produce distinctive receptivities to racial change. The changes people find acceptable, in turn, reflect the stakes that are generated for them by the racial and class organization of society. Black people raise issues that often directly affect working-class whites like Danich and Kurier. When the situation of blacks is upgraded, these people feel it first. The issue for working-class whites, then, is a *personal* one: They will feel changes in the racial order personally and directly. Gene Danich is vividly aware of the problem: He favors anything that does not affect him personally. Mrs. Kurier fears that changing the current arrangements may allow blacks to "get even." Despite their personal concerns, these two people are more receptive than the others to strategies like black power and militant leaders like Stokely Carmichael.

Middle- and upper-class whites like Harper and Wilson have other concerns, and they are receptive to other possibilities. The issues posed by blacks do not usually affect them as directly as they do working-class whites. Black demands barely touch Harper. Militancy inconveniences Wilson and makes his job more difficult, but it does not "cost" him anything directly. Thus, for middle-class whites the issue is not a personal one. They feel involved only to the extent that blacks become a "social" problem. Their

[3] I am not suggesting that middle-class life in America is without its consstraints. This characterization of Wilson's situation is his, not mine.

lack of personal involvement is not translated into neutrality toward black power and militant leaders, however. They are not receptive to either one. Harper and Wilson feel most comfortable with strategies that promote and encourage individual effort. Both agree that blacks need to develop pride in themselves and learn how to work hard. Each feels that his personal experience validates this strategy.

These observations contain an apparent paradox. The two people most personally affected by racial change are the least hostile to militant strategies; the two people least affected are the most hostile. The paradox disappears when we consider what is at stake for each group, which also tells us something about how receptive each is to racial change.

Danich and Kurier are concerned about problems affecting them directly; they are defending personal interests. Blacks can do pretty much what they please, as long as it does not involve them directly. Harper and Wilson, on the other hand, are *not* defending their personal interests; that is not what is at stake for them. They are defending the principle of individualism. They do not object to the black power strategy because of the personal consequences it might have for them: Their class position insulates them from most of the direct effects. Their basic objection to a strategy like black power is that it violates the principle of individualism that guides and justifies their lives. Each of these men is convinced that America does not recognize color, it recognizes only individual achievement; They are deeply committed to it, and they want it to continue. Strategies like black power evoke group solutions to problems that Harper and Wilson attribute to individual deficiencies. Group solutions, however, do more than that: They attack the very basic belief that individuals can succeed if they try hard enough. That is why militant leaders and strategies "burn up" Wilson; that is why Harper rejects militancy with the accurate observation that agitators want to "upset our way of life."

This explains how people who appear the least affected by potential change can be the most hostile to militant strategies. Harper and Wilson actually have more at stake than Danich and Kurier. Their principals are at issue. It is not just a question of immediate personal interest. There is no way group strategies can avoid bumping into the principles of individualism to which these men subscribe. In contrast, the same strategy need not necessarily collide with the personal interests of Danich and Kurier. When it does, it is opposed; when it does not, the problem is minimized.

Another reason why Danich and Kurier are more receptive to black demands is perhaps attributable to the downward pushes of class. Evidently one aspect of working-class experience in America is a heightened awareness of inequality. Along with Wilson, the other person of working-class origin, Danich and Kurier are the most conscious of the inequalities experienced by blacks. Gene would like to see equality achieved in America, and he has concrete ideas about what it would look like. Darlene has similar desires. Nevertheless, neither of them is particularly optimistic about the possibilities. Both are aware of the many obstacles that block the way: They are conscious of power differences and the differences these make in accomplishing something approximating equality. Working-class people like Danich and Kurier, then, recognize and acknowledge differential power and relate these differentials to racial problems. Recognizing that power is involved, they realize there is little blacks can do as individuals to change the situation. Thus they are sensitive to the limits of individual solutions and the advantages of group strategies. Middle-class people, on the other hand, deny that inequality even exists. For Harper there is no issue: Equality is already a fact. While Wilson recognizes that people are treated differently, he argues this is not a function of inequality. It occurs because people are born with different capabilities. He says there is no such thing as equality. Since Danich and Kurier recognize inequality and attribute it in part to differences in power, under certain conditions they are willing to accept group solutions that involve militancy and invoke power.

But what of the young people, like Roberta, from the counterculture community? How do their racial and class experiences come together in the possibilities they envision for racial change? Roberta combines elements of the stance taken by Danich and Kurier with elements of the Harper—Wilson thrust. Like working-class whites, people in Roberta's situation are directly affected by the actions of black people. Most of them have decided to temporarily give up class-based advantage. They therefore feel the racial pushes from below in much the same way as do working-class people. They are defined by blacks and acted toward as a group. Thus the issue for people like Roberta, with Danich and Kurier, is a personal one and that is the way Roberta sees it: She resents being "hassled by spades." Unlike working-class whites, however, Roberta is not receptive to strategies such as black power. She finds it a "drag." Blacks should be "above" issues like racism and "ignore" the people who dislike them. Like middle-class whites, Roberta is most receptive to individual rather than group strategies for change. In this respect, she sounds a great deal like Harper and Wilson. Roberta may have been able to give up the advantages of class; she certainly has not been able to give up its ideology.

There is a powerful irony contained in her situation. On the surface, people like Roberta appear the least prejudiced of all, and the most interested in creating a new world. The opposite, however, may be in fact the case. Unlike the others, Roberta is defending *both* her personal interests *and* the principles of individualism; she does one in terms of the other. Given the peculiar way in which she experiences race and class, she resists changes that have negative personal consequences and that challenge the principles by which she organizes her life. Thus she may have the most at stake and be the least sympathetic to racial changes.

Does this mean that people like Danich and Kurier, who are the most receptive, are therefore allies of black people in their assault on inequality? The answer is clearly, no. They are sympathetic to group strategies for change; they do not, however, include themselves in the group needing changes. Since working-class people experience the squeezes of class in individual terms, they do not explicitly see themselves as part of a group, much less one that might include blacks. Thus they cannot imagine that the upward push of blacks might not directly conflict with their personal interests. When they feel no conflict they do not oppose blacks, but they cannot see how they can better their own situation if blacks do too. People like Gene and Darlene realize that resources are limited and that they cannot link their problems with the ones experienced by blacks. The problem is not that they have a blind spot, however. Because their lives are demarcated along both racial and class lines, they cannot afford to reduce one to the other. Given their situation, *that* would be irrational.

There is yet another feature of American life that complicates the potential for victims of inequality to direct their energies toward its sources instead of one another. Neither Danich nor Kurier expresses the same kind of commitment to individualistic principles as do Harper, Roberta, and Wilson. Gene and Darlene find group strategies for social problems acceptable under some conditions, but, like the other three, they are committed to the notion that people should be autonomous and independent. They strongly subscribe to this aspect of America's creed and culture. Gene thinks people should be "self-sufficient"; men should have "control over" their work; the job should involve responsibility and initiative. Darlene is firmly convinced that people should have the "freedom" to move wherever they please; people should have their "own rights" to decide what is done with their property. White working-class people like Gene Danich and Darlene Kurier are not only committed to these ideals, they have a stake in them as well. If the ideals did not exist and have meaning for them, they would be without hope for the future. They would be unable to see a way out from under the downward pushes of class for either themselves or their children. They would have to resign themselves to the present. Danich and Kurier want these ideals to be a reality. It helps them experience class in individual and thus escapable terms.

Black people threaten and challenge these ideals, and thereby Danich and Kurier, on two levels. One: They stand as a living refutation of the ideals. Their situation is testimony that the ideals are applied selectively. Danich and Kurier are aware of this. Blacks, then, open the ideals to suspicion. Two: When blacks make demands on society, they often invoke past denials they have experienced rather than the independent ideals espoused by Danich and Kurier. Blacks, then, are asking to be rewarded on the basis of criteria that conflict with the ideals to which these people are committed. If black people were rewarded on this basis, it would give them some advantages relative to working-class whites. It would do even more than that, however. In effect, it would say to people that the cultural currency they have invested in has been devalued; the rules of the game have been changed. That is something Danich and Kurier will not tolerate; they have too much of themselves invested. Thus they will only support changes that leave intact the cultural rules for competition. Everything else affects them too personally. A radical break with crucial aspects of American culture is therefore necessary for the Daniches and Kuriers to become involved with blacks in a thoroughgoing assault on inequality. There is however, very little in their experience that would support this kind of departure.

Conclusion

This is the situation within which racial sentiments are defined, the context within which racial attitudes exist. White people's sentiments toward blacks are not only forged in this context; they reflect it as well. If they oppose black demands for increased equality, it is not because of their personal predispositions or "prejudices." Their refusal is based primarily on their acceptance of American cultural standards. The people with whom we spoke are concerned about the consequences that racial changes will have for American norms and social institutions. They do not oppose demands raised by blacks in racial terms. Their opposition is based on an *acceptance* of and stake in standards and institutional priorities rather than a *rejection* of black people. If anything, they are more concerned about the things black people *lack* — money, education, middle-class values and aspirations — than about black people per se. In some instances, they seem more concerned about what is happening to them than they are about blacks. William Simon and John Gagnon put it the following way:

> Change itself becomes the enemy. Much of the current racism may derive not so much from the factors we once associated with prejudice but with the increasing complications that the image of the Negro community now represents the most powerful symbol of "disruptive" changes in their lives (sic) [1970: 49].

Lipset and Raab found this feeling among Wallace voters in 1968: ". . . it can best be seen as a backlash against change in which there is an almost absolute congruence between the backlash against dreaded change and the back-lash targetry, that is, the change bearers" (1970: 341). They conclude that "the nativist bigotry of such whites finds its genesis not so much in hatred of Negroes, but in the felt dimunition of their own status" (1970: 510).

The distinctive feature of racist thinking, then, is not hatred. What sets it off from other thinking is that it justi-fies policies and institutional priorities that perpetuate racial inequality, and it does so in distinctively American terms. It is not race to which people refer; instead they speak of "larger" societal interests and values, or the ina-bility of blacks — for reasons for which they assume little responsibility — to compete with whites on equal terms.

I do not question the motives of the people expressing these sentiments. In fact, I am willing to grant that in some instances their intentions may be quite noble: They might actually want to see blacks achieve equality. Their motives, however, are irrelevant. Their thinking is based upon assumptions, and their competing priorities are judged within a framework, that usually insure that they will respond to issues raised by blacks in ways that continue their position of social advantage and therefore maintain their privileges. Their assumptions largely determine their solutions. Given the racial and class organization of Amer-ican society, there is only so much people can "see." The positions they occupy in these structures limit the range of their thinking. The situation places barriers on their imag-inations and restricts the possibilities of their vision.

The racist nature of their thinking is not minimized by the fact that white people are often unaware of the extent to which their advantaged position is based on race. The consequence is the same as if they were conscious of it.

The subordinate position of black people is justified and the advantaged situation of whites is maintained even though nonracial terms are invoked in the reasoning. Racism, then, need not be distinct, in its content or emotional loading, from the more routine forms of competitive behavior white people engage in with other whites. A distinctive content or kind of emotional loading is not what makes certain sentiments "racist." A position is racist when it defends, protects, or enhances social organization based on racial advantage. Racism is determined by the *consequences* of a sentiment, not its surface qualities. Sometimes it is expressed in crude terms but, as this study shows, often it is not. White racism is what white people *do* to protect the special benefits they gain by virtue of their skin color.

Racism is thus indivisible from American life. Americans are racist "because they acquiesce in the large cultural order which continues the work of racism" (Kovel, 1970: 212). This is what Joel Kovel refers to as "metaracism," or "the pursuit of consciously non-racist behavior in the interests of furthering the destructive work of culture" (1970: 215). Racism, then, exists to the extent that people sell part of themselves to the existing culture and become a means to its end.

Appendix: interview guide

Part One. General questions.

A *Background*
1 Age
2 Birthplace
3 Current job or source of income
4 Marital Status

B *Work*
1 Can you tell me the most important jobs you've had?
2 What would be the ideal way to make that kind of living?
3 Is there any kind of work that you could get that you'd refuse to take? What kinds?
4 Does a man need the right kind of work to really be a man?
   a What kind of job would make you feel most like a man?
   b Least like a man?
5 How do you get along with your fellow workers? With your supervisors?

C *The family (male–female relations)*
1 What was your family like? How did people get along? Occupations of mother and father? What member of your family influenced you the most when you were growing up?

    2 What adult — family member or outside — did you admire the most when you were growing up?

    3 What do you think most women expect from a man?

    4 What do you expect from the women you go with?

    5 Is it easier for men to get along with women or with other men? (How about for yourself?)

    6 Do you think women have too much power?

    7 Would you say most of the women you know help build a man up or do you think they let him down?

    8 How does a real man treat a woman?

    9 What's the best way to get along with a woman?

D *Police*

    1 What do you think the proper role of the police is? In other words, what do you think their job is?

    2 How well do you think they live up to this role?

    3 There's been a lot of talk lately about "law and order." What does that phrase mean to you?

    4 Do you think that there are situations in which it is proper to violate laws? What kinds of situations?

E *Schools*

    1 How did you do in school?

    2 What do you think your teachers thought about you? What kinds of expectations did they have of you?

    3 What do you think education is all about? What do you think it should do, what kinds of things should it teach?

    4 In terms of this, how would you evaluate our present educational system?

Part Two. Race questions.

A *Experience and contact*

    1 When did you first learn that there was a white and a black race in this country?

    2 Do you remember your first contact with colored people?

When? What kind of relation?

3 Were there Negroes:
   a In your neighborhood where you grew up?
   b Who worked in your parent's house?
   c In your grade or elementary school?
   d Junior high or high school, college?
   e With you in the military?
   f On jobs you've worked?

Note: For each *yes*, ask about frequency of contact, how close a relationship, how the other whites and you particularly got along with them, what you thought about Negroes then.

4 At present, do you know any Negro people on a personal level? Would you like to have more Negro friends?

5 At present what is the situation with respect to the races where you work? (Or where you go to school?)
   a How many employed? Is this the right amount? Why not more?
   b What kinds of jobs? Is this okay?
   c How would you feel about more Negroes? 20% of plant, office, school, etc.? 40% 60%
   d Would you have any objection about having a Negro boss? Secretary? etc.
   e Is anybody trying to change the racial balance where you work?

Note: Then ask the same parallel questions about the neighborhood where you live.

6 Let's say your company was going to employ a Negro to work in the same job as yours, right along with you — could you describe the ideal characteristics of this man (or woman)?

7 If you were to have a Negro family as a neighbor could you describe the kind of man you'd like to see; then what the wife would be like, the children?

8 Are most people you know prejudiced or unprejudiced?

9 When was the last time you talked about Negroes and race problems? When and where, what group? What was the discussion about — and what did you say? How often do you talk about these things?

B *Attitudes toward contemporary race issues*

  1 In general, how do you think Negroes have been treated in this society? Do they have any legitimate grievances, in your opinion?

  2 In the last few years, do you think there has been much progress in race relations? If yes, some examples of this progress. If no, why not, why do you feel this way?

  3 Do you enjoy watching TV programs that deal with racial news or documentaries?

  4 What about the riots?
     a How do you feel about them?
     b What do you think causes them?
     c What should be done about them?

  5 What do you think about black power? What do you think it means?

  6 What's your general opinion about:
     a Martin Luther King
     b Malcolm X
     c Stokely Carmichael
     d The Black Panther Party
     Is there any Negro leader or organization whose position you would generally go along with?

  7 How did you feel about King being shot? How did you feel about Kennedy? (RFK) Did you watch their funerals on TV?

  8 What colored person in America do you admire most?

  9 Are the black leaders and organizations going about things right?

  10 In your opinion, is the rate of unemployment among Negroes higher than that of whites, lower, or about the same? If higher — why do you think this situation exists?

  11 Have you heard anything about programs to give special preference to Negroes in getting jobs or getting into schools? This is sometimes called preferential treatment. What do you think about it?

  12 What do you think should be done about the Negro ghettos?

  13 How do you feel about these proposals that some people have suggested?
     a That the Negro community in the ghetto areas (e.g.,

Hunters Point, Fillmore, Oakland) run their own schools.

b That the ghetto set up its own independent black police force and keep city police out of the Negro areas.

c That ghetto districts secede from the city and become independent townships so they could run their own affairs.

14 Do you think a race war is possible in this country? What will you do if this happens?

15 What is the meaning of integration to you?

C *Images of black people*

1 Have you noticed any differences in the ways Negroes have been acting recently?

2 Do you think Negroes have been getting out of line recently? If yes

a How so?

b Do you think Negroes are all right as long as they stay in their place?

c What do you mean by that?

d What's their place?

3 Have you noticed any change in the way Negroes are wearing their hair lately? If yes, what do you see, and what do you think about it?

4 There are a lot of different words that people use to refer to the Negro group.

a How many of them can you think of?

b What term do you usually use?

1 When a Negro is present.

2 When you're with friends or family.

5 Have you noticed any changes in the use of words for Negroes? What do you think of calling them "blacks," as many young Negroes are today insisting? What do you think of the term, Afro-American?

6 Do you feel any different about Negroes who are light-skinned than about those who are black?

7 Do you think black men prefer white women?

8 Do you think Negroes are basically the same as white people, or do you think they are different in some ways? If same, why do you say that? If different, how different?

9 Do you think Negro people are pretty much the same, or do you think there are different types of Negro Americans?

   a If same, how so — what are they like?

   b If different, what are these types, how does the Negro group differ within?

10 Do you think white people would act the same way as Negroes if whites were in the same situation as blacks?

11 Do you think Negroes as a group are making it as well as immigrants and other minority groups made it? Why?

D White identity and racism

1 Do you think of yourself in terms of any nationality? What? Do you think of yourself in terms of any color or race?

2 Have you ever thought about having white skin? How often? What do you think about it? Ever feel good or bad about not being born brown, black, or yellow? Do you ever wish you were a Negro or a Mexican? Why or why not?

3 What does it mean to you to be a white man? Or woman? Are you proud to be white today? Do you think it's made any difference in your life, being white?

4 Lately there has been a lot of talk about *racism*. What do you think racism is?

5 The U.S. Riot Commission Report (Kerner Commission) said America is a racist society. Do you think this is a fair statement?

6 Do you consider yourself a racist or not?

7 Does it make any difference in your life that there are black people living in this country and in this area?

   a If no difference, why not?

   b If yes, what difference does it make?

8 Have you heard the term "honky?" What do you think it means? How would you feel if you were called a "honky?"

References

Adorno, T. W., E. Frenkel-Brunswick, D. S. Levinson, and R. N. Sanford (1950). *The Authoritarian Personality*. New York: Harper & Row.

Allport, G. (1958). *The Nature of Prejudice*. Garden City, N.Y.: Doubleday.

and B. M. Kramer (1946). "Some Roots of Prejudice." *Journal of Psychology*. 22 (July): 10–12.

Baran, P. and P. Sweezy (1966). *Monopoly Capital*. New York: Monthly Review Press.

Baron, H. (1969). "The Web of Urban Racism," in Knowles and Prewitt (eds.), *Institutional Racism*. Englewood Cliffs, N.J.: Prentice-Hall.

(1971). "The Demand for Black Labor: Historical Notes on the Political Economy of Racism." *Radical America*. 5 (March-April): 1–46.

Becker, G. (1957). *The Economics of Discrimination*. Chicago: University of Chicago Press.

Bendix, R. (1956). *Work and Authority in Industry*. Berkeley: University of California Press.

Bettelheim, B. and M. Janowitz (1964). *Social Change and Prejudice*. New York: Free Press.

Blalock, H. M. (1967). *Toward a Theory of Minority-Group Relations*. New York: Wiley.

Blau, P. and O. D. Duncan (1967). *The American Occupational Structure*. New York: Wiley.

Blauner, R. (1972a). *Racial Oppression in America*. New York: Harper & Row.

(1972b). "Racial Capitalism: The Dynamics of Race and Class." Mimeo.

(1972c). "Marxist Theory, Nationality and Colonialism." Mimeo.

and D. Wellman (1973). "Toward the Decolonization of Social Research," in J. Ladner (ed.), *The Death of White Sociology*. New York: Random House.

Bloch, H. (1969). *The Circle of Discrimination*. New York: New York University Press.

Blumer, H. (1958a). "Research Trends in the Study of Race Relations." *International Social Science Bulletin*. 10(3): 403–47.

(1958b). "Race Prejudice as a Sense of Group Position." *Pacific Sociological Review*. 1 (Spring): 3–6.

(1969). *Symbolic Interactionism: Perspective and Method*. Englewood Cliffs, N.J.: Prentice-Hall.

Brooks, T. (1966). "No! Says the P.B.A." *New York Times Magazine*. (October 16): 36–7+.

Campbell, A. (1972). *White Attitudes Toward Black People*. Ann Arbor, Mich.: Institute for Social Research.

Carmichael, S. and C. Hamilton (1967). *Black Power*. New York: Vintage.

Caton, W., Jr. (1960–61). "The Functions and Dysfunctions of Ethnocentrism." *Social Problems*. 8 (Winter): 201–11.

Cavan, R., P. Hauser, and S. Stouffer (1930). "A Note on the Statistical Treatment of Life History Material." *Social Forces*. 9 (December): 200–3.

Cohen, A. and H. Hodges, Jr. (1963). "Characteristics of the Lower-Blue-Collar-Class." *Social Problems*. 10 (Spring): 303–33.

Coles, Robert (1971). *Children of Crisis*. Volumes 2 and 3. Boston: Little, Brown.

Cooley, C. (1918). *Social Process*. New York: Scribner.

Cox, O. C. (1959). *Caste, Class and Race*. New York: Monthly Review Press.

Cramer, M. R. (1963). "School Desegregation and New Industry: The Southern Community Leader's Viewpoint." *Social Forces*. 41 (May): 384–9.

Cruse, H. (1969). *Rebellion or Revolution*. New York: Morrow.

Cutright, R. (1965). "Negro Subordination and White Gains." *American Sociological Review*. 30 (February): 110–12.

Davis, A., B. Gardner, and M. Gardner (1941). *Deep South*. Chicago: University of Chicago Press.

Denzin, N. (1970). *The Research Act*. Chicago: Aldine.

Deutsch, M. and M. E. Collins (1951). *Interracial Housing*. Minneapolis: University of Minnesota Press.

Dollard, J. (1957). *Caste and Class in a Southern Town*. Garden City, N.Y.: Doubleday.

Douglas, Jack (1967). *The Social Meaning of Suicide*. Princeton, N.J.: Princeton University Press.

Drake, S. C. and H. Cayton (1945). *Black Metropolis*. New York: Harcourt Brace Jovanovich.

DuBois, W. E. B. (1940). *Dusk of Dawn*. New York: Harcourt Brace Jovanovich.

Erskine, H. G. (1962). "The Polls: Race Relations." *Public Opinion Quarterly*. 26 (Spring): 138–48.

Fredrickson, G. M. (1971). "Toward a Social Interpretation of the Development of American Racism," in N. Huggins, M. Kilson, and D. Fox (eds.), *Key Issues in the Afro-American Experience*. New York: Harcourt Brace Jovanovich.

Frenkel-Brunswick, D. (1948). "A Study of Prejudice in Children." *Human Relations*. 1: 295–306.

Focus. (1972). Publication of the International Brotherhood of Teamsters.

Garfinkel, H. (1967). *Studies in Ethnomethodology*. Englewood Cliffs, N.J.: Prentice-Hall.

Genovese, E. (1969). "Materialism and Idealism in the History of Negro Slavery in the Americas," in L. Foner and E. Genovese (eds.), *Slavery in the New World*. Englewood Cliffs, N.J.: Prentice-Hall.

(1971). "Nationality and Class in Black America," in *In Red and Black: Marxian Explorations in Afro-American and Southern History*. New York: Pantheon.

Giddings, F. (1908). *The Principles of Sociology* New York: Macmillan.

Gitlin, Todd (1975). "Lower-Class Racism: Its Phenomenology and Transcendence." Unpublished paper.

Gittell, M. (1969). "Urban School Reform in the 1970's," in M.
    Berube and M. Gittell (eds.), *Confrontation at Ocean
    Hill-Brownsville*. New York: Praeger.
Glenn, N. (1963). "Occupational Benefits to Whites from the Sub-
    ordination of Negroes." *American Sociological Review*. 28
    (June): 446–7.
    (1966). "White Gains from Negro Social Subordination." *Social
    Problems*. 14 (Fall): 159–78.
Hamilton, R. (1972). *Class and Politics in the United States*. New
    York: Wiley.
Hammond, Phillip (1964). *Sociologists at Work*. New York: Basic
    Books.
Heer, D. (1959). "The Sentiment of White Supremacy: An Ecolog-
    ical Study." *American Journal of Sociology*. 64 (May):
    592–8.
Jacobs, Jerry. (1967). "A Phenonological Study of Suicide Notes."
    Social Problems. 15 (Summer): 60–72.
Kahn, L. A. (1951). "The Organization of Attitudes Toward the
    Negro as a Function of Education." *Psychological Monographs*.
    65 (131): 1–59.
Kaplan, A. (1964). *The Conduct of Inquiry*. San Francisco:
    Chandler.
Keniston, K. (1965). *The Uncommitted*. New York: Harcourt Brace
    Jovanovich.
    (1968). *Young Radicals*. New York: Harcourt Brace Jovanovich.
Kitano, H. and R. Daniels (1970). *American Racism: Exploration of
    the Nature of Prejudice*. Englewood Cliffs, N.J.: Prentice-Hall.
Kovel, Joel (1970). *White Racism: A Psychohistory*. New York:
    Pantheon.
Lemert, E. (1958). "The Behavior of the Systematic Check Forger."
    Social Problems. 6 (Fall): 141–8.
Levin, J. (1975). *The Functions of Prejudice*. New York: Harper &
    Row.
Lifton, R. (1961). *Thought Reform and the Psychology of Totalism*.
    New York: Norton.
    (1967). *Death in Life: Survivors of Hiroshima*. New York:
    Random House.
    (1974). "On Psychohistory," in R. Lifton (ed.), *Exploration in
    Psychohistory*. New York: Simon and Schuster.

Lipset, S. M. (1959). "Democracy and Working Class Authoritarianism." *American Sociological Review*. 24 (August): 482–501.

and Earl Rabb (1970). *The Politics of Unreason*. New York: Harper & Row.

Lofland, J. (1966). *Doomsday Cult*. Englewood Cliffs, N.J.: Prentice-Hall.

Merton, R. (1949). "Discrimination and the American Creed," In R. MacIver (ed.) *Discrimination and National Welfare*. New York: Harper & Row.

(1961). *Social Theory and Social Structure*. New York: Free Press.

Mills, C. W. (1961). *The Sociological Imagination*. New York: Evergreen.

Moynihan, Daniel P. (1965). *The Negro Family: A Case for National Action*. Washington, D.C.: U.S. Department of Labor.

Myrdal, G. (1944). *An American Dilemma*. New York: Harper & Row.

Nation. (1966). "Symbol of the Backlash: The Question of the Civilian Review Board." 203 (November 7): 468.

Newman, W. (1973). *American Pluralism: A Study of Minority Groups and Social Theory*. New York: Harper & Row.

New Yorker. (1966). "Election Night: Defeat of the Civilian Review Board." 42 (November 9): 50–1.

Noel, D. (1972). "Slavery and The Rise of Racism," in D. Noel (ed.), *The Origins of American Slavery and Racism*. Columbus: Merrill.

Park, R. (1950). "The Basis of Race Prejudice," in R. Park, *Race and Culture*. New York: Free Press.

and E. W. Burgess (1924). *Introduction to the Science of Sociology*. Chicago: University of Chicago Press.

Parsons, T. (1953). "Revised Analytical Approach to the Theory of Social Stratification," in R. Bendix and S. M. Lipset (eds.), *Class, Status and Power*. New York: Free Press.

Raab, E. (1962). "Introduction," *American Race Relations*. New York: Anchor.

and S. M. Lipset (1962). "The Prejudiced Society," in E. Raab (ed.), *American Race Relations Today*. Garden City, N.Y.: Doubleday.

Reich, M. (1972). "The Economics of Racism," in R. Edwards, M.

Reich, and T. Weisskopf (eds.), *The Capitalist System*. Englewood Cliffs, N.J.: Prentice-Hall.

Reitzes, D. (1964). "Behavior in Urban Race Contacts," in E. W. Burgess and D. J. Bogue (eds.), *Contributions to Urban Socio logy*. Chicago: University of Chicago Press.

Rose, A. (1956). "Intergroup Relations vs. Prejudice." *Social Problems*. 4 (October): 173–76.

Ross, E. A. (1921). *Principles of Sociology*. New York: The Century Col.

Roucek, J. (1956). "Minority-Majority Relations in Their Power Aspects." *Phylon*. 9 (1): 24–31.

Ryan, William (1971). *Blaming the Victim*. New York: Pantheon.

Schatzman, L. and A. Strauss (1973). *Field Research: Strategies for a Natural Sociology*. Englewood Cliffs, N.J.: Prentice-Hall.

Schermerhorn, R. (1956). "Power as a Primary Concept in the Study of Minorities." *Social Forces*. 35 (October): 53–6.

——— (1970). *Comparative Ethnic Relations: A Framework for Theory and Research*. New York: Random House.

Schuman, H. and J. Harding (1964). "Prejudice and the Norm of Rationality." *Sociometry*. 27 (September): 353–71.

Selznick, G. and S. Steinberg (1969). *The Tenacity of Prejudice*. New York: Harper & Row.

Sennett, R. and J. Cobb (1972). *The Hidden Injuries of Class*. New York: Random House.

Shaw, C. (1966). *The Jack Roller*. Chicago: University of Chicago Press.

Sheatsley, P. (1966). "White Attitudes Toward the Negro," in T. Parsons and K. Clark (eds.), *The Negro American*. Boston: Beacon.

Shibutani, T. and K. Kwan (1965). *Ethnic Stratification*. New York: Macmillan.

Siegel, P. (1965). "The Cost of Being Negro." *Sociological Inquiry*. 35 (Winter): 41–57.

Simon, W. and J. Gagnon (1970). "Working-Class Youth: Alienation Without an Image," in L. Howe (ed.), *The White Majority*. New York: Vintage Books.

Simpson, G. and M. Yinger (1965). "The Sociology of Race Relations," in R. Merton, L. Broom, and L. Cottrel, Jr. (eds.),

Sociology Today. New York: Basic Books

(1972). *Racial and Cultural Minorities: An Analysis of Prejudice and Discrimination*. New York: Harper & Row.

Stewart, D. and T. Hoult (1959). "A Social-Psychological Theory of the Authoritarian Personality." *American Journal of Sociology*. 65 (November): 274–9.

Sumner, W. (1906). *Folkways*. Boston: Ginn.

Sutherland, E. H. (1937). *The Professional Thief, by a Professional Thief*. Chicago: University of Chicago Press.

Swartz, M. (1961). "Negative Ethnocentrism." *Journal of Conflict Resolution*. 5 (March): 75–81.

Tabb, W. (1970). *The Political Economy of the Black Ghetto*. New York: Norton.

Thomas, W. I. (1904). "The Psychology of Race Prejudice." *American Journal of Sociology*. 9 (March): 593–611.

and F. Znaniecki (1927). *The Polish Peasant*. New York: Knopf.

Thurow, L. (1969). *Poverty and Discrimination*. Washington, D.C.: Brookings Institution.

van den Berghe, P. (1967). *Race and Racism*. New York: Wiley.

Vander Zanden, J. (1959). "The Ideology of White Supremacy." *Journal of the History of Ideas*. 20 (June–September): 385–402.

(1965). *Race Relations in Transition*. New York: Random House.

Wilson, W. (1973). *Power, Racism, and Privilege*. New York: Macmillan.

Index

Adorno, T. W., 2, 34
Allport, G., 2, 26, 27n
American Creed: faith in, 163—4,
190; laissez-faire ideology of, 166;
racism and, 23—6, 126, 137, 233;
see also ideology
anti-Semitism, 80—1
attitudes: differences among, 222—5;
inconsistencies in, 11—12;
measurement of, 24—5; prejudice
and, 5, 10; psychology and, 14;
racism and, 4, 20—3
authoritarianism: concept of, 102;
groups and, 2—3; racism and, 27

banks, hiring policies of, 181
Baran, P., 19
Bendix, R., 15
Bergman, Lincoln, 194
Bettelheim, B., 9
Black Panther party, 74, 90, 101,
103, 154, 158
black power: criticized, 154—5,
184—6, 224, 228; perspectives of,
57; working class and, 90, 93, 104
black studies departments, 8, 187—8
Blalock, H., 36
Blauner, R.: on academic norms, 8;
on colonialism, 60; cn industrial
society, 17; manhood orientations,
49, 52n; on Marxism, 19; on
racial stratification, 35n, 37
Blumer, Herbert, 23, 43, 63, 72

Brooklyn (N.Y.), 7
Brooks, T., 8
Burgess, Ernest, 70
businessmen: attitudes of, 11—12,
138, 160—3; racial exploitation
by, 103
busing: ambivalence toward, 121,
223; Gallup poll and, 3, 11; mid
dle class and, 8, 32, 33; working
class and, 90, 96

Campbell, A., 3, 11
capitalism, prejudice and, 22
Carmichael, Stokely: criticized, 120,
154, 223; on racial stratification,
35n; working-class attitude toward, 91—6, 104—5, 106
caste: persistence of, 10; studies of,
9, 28
Caton, W., Jr., 34
Cayton, H., 17
Chicago, 10, 17, 99
childhood: prejudice in, 26; racial
experiences in, 112—13, 134, 144,
190, 197—9; segregation in,
84—5, 111
children, interracial, 97—8
church organizations, 52
cities: racial attitudes in, 3, 11; riots
in, 98—9
civil rights, conflict with property
rights, 13
civil rights movement: activists of,

civil rights movement (*cont.*)
194; defeat of, 207; in South, 38;
as threat, 111, 118, 124
civil service, 176
Civil War, 38
civilian review boards, 7
class: caste and, 9—10, 28; persistence of, 215; racial attitudes and,
2—4, 15, 30, 62—3, 225—8, 232;
racial stratification and, 35, 144,
164—7; *see also* middle class,
working class
Cobb, Jonathan, 64—5, 73
Coles, Robert, 64—5, 68—9, 70
colleges and universities, racial attitudes in, 8, 199—200
Collins, M. E., 9
Constitution (U.S.), 25, 158
courts, 92, 130
Cox, Oliver, 22
Cramer, M. R., 11
Cuba, 92

Davis, A., 9, 17
Democratic Party Convention
(1968), 10
Denzin, N., 70
desegregation, *see* integration
Detroit, 158
Deutsch, M., 9
Dollard, J., 9, 17, 28
Douglas, Jack, 70
Drake, St. Clair, 17
drugs, 201, 204, 206
DuBois, W. E. B., 28—9, 35n

East Harlem, 7
education: instrumental view of, 188;
opportunity of, 90—1, 121, 146,
177—8; racial attitudes and, 31,
33, 118; as solution, 124—6,
133—4, 222; *see also* schools
egalitarianism: liberalism, 33; racial
attitudes and, 23—6, 34, 39, 132;
working class and, 92
employment: opportunity and, 11,
147; as solution, 159, 222
Erikson, E., 70
Erskine, H. G., 9
ethnocentrism: beliefs of, 27;
measures of, 2

family: authority and, 70, 191; racial
feelings in, 87, 117—18; *see also*
childhood
fire protection, 99
firearms, 101—2
franchise, *see* voting
Frederickson, G. M., 39
"Free Huey" demonstrations, 156
Free Speech Movement, 187
Frenkel-Brunswick, D., 26
Freud, S., 70
Frye, Hardy, 108

Gagnon, John, 234—5
Gallup poll: busing and, 3, 11; racial
feelings and, 10
Garfinkel, H., 70
General Equivalency High School
Diploma, 81, 146
Genovese, Eugene, 20
ghettos, creation of, 17
Giddings, F., 16
Gittell, M., 7
Goldwater, Barry, 10
Great Depression, 141—2, 172
groups: positions of, 23, 36—7;
strategies of, 224
Guttman scale, 24

Hamilton, R., 11, 31
Hammond, Phillip, 47, 48n
Harding, J., 24, 27
Head Start program, 110, 124
high schools: experiences in, 80—1,
114, 135, 183; integration of, 96;
segregation in, 85—6
hippies, 196
Hoult, T., 2
housing: assistance in, 162; integration of, 9, 32, 33; open housing
ordinance, 127; segregation in,
11, 89; *see also* neighborhoods
human rights, 132

ideology: defends interests, 37, 221;
racism and, 20—7, 154—7; *see
also* American Creed
indentured servants, 38, 184
Indians, 88
individualism, 228—34
industrial society: racial divisions in,

252   Index

industrial society (*cont.*)
  16—20; South and, 40
institutions: changes in, 42, 216;
  race relations and, 8
integration of schools, 3, 11, 32, 223
intermarriage: fears of, 21—2, 117,
  122; opposed, 92—3, 96—7, 115
International Longshoremen's and
  Warehousemen's Union (ILWU),
  76, 83
interviews: race and, 74—6, 110;
  techniques of, 54—5

Janowitz, M., 9
Japanese, 113, 114, 122
Johnson, Lyndon, 159

Keniston, K., 70
Kerner Commission, *see* President's
  Commission on Civil Disorders
King, Martin Luther: admired, 120;
  assassination of, 207; criticized,
  158; working-class view of, 92—5,
  105
Kiwanis Clubs, 52
Korean War, 145
Kovel, Joel, 236
Kramer, B. M., 26
Kwan, K., 36

labor force, black mobility in, 32
labor unions, 52, 119, 128
language, 179, 201
law and order, 101, 157
Lemert, E., 70
Levin, Jack, 21
liberalism: egalitarianism and, 33;
  prevalence of, 219—20
Lifton, Robert, 70
Lipset, S. M., 22, 27n, 235
Lofland, J., 70

Malcolm X, 91, 92, 105
March on Washington, 93
Marine Corps, 81—2, 85—6, 145—6
Marxism: perspective of, 22; and
  race, 19—20
Merton, R., 12, 47n
middle class: inequality denied by,
  230; opposes black demands, 13;
  opposes busing, 8; race relations

and, 2, 29—30, 41, 60; rejection
  of, 212; tolerance in, 31, 220
militancy, *see* black power
Mills, C. Wright, 69
miscegenation, *see* intermarriage
mobility: achievement and, 18, 152
  —4; blacks and, 17, 32, 139—41,
  161, 164—6; discrimination and,
  108—9; effect on racism, 227;
  geographic, 40
modernization, 19
Moynihan, D. P., 56—7
Myrdal, G., 9, 17, 21, 28, 136

National Guard, 119
National Institute for Mental Health
  (NIMH), 49
National Opinion Research Center
  (NORC), 24
neighborhoods: busing and, 121;
  racial organization of, 11, 12, 89,
  126, 129, 142, 150—51, 185, 205
New York City, schools in, 7
Newman, W., 36
Newton, Huey, 74, 156
Noel, D., 39

Ocean Hill-Brownsville, 7
open enrollment, 8
opinion polls, 10
Orientals, 84

Papillon, Alex, 74
Park, Robert, 9, 17, 27, 70
Parsons, Talcott, 17—18
paternalism, 148, 197, 198
Peace Corps, 188
peer pressure, 114
personality, *see* psychology
police: brutality of, 103, 120, 154;
  harrassment by, 204; racial
  minorities and, 7, 8, 99—101,
  103, 119
Postal Service (U.S.), 108
prejudice: attitudes of, 5; distinguished from racism, 3—4, 10
  —12, 27, 33—4; measures of, 26;
  studies of, 9
President's Commission on Civil Disorders (Kerner Commission), 186
Price, Edward, 169

privilege, racism as strategy for maintaining, 40—4, 60—1, 193, 217, 218, 235
professionals, 8, 33
property rights: conflict with civil rights, 13, 127, 131, 233; police and, 100; working class and, 106
psychology: prejudice and, 26—7; racist attitudes and, 14; tolerance and, 30
public housing, see housing
Puerto Ricans, 7, 84
Pullman car workers, 186

Raab, E., 22; quoted, 216, 235
race relations: American Creed and, 23—7, 125, 137; class and, 2—4, 15—20, 35—44, 225—8; feelings and, 6, 84, 116, 136—7, 177; ideology and, 20—7; inconsistencies in, 12; irrationality in, 14, 27—9; liberal view of, 29—30, 190—3; military and, 85—6, 115; paternalism, 197; separation, 187
racism: defined, 39, 221—2; dominant groups and, 58
rape, 205
real estate companies, 89
Reitzes, Dietrich, 22
riots: causes of, 189, 209; deplored, 157, 162; as threat, 111, 119, 124, 207; working-class views of, 90, 95, 98—9
Rose, Arnold, 22
Roucek, J., 29
Rubin, Jerry, 187
Rusk, Dean, 122
Russian revolution, 28—9
Ryan, William, quoted, 217

sampling, 55—6
San Francisco, 49, 194
Schatzman, L., 45, 47
Schermerhorn, R., 29, 36
schools: decentralization of, 7; integration of, 3, 11, 12, 32, 104, 121, 158, 198; segregation in, 85; see also high schools, colleges, and universities
Schuman, H., 24, 27
Seale, Bobby, 74

Selznick, G., 13—14
Sennett, Richard, 64—5, 73, 226n
sexuality, 50, 97, 201
Shaw, C., 70
Sheatsley, P., 9, 24, 32
Shibutani, T., 36
Simon, William, 234—5
Simpson, G., 4, 18
slavery, 38, 50
Social Darwinism, 166
South Africa, 36—7
sports, 84—5
Steinberg, S., 13—14
Steward, D., 2
stigma, 142—3
stratification, see class
Strauss, A., 45, 47
Student Nonviolent Coordinating Committee, 91, 109, 209
students, see youth
suburbs, racial attitudes and, 3
Sumner, W., 16
Supreme Court (U.S.), 25, 158, 198
Sutherland, E. H., 71
Swartz, M., 34
Sweezy, P., 19

Tawney, R. H., quoted, 220
tax policies, 162, 182—3
teachers, race and, 7
television, race and, 1—2, 87, 90, 92
Thomas, W. I., 9, 16, 27, 70
tolerance: liberalism and, 31—2; personality and, 30
Tuskegee (Alabama), 108
Tyler, Gus, quoted, 217

unemployment, 126
universities, see colleges and universities
University of California (Berkeley), 109, 195
University of Chicago, 70
University of Michigan Survey Research Center, 3

van den Berghe, P., 36
Vander Zanden, J., 27n, 38
Veterans Administration, 108
Vietnam, 88, 123
violence, see riots

voting, 119, 125, 132

Watts, 99, 158
welfare, 110, 141, 144, 204
Wilson, W., 36–7, 43n
working class: assembly lines and, 82;
    awareness of inequality in, 230;
    bourgeois orientation of, 106;
    caricature of, 1; inconsistent atti-
    tudes in, 11, 60; racism of, 6, 42,

102–7, 228; tolerance in, 31
World War II, interracial contact and,
    115, 122, 135

Yinger, M., 4, 18
youth: college students, 60; liberal-
    ism among, 220; prejudice among,
    9, 117

Znaniecki, F., 70